P. Kropotkin

In Russian and French Prisons

P. Kropotkin

In Russian and French Prisons

ISBN/EAN: 9783744751971

Printed in Europe, USA, Canada, Australia, Japan

Cover: Foto ©ninafisch / pixelio.de

More available books at **www.hansebooks.com**

IN

RUSSIAN AND FRENCH PRISONS.

BY

P. KROPOTKINE.

WITH A PLAN OF THE ST. PETERSBURG FORTRESS.

London:
WARD AND DOWNEY,
12, YORK STREET, COVENT GARDEN.

MDCCCLXXXVII.

CONTENTS.

CHAPTER	PAGE
INTRODUCTORY	1
I.—MY FIRST ACQUAINTANCE WITH RUSSIAN PRISONS	8
II.—RUSSIAN PRISONS	24
III.—THE FORTRESS OF ST. PETER AND ST. PAUL	84
IV.—OUTCAST RUSSIA	124
V.—THE EXILE IN SIBERIA	154
VI.—THE EXILE ON SAKHALIN	202
VII.—A FOREIGNER ON RUSSIAN PRISONS	227
VIII.—IN FRENCH PRISONS	257
IX.—ON THE MORAL INFLUENCE OF PRISONS ON PRISONERS	299
X.—ARE PRISONS NECESSARY?	338

APPENDIX A.—Trial of the Soldiers accused of having carried Letters from the Alexis Ravelin . . . 373

PAGE

APPENDIX B.—On the part played by the Exiles in
the Colonization of Siberia . 377

APPENDIX C.—Extract from a Report on "Administrative Exile," read by
M. Shakéeff at the Sitting of
the St. Petersburg Nobility on
February 17, 1881 . . 379

APPENDIX D.—On Reformatories for Boys in France 382

INDEX 383

IN RUSSIAN AND FRENCH PRISONS.

INTRODUCTORY.

IN our busy life, preoccupied as we are with the numberless petty affairs of everyday existence, we are all too much inclined to pass by many great evils which affect Society without giving them the attention they really deserve. If sensational "revelations" about some dark side of our life occasionally find their way into the daily Press; if they succeed in shaking our indifference and awaken public attention, we may have in the papers, for a month or two, excellent articles and letters on the subject. Many well-meant things may then be said, the most humane feelings expressed. But the agitation soon subsides; and, after having asked for some new regulations or laws, in addition to the hundreds of thousands of regulations and laws already in force; after having made some microscopic attempts at combating

B

by a few individual efforts a deep-rooted evil which ought to be combated by the combined efforts of Society at large, we soon return to our daily occupations without caring much about what has been done. It is good enough if, after all the noise, things have not gone from bad to worse.

If this remark is true with regard to so many features of our public life, it is especially so with regard to prisons and prisoners. To use Miss Linda Gilbert's—the American Mrs. Fry's—words, " After a man has been confined to a felon's cell, Society loses all interest in and care for him." Provided he has "bread to eat, water to drink, and plenty of work to do," Society considers itself as having fulfilled all its duties towards him. From time to time, somebody acquainted with prisons starts an agitation against the bad state of our jails and lock-ups. Society recognizes that something ought to be done to remedy the evil. But the efforts of the reformers are broken by the inertia of the organized system; they have to fight against the widely-spread prejudices against all those who have fallen under the ban of the law; and soon they are left to themselves in their struggle against an immense evil. Such was the fate of John Howard, and of how many others? A few kindhearted and energetic men and women continue, of course, amidst the general indifference, to do their work of improving the condition of prisoners, or rather of mitigating the bad effects of prisons on their inmates. But, guided as they are merely by philanthropic feeling, they seldom venture to criticize the principles of penal institutions; still less do they search for the causes which every year bring millions of human beings within the enclosure of prison walls. They try to mitigate the evil; they seldom attempt to grapple with it at its source.

Every year something like a hundred thousand men, women, and children are locked up in the jails of Great Britain alone—very nearly one million in those of the whole of Europe. Nearly 1,200,000*l*. of public money are spent every year, in this country alone, for convict and local prisons; very nearly ten millions in Europe—not to speak of the expenses involved by the maintenance of the huge machinery which supplies prisons with inmates. But, apart from a few philanthropists and professional men, who cares about the results achieved at so heavy an expenditure? Are our prisons

worth the enormous outlay in human labour
yearly devoted to them? Do they guarantee
Society against the recurrence of the evils
which they are supposed to combat?

Having had in my life several opportunities
of giving more than a passing attention to
these great questions, I have thought that it
would be useful to put together the observa-
tions which I have been enabled to make on
prisons and the reflections they have suggested.

My first acquaintance with prisons and exile
was made in Siberia, in connection with a
committee for the reform of the Russian penal
system. There I had the opportunity of learning the state of things with regard both to
exile in Siberia and to prisons in Russia, and
then my attention was attracted first to the
great question of crime and punishment. Later
on, in 1874 to 1876, I was kept, awaiting trial,
nearly two years in the fortress of Peter and
Paul at St. Petersburg, and could appreciate
the terrible effects of protracted cellular confinement upon my fellow-prisoners. Thence I
was transferred to the newly-opened House of
Detention, which is considered as a model
prison for Russia, and thence again to a military
prison at the St. Petersburg Military Hospital.

When in this country, I was called upon, in
1881, to describe the treatment of political
prisoners in Russia, in order to *tell the truth*
in the face of the systematic misrepresentation
of the matter by an admirer of the Russian
Government. I did so in a paper on the Russian Revolutionary Party, which appeared in the
Fortnightly Review, June, 1831. None of the
facts revealed in this paper have been contradicted by the Russian agents. Attempts were,
however, made to circulate in the English press
accounts of Russian prisons, representing them
under a somewhat smiling aspect. I was thus
compelled to give a general description of
prisons and exile in Russia and Siberia, and
did so in a series of four papers, which appeared
in the *Nineteenth Century*. Refraining as much
as possible from complaints of the treatment
undergone by our political friends in Russia,
I preferred to give an idea of the general
state of Russian prisons, of exile to Siberia,
and of its results; and told the unutterable
sufferings which scores of thousands of common-
law prisoners are enduring in the jails throughout Russia, on their way to Siberia, and in the
immense penal colony of the Russian Empire.
In order to complete my own experience, which

might have been out of date, I consulted the bulky Russian literature which has been devoted of late to the subject. The perusal of this literature convinced me that things have remained in very nearly the same state as they were five-and-twenty years ago; but I also learned from it that although the Russian prison authorities are very anxious to have mouthpieces in West Europe, in order to circulate embellished accounts of their humane endeavours, they do not conceal the truth either from the Russian Government or from the Russian reading public, and both in official reports and in the Press they represent the prisons as being in the most execrable condition. Some of these avowals will be found in the following pages.

Later on, that is, in 1882 to 1886, I spent three years in French prisons; namely, in the *Prison Départementale* of Lyons, and the *Maison Centrale* of Clairvaux. The description of both has been given in a paper contributed last year to the *Nineteenth Century*. My sojourn of nearly three years at Clairvaux, in close neighbourhood with fourteen hundred common-law prisoners, has given me an opportunity of obtaining a personal insight into the results achieved by detention in this prison, one of the best in France, and, as far as my information goes, in Europe. It induced me to treat the question as to the moral effects of prisons on prisoners from a more general point of view, in connection with modern views on crime and its causes. A portion of this inquiry formed the subject of an address delivered in December last, before the Edinburgh Philosophical Institution.

While thus reprinting some review articles, I have completed them with more recent information and data, mostly taken from official Russian publications; and whilst eliminating from them the controversial element, I have also eliminated all that cannot be supported by documents which can be published now without causing harm to anybody of our friends in Russia. The newly-added chapter on exile to Sakhalin will complete the description of the Russian penal institutions. I take advantage of this opportunity to express my best thanks to the editor of the *Nineteenth Century* for his kind permission to reprint the articles published in his review.

CHAPTER I.

MY FIRST ACQUAINTANCE WITH RUSSIAN PRISONS.

My first acquaintance with Russian prisons was made in Siberia. It was in 1862. I had then just arrived at Irkutsk—a young Lieutenant of Cossacks, not fully twenty years of age,—and a couple of months after my arrival I was appointed secretary to a committee for the reform of prisons. A few words of explanation are necessary, I suppose, for my English readers.

The education I had received was only what a military school could give. Much of our time had been devoted, of course, to mathematics and physical sciences; still more to the science of warfare, to the art of destroying men on battle-fields. But we were living, then, in Russia at the time of the great revival of thought which followed in our country the Crimean defeat; and even the education in military schools felt the influence of this great movement. Something superior to mere militarism penetrated even the walls of the *Corps des Pages*.

The Press had received some freedom of expression since 1859, and it was eagerly discussing the political and economic reforms which had to shake off the sad results of twenty-five years of military rule under Nicholas I.; and echoes of the intense intellectual activity which was agitating the outer world reached our class-room. Some of us were reading a good deal to complete our education. We took a warm interest in the proposed rebuilding of our institutions, and lively discussions on the emancipation of Serfs, on the reforms in administration, were carried on between lessons on tactics and military history. The very next day after the long-expected and often delayed emancipation of Serfs had been promulgated, several copies of the bulky and incoherently-worded *Polozhenie* (Emancipation Act) were busily studied and briskly commented upon in our small sunny library. The Italian Opera was forgotten for guesses as to the probable results and meaning of the emancipation. Our teachers, too, fell under the influences of the epoch. History, and especially the history of foreign literature, became, in the lectures of our professors, a history of the philosophical, political, and social growth of humanity. The dry principles of J. B. Say's "Political Economy," and the commentaries upon Russian civil and military law, which formerly were considered as a useless burden in the education of future officers, became endowed with new life in our classes, when applied to the present needs of Russia.

Serfdom had been abolished, and a series of reforms which were to culminate in constitutional guarantees, preoccupied the minds. All had to be reformed at once. All had to be revised in our institutions, which are a strange mixture of legacies from the old Moscow period, with Peter I.'s attempts at creating a military State by orders from St. Petersburg, with the depravity bequeathed by the Courtiers of the Empresses, and Nicholas I.'s military despotism. Reviews and newspapers were fully devoted to these subjects, and we eagerly read them.

It is true that Reaction had already made its appearance on the horizon. On the very eve of the liberation of the Serfs, Alexander II. grew frightened at his own work, and the Reactionary Party gained some ground in the Winter Palace.

Nicholas Milutine—the soul of the emancipation of the Serfs in bureaucratic circles—had been suddenly dismissed, a few months before the promulgation of the law, and the work of the Liberal Emancipation Committees had been given over, for revision in a sense more favourable to the nobility, to new committees chiefly composed of Serf-proprietors of the old school,— the so-called *kryepostniki*. The Press began to be muzzled; free discussion of the Emancipation Act was prohibited; the paper of Aksakoff— he was Radical then and advocated the summons of a Zemskoye Sobranie, and was not opposed to the recall of Russian troops from Poland—was suppressed number after number. The small outbreak of peasants at Kazan, and the great conflagration at St. Petersburg in May, 1862 (it was attributed to Poles), still reinforced the reaction. The series of political trials which were hereafter to characterize the reign of Alexander II. was opened by sentencing our poet and publicist, Mikhailoff, to hard-labour.

The wave of reaction, however, had not in 1862 yet reached Siberia. Mikhailoff, on his way to the Nertchinsk mines, was fêted at a dinner by the Governor of Tobolsk. Herzen's

Kolokol ("The Bell") was smuggled and read everywhere in Siberia; and at Irkutsk I found, in September, 1862, a society animated by the great expectations which were already beginning to fade at St. Petersburg. "Reforms" were on all lips, and among those which were most often alluded to, was that of a thorough reorganization of the system of exile.

I was nominated aide-de-camp to the Governor of Transbaikalia, General Kukel, a Lithuanian, strongly inspired with the Liberal ideas of the epoch; and next month we were at Tchita, a big village recently made capital of Transbaikalia.

Transbaikalia is the province where the well-known Nertchinsk mines are situated. All hard-labour convicts are sent there from all parts of Russia; and therefore exile and hard-labour were frequently the subject of our conversations. Everybody there knew the abominable conditions under which the long foot-journey from the Urals to Transbaikalia used to be made by the exiles. Everybody knew the abominable state of the prisons in Nertchinsk, as well as throughout Russia. It was no sort of secret. Therefore, the Ministry of the Interior undertook a thorough reform of prisons in Russia and Siberia, together with a thorough revision of the penal law and the conditions of exile.

"Here is a circular from the Ministry," the Governor once said to me. "They ask us to collect all possible information about the state of prisons and to express our opinions as to the reforms to be made. There is no one here to undertake the work: you know how fully we are all occupied. We have asked for information in the usual way, but receive nothing in reply. Will you take up the work?" I objected, of course, that I was too young and knew nothing about it. But the answer was: "Study! In the Journal of the Ministry of Justice you will find, to guide you, elaborate reports on all possible systems of prisons. As to the practical part of the work, let us gather, first, reliable information as to where we stand. Then we all, Colonel P., Mr. A., and Ya., and the mining authorities also—will help you. We will discuss everything in detail with people having practical knowledge of the matter; but gather, first, the data—prepare material for discussion."

So I became secretary to the local committee for the reform of prisons. Needless to say how happy I was to accept the task: I set to work with all the energy of youth. The circular of the Ministry filled me with joy. It was couched in the most elegant style, and the Ministry incisively pointed out the chief defects of Russian prisons. The Government was ready to undertake the most thorough reform of the whole system in a most humane spirit. The circular went on to mention the penitentiary systems in use in Western Europe; but none of them satisfied the Ministry, and it advocated a return "to the great principles laid down by the illustrious grandmother and grandfather of the now happily reigning Emperor." For a Russian mind this allusion to the famous instructions of Catherine II., written under the influence of the Encyclopedists, and to the humanitarian tendencies professed during the earlier years of Alexander I.'s reign, conveyed a whole programme. My enthusiasm was simply doubled by the reading of the circular.

Things did not go, however, so smoothly. The mining authorities under whom the exiles are working in the Nertchinsk mines did not care so much about the great principles of Catherine II. and were, I am afraid, of the opinion that the less things were reformed, the better. The repeated demands for information issued by the Governor left them quite unmoved —they depend directly upon the Cabinet of the Emperor at St. Petersburg, not upon the Governor. Obstinate silence was their answer until they finally sent in a pile of papers, covered with figures, from which nothing could be obtained, not even the cost of maintenance of convicts, nor the value of their labour.

Still, at Tchita there were plenty of men thoroughly acquainted with the hard-labour prisons, and some information was gladly supplied by several mining officers. It appeared that none of the silver-mines where exiles were kept could be worked with any semblance of profit. So also with many gold-mines. The mining authorities were anxious to abandon most of them. The arbitrary despotism of the directors of prisons had no limits, and the dreadful tales which circulated in Transbaikalia about one of them—Razghildeeff—were fully confirmed. Terrible epidemics of scurvy swept away the prisoners by hundreds each year, that a more active extraction of gold was ordered from St. Petersburg, and the underfed convicts were compelled to overwork. As to the buildings and their rotten condition, the overcrowding therein, and the filth accumulated by generations of overcrowded prisoners, the reports were really heartbreaking. No repairs would do, the whole had to undergo a thorough reform. I visited a few prisons, and could but confirm the reports. The Transbaikalian authorities insisted, therefore, on limiting the number of convicts sent to the province; they pointed out the material impossibility of providing them not only with work, but even with shelter.

Things were no better with regard to the transport of exiles. This service was in the most deplorable condition. An engineer, a honest young man, was sent to visit all *étapes* —the prisons where the convicts stop to rest during the journey—and reported that all ought to be rebuilt; many were rotten to the foundation; none could afford shelter for the mass of convicts sometimes gathered there. I visited several of them, saw the parties of convicts on their journeys, and could but warmly advocate the complete suppression of this terrific punishment inflicted on thousands of men, women, and children.

As to the local prisons, destinated to be lock-ups, or houses of detention for the local prisoners, we found them overcrowded to the last extent in ordinary times, and still more so when parties of convicts were stopped on the journey by inundations or frosts—Siberian frosts. They all answered literally to the well-known description of Dostoievsky in his "Buried Alive."

A small committee, composed of well-intentioned men whom the Governor convoked from time to time at his house, busily discussed what could be done to improve affairs without imposing a new and heavy burden on the budget of the State and the province. The conclusions unanimously arrived at were: that exile, as it is, is a disgrace to humanity; that it is a quite needless burden for Siberia; and that Russia herself must take care of her own prisoners, instead of sending them thither. For that purpose, not only the penal code and the judicial procedure ought to be revised at once, as promised in the Ministerial circulars, but also within Russia herself some new system of penal organization ought to be introduced.

The committee sketched such a system where cellular imprisonment was utterly condemned, and the subdivision of the prisoners into groups of from ten to twenty in each room, short sentences, and productive and well-paid work in common were advocated. An appeal was to be made to the best energies of Russia in order to transform her prisons into reformatories. Transbaikalia was declared ready to transform her own prisons on these lines without imposing any fresh expenses upon the budget of the Empire. The kinds of work which could be done by prisoners were indicated, and the conclusion was that prisons ought to, and might, support themselves if properly organized. As to the new men and women necessary for such a reorganization of penal institutions on new principles, the Committee was sure of finding them; and while an honest jailer under the present system is very rare, there was no doubt that a new departure in the penal system would find no lack of new honest men.

I must confess that at that time I still believed that prisons could be reformatories, and that the privation of liberty is compatible with moral amelioration . . . but I was only twenty years old.

All this work took several months. And by this time Reaction became more and more in favour at the Winter Palace. The Polish in-

My first Acquaintance with Russian Prisons. 19

surrection gave to Reactionaries the long-expected opportunity for throwing off their masks and for openly advocating a return to the old principles of the time of Serfdom. The good intentions of 1859-62 were forgotten at the Court; new men came into favour with Alexander II. and were admirably successful in working upon his feeble character and his fears. New circulars were sent out by the Ministries; but these circulars—couched in a far less elegant and far more bureaucratic style—mentioned no more reforms, and insisted, instead, on the necessity of strong rule and discipline.

One day the Governor of Transbaikalia received an order to leave his post at once and return to Irkutsk, where he was left *en disponibilité*. He had been denounced: he had treated the exiled Mikhailoff too well; he had permitted him to stay on a private mine in the district of Nertchinsk; he sympathized too much with the Poles. A new Governor came to Transbaikalia, and our report on prisons had to be revised again. The new Governor would not sign it. We fought as much as we could to maintain its conclusions. We made concessions as to the style, but we insisted on the general conclusions of the report, and we did this so firmly that finally the Governor signed it and sent it to St. Petersburg.

What has become of it since? Surely it is still lying in some portfolios at the Ministry. For the next ten years the reform of prisons was completely forgotten. In 1872, however, new committees were nominated for the same purpose at St. Petersburg, and again in 1877-78, and on several succeeding occasions. New men elaborated new schemes; new reports were written criticizing again and again the old system. But the old system remains untouched. Nay, the attempts at making a new departure have been, by some fatality, mere returns to the old-fashioned type of a Russian *ostrog*.

True, several central prisons have since been erected in Russia, and hard-labour convicts are kept there before being sent to Siberia, for terms varying from four to six years. To what purpose? Probably to reduce their numbers by the awful mortality in these places. Seven such prisons have been erected of late—at Wilno, Simbirsk, Pskov, Tobolsk, Perm, and two in the province of Kharkoff. But—official reports say so—they have been modelled on the

My first Acquaintance with Russian Prisons. 21

very same type as the prisons of old. "The same filth, the same idleness of the prisoners, the same contempt for the most primary notions of hygiene," says a semi-official report. All together they contained an aggregate of 2464 men in 1880—too much for their capacity, too little to noticeably diminish the numbers of hard-labour convicts transported to Siberia. A new and terrible punishment inflicted on the convicts to no purpose,—that is all that they have accomplished after having swallowed millions from the budget.

Exile, in the meantime, remains very much what it was in 1862. Only one important modification has been introduced. It proved cheaper to transport the nearly 20,000 people yearly sent to Siberia (two-thirds of them without trial) on horses between Perm and Tumen [1] —that is from the Kama to the basin of the Obi—and thence on barges towed by steamers to Tomsk, instead of sending them on foot. And so they are transported now. Besides, the extraction of silver from the Nertchinsk mines having been nearly abandoned, no exiles are sent to these most unhealthy mines, some of

[1] The Siberian railway being now opened along the whole of this distance, they will be transported by rail.

which, like Akatui, were in the worst repute. But a scheme is now afloat for reopening these mines; and in the meantime a new hell, worse than Akatui, has been devised. Hardlabour convicts are sent now to die on the Sakhalin island.

Finally, I must mention that new *étapes* have been built on the route, 2000 miles long, between Tomsk and Sryetensk, on the Shilka,— this space being still traversed on foot by the exiles. The old *étapes* were falling to pieces; it was impossible to repair these heaps of rotten logs, and new *étapes* have been erected. They are wider than the old ones, but the parties of convicts being also more numerous, the overcrowding and the filth in these *étapes* are the same as of old.

What further "improvements" can I mention in glancing over these five-and-twenty years? I was nearly going to forget the House of Detention at St. Petersburg, the showprison for foreigners, with 317 cells and several rooms for keeping an aggregate of 600 men and 100 women awaiting trial. But that is all. The same old, dark and damp, and filthy lockups—the *ostrogs*—may be seen at the entrance of each provincial town in Russia; and all has remained in these *ostrogs* as it was twenty-five years ago. Some new prisons have been erected here and there, some old ones have been repaired; but the system, and the treatment of prisoners, have remained unaltered; the old spirit has been transported in full in the new buildings; and to see a new departure in the Russian penal institutions we must wait for some new departure in Russian life as a whole. At present, if there is some change, it is not for the best. Whatever the defects of the old prisons, there was still a breath of humanitarianism in 1862, which penetrated in a thousand ways, even into the jails. But now, the openly-avowed ideal of Alexander III. being his grandfather Nicholas, the Administration, too, seek their ideals in the old drunken soldiers patronized by the " Gendarme of Europe." " Keep Russia *in urchin-gloves!* " they say at the Gatchina Palace; " Keep them in urchin-gloves! " they repeat in the prisons.

CHAPTER II.

RUSSIAN PRISONS.

It is pretty generally recognized in Europe that altogether our penal institutions are very far from being what they ought, and no better indeed than so many contradictions in action of the modern theory of the treatment of criminals. The principle of the *lex talionis*— of the right of the community to avenge itself on the criminal—is no longer admissible. We have come to an understanding that society at large is responsible for the vices that grow in it, as well as it has its share in the glory of its heroes; and we generally admit, at least in theory, that when we deprive a criminal of his liberty, it is to purify and improve him. But we know how hideously at variance with the ideal the reality is. The murderer is simply handed over to the hangman; and the man who is shut up in a prison is so far from being bettered by the change, that he comes out more resolutely the foe of society than he was when he went in. Subjection, on disgraceful terms, to humiliating work gives him an antipathy to all kinds of labour. After suffering every sort of humiliation at the instance of those whose lives are lived in immunity from the peculiar conditions which bring man to crime—or to such sorts of it as are punishable by the operations of the law—he learns to hate the section of society to which his humiliation belongs, and proves his hatred by new offences against it.

If the penal institutions of Western Europe have failed thus completely to realize the ambitious aim on which they justify their existence, what shall we say of the penal institutions of Russia? The incredible duration of preliminary detention; the disgusting circumstances of prison life; the congregation of hundreds of prisoners into small and dirty chambers; the flagrant immorality of a corps of jailers who are practically omnipotent, whose whole function is to terrorize and oppress, and who rob their charges of the few coppers doled out to them by the State; the want of labour and the total absence of all that contributes to the moral welfare of man; the cynical contempt for human dignity, and the physical degradation of prisoners—these are the elements of prison life in Russia. Not that the principles of Russian penal institutions are worse than those applied to the same institutions in Western Europe. I am rather inclined to hold the contrary. Surely, it is less degrading for the convict to be employed in useful work in Siberia, than to spend his life in picking oakum, or in climbing the steps of a wheel; and—to compare two evils—it is more humane to employ the assassin as a labourer in a gold-mine and, after a few years, make a free settler of him, than quietly to turn him over to a hangman. In Russia, however, principles are always ruined in application. And if we consider the Russian prisons and penal settlements, not as they ought to be according to the law, but as they are in reality, we can do no less than recognize, with all efficient Russian explorers of our prisons, that they are an outrage on humanity.

One of the best results of the Liberal movement of 1859—1862 was the judicial reform. The old law-courts, in which the procedure was in writing, and which were real sinks of corruption and bribery, were done away with. Trial by jury, which was an institution of old

Russia, but had disappeared under the Tsars of Moscow, was reintroduced. Peasant-courts, to judge small offences and disputes in villages according to the unwritten customary law, had already been established by the Emancipation Act of 1861. The new law of Judicial Procedure, promulgated in 1864, introduced the institution of justices of peace, elected in Russia, but nominated by Government in the Lithuanian provinces and in Poland. They had to dispose of smaller criminal offences, and of all civil disputes about matters not exceeding 30*l*. in value. Appeal against their decisions could be made to the District Gathering of Justices of the Peace, and eventually to the Senate.

All cases implying a privation of civil rights were placed under the jurisdiction of Courts of Justice, sitting with open doors, and supported by a jury. Their decisions could be carried to Courts of Appeal, and cases decided by verdicts of jurors could be brought before Courts of Cassation. The preliminary investigation, however, still remained private, that is (in conformity with the French system, as opposed to the English), no counsel was admitted to the prisoner during the preliminary examination; but provisions were made to guarantee the independence of the examining magistrates. Such were, in a few words, the leading features of the new organization of justice under the law of 1864. As to its general spirit it is only fair to say that—apart from the preliminary inquiry—it was conceived in accordance with the most Liberal ideas now current in the judicial world of Europe.

Two years after the promulgation of this law, the most shameful feature of the old Russian penal code—punishment by the *knut* and branding-iron—was abolished. It was high time. Public opinion was revolted by the use of these relics of a barbarous past, and it was so powerful at that time that governors of provinces refused to confirm sentences that enjoined the use of the *knut;* while others—as I have known in Siberia—would intimate to the executioner that unless he merely cracked the terrible instrument of torture in the air, barely touching his victim (an art well known and very profitable to executioners), "his own skin should be torn to pieces." Corporal punishment was thus abolished, but not completely. It remained in the villages (the peasant-courts being still empowered to administer flogging), in the army, and in the convict-prisons. Only women could no longer be submitted to flogging as long as not deprived of their civil rights.

But, like all other reforms of that period, the benefits of these two great changes were to a great extent paralyzed by subsequent modifications, or by leaving them uncomplete. The old penal code, containing a scale of punishments in flagrant disagreement with the state of prisons, was still maintained. Twenty years have elapsed since a thorough revision of the code was promised; committee has succeeded committee; last year again the newspapers reported that the revision of the code had been terminated, that the sentences would be shortened, and that the barbarous provisions introduced in 1845 would be abolished. But the code remains still what it was when it issued from the hands of Nicholas I.'s committees; and we may still read in the revised edition of 1857, § 799, that convicts can be punished by five to six thousand strokes of the whip, and by being riveted to a wheel-barrow for terms varying from one to three years.

As to the judicial reform, it had hardly become law ere it was ruined by ministerial circulars. First of all, years passed and in thirty-nine provinces out of seventy-two the old courts were maintained, and progress in any suit, as well as the final decision, could be obtained only by *vzyatki*, that is, by bribery. Until 1885, the old system remained in operation over the whole of Siberia. And when the law of 1864 was extended to three Siberian provinces, it was so mutilated as to lose precisely its best features. A jury is still a *desideratum* beyond the Urals. The Lithuanian provinces, Poland, and the Baltic provinces, as also several provinces in the north and in the south-east (Arkhangelsk included) remain still under the old jurisdiction; while Wilno and Minsk received the new law quite mutilated by the reactionary proclivities of the present rulers.

As to the Russian provinces where the law has been in force since 1864, all that could be devised to attenuate its good effects—short of actual repeal, has been done. The examining magistrates (*juges d'instruction*) have never enjoyed the independence bestowed on them by the new law; and this was managed by means of a very simple stratagem: no examining magistrates were nominated, and those to whom their work was entrusted were nominated merely *ad interim*. So the Ministry could displace and discharge them at will. The judges have been made more and more dependent upon the Minister of Justice, whose nominees they are, and who has the right to transfer them from one province to another— from St. Petersburg, for instance, to Siberia. The institution of sworn advocates, uncontrolled by criticism, has degenerated; and the peasant whose case is not likely to become a *cause célèbre*, has not the benefits of a counsel, and is completely in the hands of a creature like the procureur-impérial in Zola's novel. Freedom of defence was trampled under foot, and the few advocates, like Urusoff, who have indulged in anything approaching to free speech in the trial of political prisoners, have been exiled merely by order of the Third Section.

Independent jurors are, of course, impossible in a country where the peasant-juror knows that he may be beaten by anything in uniform at the very doors of the court. As for the verdicts of the juries, they are not respected at all if they are in contradiction with the opinions of the governor of the province; and the acquitted may be seized as they leave the dock, and imprisoned anew, on a simple order of the Administrative. Such, for instance, was the case of the peasant Borunoff. He came to St. Petersburg on behalf of his fellow-villagers to bring a complaint to the Tsar against the authorities, and he was tried as a "rebel." He was acquitted by the court; but he was re-arrested on the very flight of steps outside, and exiled to the peninsula of Kola. Such, too, was the case of the *raskolnik* (nonconformist) Tetenoff, and several more. As to Vera Zassoulitch, who also was acquitted by the jury, the Government ordered her re-arrest at the very doors of the court, and re-arrested she would have been if her comrades had not rescued her, leaving one dead in the riot which ensued.

The Third Section, the courtiers, and the governors of provinces look on the new courts as mere nuisances, and act accordingly. A great many cases are disposed of by the Executive *à huis clos*, away from examining magistrates, judges, and jurors alike. The preliminary inquiry, in all cases in which a "political meaning" is discovered, is simply made by gendarmerie-officers, sometimes in the presence of a procureur who accompanies them in their raids. This procureur—an official in civil dress, attached to the blue uniforms of the gendarmes—is a black sheep to his colleagues; his function is to assist, or appear to assist, at the examination of those arrested by the secret police, and thus give an aspect of lawfulness to its proceedings. Sentence and punishment are often awarded by the Department of States' Police (which is but another name for the Third Section) or the Executive; and a punishment as terrible as exile—may be for life—within the Arctic circle in Siberia is pronounced on mere reports of the gendarmerie officers. In fact, Administrative Exile is resorted to in all cases when there is not the slightest indication which could lead to condemnation, even by a packed court. "You are exiled to Siberia, *because* it is impossible to commit you for trial, there being no proofs against you,"—such is the cynical form in which the announcement is made to the prisoner. "Be happy that you have escaped so cheap"—they add; and people are sent for five, ten, fifteen years to some small borough of 500 inhabitants within or in the vicinity of the Arctic circle. In this category are included not only the cases of political offenders who

D

are supposed to belong to some secret society, but also those of religious dissenters; of people who frankly speak out their opinions on Government; writers whose romances are considered " dangerous;" almost all persons accused of " disobedience " and " turbulent character;" workmen who have been most active in strikes; those accused of verbal " offences against the Sacred Person of his Majesty the Emperor," under which head 2500 people were arrested in 1881 in the course of six months; in short, all those cases which might tend—to use the official language—" to the production of excitement in the public mind " were they brought before a court.

As to political trials, only the early revolutionary societies were tried under the law of 1864. Afterwards, when the Government perceived that the judges would not send to hard labour those political offenders who were brought before them, merely because they were suspected of being acquainted with revolutionists, the political cases were tried by packed courts, that is, by judges nominated especially for that purpose. To this rule the case of Vera Zassoulitch was a memorable exception. She was tried by a jury, and acquitted. But, to quote Professor Gradovsky's words in the *Golos* (suppressed since)—"It is an open secret in St. Petersburg that the case would never have been brought before a jury but for certain 'quarrels' between the Prefect of the Police on the one side, and the Third Section and the Ministers of Justice and the Interior on the other,—but for certain of those *jalousies de métier* without which, in our disordered state of existence, it would often be impossible for us so much as to breathe." In plain words, the courtiers quarrelled, some of them considered that it would be advantageous to discredit Trepoff, who was then omnipotent in the counsels of Alexander II., and the Minister of Justice succeeded in obtaining permission from the Emperor that Vera Zassoulitch should be sent before a jury : he surely did not expect that she would be acquitted, but he knew that the trial would render it impossible for Trepoff to remain Prefect of the Police at St. Petersburg.

It is, again, to a like *jalousie de métier*, that we were indebted for a public trial on the most scandalous affair of Privy Councillor Tokareff, General-Lieutenant Loshkareff, and their accomplices : Sevastianoff, chief of the Administration of Domains in Minsk, and Kapger, chief of Police in the same province. These personages, of whom Tokareff was Governor of Minsk, and Loshkareff was a member of the Ministry of the Interior "for peasants' affairs," had contrived to simply steal an estate of 8000 acres belonging to the peasants of Logishino, a small town in Minsk. They managed to buy it from the Crown for the nominal sum of 14,000 roubles (1400*l*.) payable in twenty yearly instalments of 700 roubles each. The peasants, robbed of land that belonged to them, applied to the Senate, and the Senate recognized their rights. It ordered the restoration of the land; but the *ukaze* of the Senate was "lost," and the chief of the Administration of Domains feigned ignorance of the decision of the Senate. In the meantime the governor of the province exacted from the peasants 5474 roubles as a year's rent, (for the estate which he had bought for twenty yearly payments of 700 roubles each). The peasants refused to pay, and sent their delegates to St. Petersburg. But as these delegates applied to the Ministry, where General Loshkareff was powerful, they were directly exiled as "rebels." The peasants still refused to pay, and then Governor Tokareff asked for troops to exact the money. General Loshkareff, his friend, was immediately sent by the Ministry at the head of a military expedition, in order to "restore order" at Logishino. Supported by a battalion of infantry and 200 Cossacks, he flogged all the inhabitants of the village until they had paid, and then reported to St. Petersburg that he had crushed an outbreak in the Western provinces. He did better. He obtained the military cross of Vladimir to decorate his friend Tokareff and the Ispravnik Kapger.

Well, this abominable affair, widely known and spoken of in Russia, would never have been brought before a court but for the Winter Palace intrigues. When Alexander III. surrounded himself with new men, the new courtiers who came to power found it desirable to crush with a single blow the party of Potapoff, which was intriguing for a return to power. It was necessary to discredit this party, and the Loshkareff affair, more than five years old, was brought before the Senate in November, 1881. All publicity was given to it, and we could then read for several days in the St. Petersburg newspapers the horrible tale of spoliation and plunder, of old men flogged nearly to death, of Cossacks exacting money with their whips from the Logishino peasants, who were robbed of their own land by the governor of the province. But, for one Tokareff condemned by the Senate, how many other Tokareffs are still peacefully enjoying the fruits of their thieving in the Western and South-Eastern provinces,—sure that none of their deeds will ever see the light of a law court; that any affair which may arise in such a court in connection with their shameful deeds will be stifled in the same way as the Tokareff affair was stifled for five years by orders emanating from the Ministry of Justice?

As to political affairs they have been completely removed from the jurisdiction of the ordinary courts. A few special judges nominated for the purpose, are attached to the Senate for judging political offenders,—if Government does not dispose of them otherwise. Most of them are sent before a court-martial; but, while the law is explicit in ordering full publicity of the proceedings of the military courts, their judgments in political cases are pronounced in absolute secrecy.

It need hardly be said that true reports of political trials in the press have never been permitted. Formerly the journals were bound to reproduce the " cooked " report published by the *Official Messenger;* but now the Government has perceived that even such reports produce a profound impression on the public mind, which is always favourable to the accused; and now the work is done in complete darkness. By the law of September, 1881, the governor-general and the governors of provinces are enabled to request " that all those cases be heard *in camera* which might produce a 'disturbance of minds' (*sic*) or disturb the public peace." To prevent the speeches of the accused, or such facts which might compromise the Government, from being divulged, nobody is admitted to the court, not even members of the Ministry of Justice—" only the wife or the husband of the accused (mostly in custody also), or the father, mother, or one of the children; but no more than one relative for each accused person." At the trial of twenty-one Terrorists at St. Petersburg, when ten people were condemned to death, the mother of Sukhanoff was the one person who enjoyed this privilege. Many cases are got rid of in such a way that nobody knows when the trials take place. Thus, for instance, we remained in ignorance of the fate of an officer of the army, son of the governor of a gaol in the St. Petersburg fortress, who had been condemned to hard labour for connection with revolutionists, until we learned it casually from an accusation read at a trial a long while posterior to his own. The public learns from the *Official Messenger* that the Tsar has commuted sentences of death pronounced on revolutionists to hard labour for life; but nothing transpires either of the trial, or of the crimes imputed to the condemned. Nay, even the last consolation of those condemned to death, the consolation of dying publicly, was taken away. Hanging will now be done secretly within the walls of the fortress, in the presence of none from the world without. The reason is, that when Rysakoff was brought out to the gallows he showed the crowd his mutilated hands, and shouted, louder than the drums, that he had been tortured after trial. His words were heard by a group of "Liberals," who, repudiating any sympathy with the Terrorists, yet held it their duty to publish the facts of the case in a clandestine proclamation, and to call attention to this flagrant offence against the laws of humanity.

Now nothing will be known of what happens in the casemates of the fortress of Paul and Peter after the trial and before the execution.

The trial of the fourteen Terrorists, amongst whom were Vera Figner and Ludmila Volkenstein, and which terminated in eight condemnations to death, was conducted in such privacy that— as an English correspondent wrote—nobody knew anything about it, even in the houses close by that in which the court-martial was sitting. Nine persons only—all courtiers anxious to see the reputed beauty of one of the accused heroines —were admitted to the court; and it was again from the correspondent of an English newspaper that the public learned that two of the condemned, namely Stromberg and Rogatchoff, were executed in greatest secrecy. The news has been since confirmed from an official source. The *Official Messenger* announced that out of eight condemnations to death six had been commuted, and that Stromberg and Rogatchoff were hanged. But that was all which transpired of this trial. Nobody could even say where the execution took place. As to those whose sentence was commuted to hard labour, all we can say is, that they have never been sent to hard labour; they have disappeared.

It is supposed that they are confined in the new State prison at Schlüsselburg. But what has become of them there—remains a secret. It transpired that several were shot for supposed, or real, "disciplinary offences." But, what has become of the remainder? None can say, not even their mothers, who make unceasing but useless efforts to discover the fate of their sons and daughters. . . .

Like atrocities being possible under the "reformed" Judicial Procedure, it is easy to foresee what may be expected from the "unreformed" prisons.

In 1861, the governors of our provinces were ordered to institute a general inquiry into the state of prisons. The inquiry was fairly made, and its results determined what was generally known: namely, that the prisons in Russia and Siberia were in the worst state imaginable. The number of prisoners in each was very often twice and thrice in excess of the maximum allowed by law. The buildings were so old and dilapidated, and in such a shocking state of filth, as to be for the most part not only uninhabitable, but beyond the scope of any theory of reform that stopped short of reconstruction.

Within, affairs were even worse than without. The system was found corrupt to the core, and the officials were yet more in need of improvement than the gaols. In the Transbaikal province where, at that time, almost all hard-labour convicts were kept, the committee of inquiry reported that the prison buildings were mostly in ruins, and that the whole system of exile had followed suit. Throughout the Empire it was recognized that theory and practice stood equally in need of light and air; that everything must be changed, alike in matter and in spirit; and that we must not only rebuild our prisons, but completely reform our prison system, and reconstitute the prison staff from the first man to the last. The Government, however, elected to do nothing. It built a few new prisons which proved insufficient to accommodate the yearly increasing numbers of prisoners; convicts were farmed out to proprietors of private gold-mines in Siberia; a new penal colony was settled on Sakhalin, to colonize an island where nobody was willing to settle freely; a new Central Board of Prisons was nominated; and that was all. The old order remained unchanged, the old mischief unrepaired. Year after year the prisons fall further into decay, and year after year the prison staff of drunken soldiers remains unchanged. Year after year the Ministry of Justice applies for money to spend in repairs, and year after year the Government is content to put it off with the half, or less than the half, of what it asks; and when it calls—during the years 1875 to 1881—for over six million roubles for the most unavoidable repairs which can no longer be postponed, can spare it no more than a paltry two and a half millions. The consequence is that the gaols are becoming permanent centres of infection, and that, according to the report of a recent committee, at least two-thirds of them are urgently in need of being rebuilt from top to bottom. Rightly to accommodate her prisoners, Russia should have to build half as many prisons again as she has. Indeed, on January 1st, 1884, there were 73,796 prisoners, and the aggregate capacity of the prisons in European Russia is only for 54,253 souls. In single gaols, built for the detention of 200 to 250 persons, the number of prisoners is commonly 700 and 800 at a time. In the prisons on the route to Siberia, when convict parties are stopped by floods, the overcrowding is still more monstrous. The Chief Board of Prisons does not, however, conceal this truth. In its report for 1882, which was published in Russia, and extracts of which have appeared in our reviews, it stated that, whereas the aggregate capacity of all prisons in the empire is only sufficient for 76,000 men, they contained on January 1st, 1882, 95,000 souls. In the prisons of Piotrokow —it reported—the space destinated for one man was occupied by five persons. In two provinces of Poland and in seven provinces of Russia the real population of the prisons was twice the amount which could nominally be contained by them at the lowest allowable cubic space, and in eleven provinces it exceeded the same at the ratio of 3 to 2.[1] In consequence of that, typhoid epidemics are constant in several prisons.[2]

The Russian prison system is thus constituted: First of all we have, in European Russia, 624 prisons or lock-ups, for cases awaiting trial, for a maximum of 54,253 inmates, with four houses of detention for 1134 inmates. If all lock-ups

[1] Yearly Report of the Chief Board of Prisons for 1882 (Russian).—*Vyestnik Europy*, 1883, vol. i.
[2] V. Nikitin, "Prison and Exile," St. Petersburg, 1880. "Our Penal Institutions," by the same, in *Russkiy Vyestnik*, 1881, vol. cliii.—Report of the Medical Department of the Ministry of Interior for 1883.

at the police-stations be added to the above, their number must be raised to 655; and in 1883, no less than 571,093 persons passed through them. In Poland there are 116 lock-ups of the same type. The political prisons at the Third Section and in the fortresses are not included in this category. Of convict depôts— for prisoners waiting transfer to their final stations—there are ten, with accommodation for 7150; with two for political convicts (at Mtsensk and Vyshniy-Volochok), with accommodation for 140. No less than 112,638 prisoners passed through these prisons in 1883, and from these figures alone it is easy to conceive the overcrowding. Then come the *ispravitelnyia arestantskiya otdeleniya*, or houses of correction, which are military organizations for the performance of compulsory labour, and which are worse than the hard-labour prisons in Siberia, though they are nominally a lighter punishment. Of these there are 33, with accommodation for 7136 (9609 inmates in 1879). In this category must be included also the 13 "houses of correction:" two large ones with accommodation for 1120 (962 in 1879), and 11 smaller ones for 435. These prisons, however, cannot receive all condemned to this kind of punishment, so that 10,000 men condemned to it remain in the lock-ups. The hard-labour cases are provided for in 17 "central prisons." Of these, there are seven in Russia, with accommodation for 2745; three in Western Siberia, with accommodation for 1150; two in Eastern Siberia, with accommodation for 1650; and one on Sakhalin Island, with accommodation for 600 (1103 inmates in 1879, 802 on January 1st, 1884). No less than 15,444 convicts were kept in these prisons in 1883. Other hard-labour convicts—10,424 in number—are distributed among the Government mines, gold-washings, and factories in Siberia; namely, at the Kara gold-washings, where there are 2000; at the Troitsk, Ust-Kut, and Irkutsk salt-works, at the Nikolayevsk and Petrovsk iron-works, at a prison at the former silver-works of Akatui, and on the Sakhalin Island. Finally, hard-labour convicts were farmed out, a few years ago, to private owners of gold-washings in Siberia, but this system has been abandoned of late. The severity of the punishment can thus be varied *ad infinitum*, according to the wish of the authorities and to that degree of revenge which is deemed appropriate.

The great majority of our prisoners (about

100,000) are persons awaiting trial. They may be recognized for innocent; and in Russia, where arrests are made in the most haphazard way, three times out of ten their innocence is patent to everybody. We learn, in fact, from the annual report of the Ministry of Justice for 1881, that of 98,544 arrests made during that year, only 49,814 cases—that is, one half —could be brought before a court, and that among these 16,675 were acquitted. More than 66,000 persons were thus subjected to arrest and imprisonment without having any serious charge brought against them; and of the 33,139 who were convicted and converted into "criminals," a very large proportion (about 15 per cent.) are men and women who have not complied with passport regulations, or with some other vexatious measure of our Administration. It must be noted that all these prisoners, three-quarters of whom are recognized as innocent, spend months, and very often years, in the provincial lock-ups, those famous *ostrogs* which the traveller sees at the entrance of every Russian town. They lie there idle and hopeless, at the mercy of a set of omnipotent gaolers, packed like herrings in a cask, in rooms of inconceivable foulness, in an atmosphere that sickens, even to insensibility, any one entering directly from the open air, and which is charged with the emanations of the horrible *parasha*— a basket kept in the room to serve the necessities of a hundred human beings.

In this connection I cannot do better than quote a few passages from the prison experiences of my friend Madame C——, *née* Koutouzoff, who has committed them to paper and inserted them in a Russian review, the *Obscheye Dyelo*, published at Geneva. She was found guilty of opening a school for peasants' children, independently of the Ministry of Public Instruction. As her crime was not penal, and as, moreover, she was married to a foreigner, General Gourko merely ordered her to be sent over the frontier. This is how she describes her journey from St. Petersburg to Prussia. I shall give extracts from her narrative without comment, merely premising that its accuracy, even to the minutest detail, is absolutely unimpeachable :—

"I was sent to Wilno with fifty prisoners— men and women. From the railway station we were taken to the town prison and kept there for two hours, late at night, in an open yard, under a drenching rain. At last we were pushed into a dark corridor and counted. Two soldiers laid hold on me and insulted me shamefully. I was not the only one thus outraged, for in the darkness I heard the cries of many desperate women besides. After many oaths and much foul language, the fire was lighted, and I found myself in a spacious room in which it was impossible to take a step in any direction without treading on the women who were sleeping on the floor. Two women who occupied a bed took pity on me, and invited me to share it with them. . . . When I awoke next morning, I was still suffering from the scenes of yesterday; but the female prisoners—assassins and thieves—were so kind to me that by-and-by I grew calm. Next night we were 'turned out' from the prison and paraded in the yard for a start, under a heavy rain. I do not know how I happened to escape the fists of the gaolers, as the prisoners did not understand the evolutions and performed them under a storm of blows and curses; those who protested—saying that they ought not to be beaten —were put in irons and sent so to the train, in the teeth of the law which says that in the cellular waggons no prisoner shall be chained.

"Arrived at Kovno, we spent the whole day in going from one police-station to the other.

In the evening we were taken to the prison for women, where the lady-superintendent was railing against the head-gaoler, and swearing that she would give him bloody teeth. The prisoners told me that she often kept her promises of this sort. . . . Here I spent a week among murderesses, thieves, and women arrested by mistake. Misfortune unites the unfortunate, and everybody tried to make life more tolerable for the rest; all were very kind to me and did the best to console me. On the previous day I had eaten nothing, for the day the prisoners are brought to the prison they receive no food; so I fainted from hunger, and the prisoners gave me of their bread and were as kind as they could be; the female inspector, however, was on duty: she was shouting out such shameless oaths as few drunken men would use. . . . After a week's stay in Kovno, I was sent on foot to the next town. After three days' march we came to Mariampol; my feet were wounded, and my stockings full of blood. The soldiers advised me to ask for a car, but I preferred physical suffering to the continuous cursing and foul language of the chiefs. All the same, they took me before their commander, and he remarked that I had walked three days and so could walk a fourth. We came next day to Wolkowysk, from whence we were to be sent on to Prussia. I and five others were put provisionally in the depôt. The women's department was in ruins, so we were taken to the men's.... I did not know what to do, as there was no place to sit down, except on the dreadfully filthy floor: there was even no straw, and the stench on the floor set me vomiting instantly. ... The water-closet was a large pond; it had to be crossed on a broken ladder which gave way under one of us and plunged him in the filth below. I could now understand the smell: the pond goes under the building, the floor of which is impregnated with sewage.

"Here I spent two days and two nights, passing the whole time at the window.... In the night the doors were opened, and, with dreadful cries, drunken prostitutes were thrown into our room. They also brought us a maniac; he was quite naked. The miserable prisoners were happy on such occurrences; they tormented the maniac and reduced him to despair, until at last he fell on the floor in a fit and lay there foaming at the mouth. On the third day, a soldier of the depôt, a Jew, took me into his room, a tiny cell, where I stayed with his wife.

... The prisoners told me that many of them were detained 'by mistake' for seven and eight months awaiting their papers before being sent across the frontier. It is easy to imagine their condition after a seven months' stay in this sewer without a change of linen. They advised me to give the gaoler money, as he would then send me on to Prussia immediately. But I had been six weeks on the way already, and my letters had not reached my people.... At last, the soldier allowed me to go to the post-office with his wife, and I sent a registered letter to St. Petersburg." Madame C—— has influential kinsfolk in the capital, and in a few days the governor-general telegraphed for her to be sent on instantly to Prussia. "My papers (she says) were discovered immediately, and I was sent to Eydtkunen and set at liberty."

It must be owned that the picture is horrible. But it is not a whit overcharged. To such of us Russians as have had to do with prisons, every word rings true and every scene looks normal. Oaths, filth, brutality, bribery, blows, hunger—these are the essentials of every *ostrog* and of every depôt from Kovno to Kamchatka, and from Arkhangel to Erzerum. Did space permit, I might prove it with a score of such stories.

Such are the prisons of Western Russia. They are no better in the East and in the South. A person who was confined at Perm wrote to the *Poryadok* :—" The gaoler is one Gavriloff ; . . . beating 'in the jaws' (*v mordu*), flogging, confinement in frozen black-holes, and starvation—such are the characteristics of the gaol. . . . For every complaint the prisoners are sent ' to the bath' (that is, are flogged), or have a taste of the black-hole. . . . The mortality is dreadful." At Vladimir, there were so many attempts at escape that it was made the subject of a special inquiry. The prisoners declared that on the allowance they received it was utterly impossible to keep body and soul together. Many complaints were addressed to headquarters, but they all remained unanswered. At last the prisoners complained to the Moscow Superior Court; but the gaoler got to hear of the matter, instituted a search, and took possession of the document. It is easy to imagine that the mortality must be immense in such prisons; but, surely, the reality surpasses all that might be imagined.

The hard-labour department of the civil

prison at Perm was built in 1872 for 120 inmates. But by the end of the same year it received 240 prisoners, of whom 90 Circassians —some of those poor victims of the Russian conquest who cannot support the rule of the Cossack whip, revolt against it, and are deported by hundreds to Siberia. This prison consists of three rooms, one of which, for instance—27 feet long, 19 feet wide, and 10 feet high—contained thirty-one inhabitants. The overcrowding was the same in the other two rooms, so that the average space was from 202 to 260 cubic feet per each man; that is, let me explain, as if a man were compelled to live in a coffin 8 feet long, 6 feet wide, and 5 feet high. No wonder that the prisoners could not live in such confinement and died. Thus, from the end of 1872 to April 15, 1874, 377 Russians and 138 Circassians entered the prison; they were compelled to live there in dreadful humidity, terrible damp and cold, without anything of the nature of a blanket; and they died in the proportion of 90 Russians and 86 Circassians in the space of fifteen months; that is, twenty-four per cent. of the Russians and sixty-two per cent. of the Circassians, not to speak, of course, of those who were sent away to die on the route to Siberia. The causes of the deaths were no special epidemics: nothing but scurvy, taking a great variety of forms, very malignant in its character, and often terminating by death.[3]

Surely, no Arctic expedition, recent or remote, has been so fatal as detention in a Russian central prison. As to the Perm depôt prison for convicts sent to Siberia, the same official publication describes it in words hardly credible: it represents it as incomparably worse. The walls are dripping, there is no question of ventilation, and it is commonly so overcrowded that in the summer every inmate has "less than 124 cubic feet (a coffin of eight feet by five and three) to live and breathe in."[4]

As to the first Kharkoff central prison, the chaplain of this prison said in 1868 from the pulpit, and the *Eparchial Gazette* of 1869 reproduced the fact, that in the course of four months, of the 500 inmates of the prison *two hundred died from scurvy*. Things were not better in the Byelgorod prison. Out of 330 inmates who

[3] There is no need to travel to Siberia to ascertain these facts. They are published in an official publication which may be consulted at the British Museum, namely, in the *Journal of Legal Medicine* published by the Medical Department of the Ministry of the Interior, 1874, vol. iii.

[4] Same official publication, vol. iii.

were kept there in 1870, 150 died in the course of the year, and forty-five in the first half of the next year out of the same number of prisoners.[5] At Kieff, the gaol was a sink of typhus fever. In one month in 1881, the deaths were counted by hundreds, and fresh batches were brought in to fill the room of those removed by death. This was in all the newspapers. Only a year afterwards (June 12, 1882), a circular from the Chief Board of Prisons explained the epidemics as follows:—" 1. The prison was dreadfully overcrowded, although it was very easy to transfer many of the prisoners to other prisons. 2. The rooms were very damp; the walls were covered with mildew, and the floor was rotten in many places. 3. The cesspools were in such a state that the ground about them was impregnated with sewage;" and so on, and so on. The Board added that owing to the same foulness other prisons were also exposed to the same epidemics.

[5] Dr. Leontovitch, in *Archiv* of Legal Medicine and Hygiene, for 1871, vol. iii.; and in *Sbornik*, published by the Medical Department of the Ministry of the Interior, 1873, vol. iii., p. 127. Shall I add that both the *Archiv* and *Sbornik* have been suppressed for their *opasnoye napravleniye*, that is, "dangerous direction"? Even official figures are dangerous to the Russian autocracy.

It might be supposed that some improvements have since been made, and the recurrence of such epidemics prevented. At least, the official publication of the Statistical Committee for 1883 would support such a supposition.[6] There remains, however, some doubt as to the accuracy of its figures. Thus, in the three provinces of Perm, Tobolsk, and Tomsk, we find only an aggregate of 431 deaths reported in 1883 among prisoners of all categories. But if we revert to another publication of the same Ministry—the Medical Report for 1883—we find that 1017 prisoners died same year in the hospitals of the prisons of the very same three provinces.[7] And even in 1883, although no special epidemics are mentioned this year, the mortality at the two Kharkoff central prisons appears to have been 104 out of 846 inmates, that is, 123 in the thousand; and the same report states that scurvy and typhus continued their ravages in most Russian prisons, and especially on the way to Siberia.

The chief prison in St. Petersburg, the so-

[6] *Sbornik Svyedeniy po Rossii* for 1883. St. Petersburg, 1886.

[7] *Otchot Medicinskago Departamenta* for 1883. St. Petersburg, 1886.

called " Litovskiy Zamok," is cleaner; but this old-fashioned, damp, and dark building should simply be levelled to the ground. The common prisoners have a certain amount of work to do. But the political ones are kept in their cells in absolute idleness; and some friends of mine— the heroes of the trial of the hundred and ninety-three who had two years and more of this prison—describe it as one of the worst they know. The cells are very small, very dark, and very damp; and the gaoler Makaroff was a wild beast pure and simple. The consequences of solitary confinement in this prison I have described elsewhere. It is worthy of notice that the common allowance for food is seven kopeks per day, and ten kopeks for prisoners of privileged classes, the price of black rye bread being four kopeks a pound.

But the pride of our authorities—the show-place for the foreign visitors—is the new " House of Detention" at St. Petersburg. It is a " model prison"—the only one of its kind in Russia—built on the plan of the Belgian gaols. I know it from personal experience, as I was detained there for three months, before my transfer to the lock-up at the Military Hospital. It is the only clean gaol for common prisoners in Russia. Clean it certainly is. The scrubbing-brush is never idle there, and the activity of broom and pail is almost demoniac. It is an exhibition, and the prisoners have to keep it bright. All the morning long do they sweep, and scrub, and polish the asphalte floor; and dearly have they to pay for the shine upon it. The atmosphere is loaded with asphaltic particles (I made a paper-shade for my gas, and in a few hours I could draw patterns with my finger in the dust with which it was coated); and this you have to breathe. The three upper stories receive all the exhalations of the floors below, and the ventilation is so bad that in the evenings, when all doors are shut, the place is literally suffocating. Two or three special committees were appointed one after the other to find out the means of improving the ventilation; and the last one, under the presidency of M. Groth, Secretary of State, reported in June, 1881, that to be made habitable, the whole building (which has cost twice as much as similar prisons in Belgium and Germany) must be completely rebuilt, as no repairs, however thorough, could make the ventilation tolerable. The cells are ten feet long and five feet wide; and at one time the prison rules obliged us to keep open the traps in our doors to the end that we might not be asphyxiated where we sat. Afterwards the rule was cancelled, and the traps were shut, and we were compelled to face as best we could the effects of a temperature that was sometimes stiflingly hot and sometimes freezing. But for the greater activity and life of the place, I should have regretted, all dark and dripping as it was, my casemate in the fortress of Peter and Paul—a true grave, where the prisoner for two, three, five years, hears no human voice and sees no human being, excepting two or three gaolers, deaf and mute when addressed by the prisoners. I shall never forget the children I met one day in the corridor of the House of Detention. They also, like us, were awaiting trial for months and years. Their greyish-yellow, emaciated faces, their frightened and bewildered looks, were worth whole volumes of essays and reports "on the benefits of cellular confinement in a model prison." As for the administration of the House of Detention, sufficient to say that even the Russian papers talked openly of the way in which the prisoners' allowances were sequestrated; so that in 1882, a committee of inquiry was appointed, when it was found that the facts were even darker than had been reported. But all this is a trifle, indeed, in comparison with the treatment of prisoners. Here it was that General Trepoff ordered Bogoluboff to be flogged because he did not take his hat off on meeting the omnipotent satrap, had the prisoners who protested in their cells knocked down and beaten, and afterwards confined several of them—for five days— in cells by the washing-rooms, among excrements, and in a temperature of 110° Fahr. (45° Celsius). In the face of these facts, what pitiful irony is conveyed in an English panegyrist's admiring remark:—" Those who wish to know what Russia *can* do, ought to visit this House of Detention"! All that Imperial Russia really *can* do, is to build prisons where the prisoners are robbed, or flogged by madmen, and edifices which must be rebuilt five years after their construction.

The great variety of punishments inflicted under our penal code may be divided broadly into four categories. The first is that of hardlabour, with the loss of all civil rights. The convict's property passes to his heirs; he is dead in law, and his wife can marry another; he may be flogged with rods, or with the *plète* (cat-o'-nine-tails) *ad libitum* by each drunken gaoler. After having been kept to hard-labour in the Siberian mines, or factories, he is settled for life somewhere in the country. The second category is that of compulsory colonization, accompanied by a complete or partial loss of civil rights, and is equivalent to Siberia for life. The third category deals with all convicts condemned to compulsory labour in the *arrestantskiya roty*, without loss of civil rights. The fourth—omitting much of less importance—consists of banishment to Siberia, without trial, and by order of the Executive merely, for life, or for an undetermined period.

Formerly, the hard-labour convicts were sent straight off to Siberia: to the mines belonging "to the Cabinet of the Emperor"—which are, in other words, the private property of the Imperial family. Some of these, however, got worked out; others were found (or represented) as so unremunerative in the hands of the Crown administration that they were sold to private persons who made fortunes with them; and Russia in Europe was compelled to take charge of her hard-labour cases herself. A few central prisons were therefore built in Russia, where convicts are kept for a time (one-third to one-fourth of their sentence) before being sent to Siberia or Sakhalin. Society at large is of course inclined to regard hard-labour convicts as the worst of criminals. But in Russia this is very far from being the case. Murder, robbery, burglary, forgery, will all bring a man to hard labour; but so, too, will an attempt at suicide; so will "sacrilege and blasphemy," which usually mean no more than dissent; so will "rebellion" —or rather what is called rebellion in Russia—which is mostly no more than common disobedience to authorities; so will any and every sort of political offence; and so will "vagrancy," that mostly means escape from Siberia. Among the murderers, too, you will find not only the professional shedder of blood —a very rare type with us—but men who have taken life under such circumstances as, before a jury, or in the hands of an honest advocate, would have ensured their acquittal. In any case, only 30 per cent. or so of the 2000 to 2500 men and women yearly sent down to hard-labour are condemned as assassins. The rest—in nearly equal proportions—are either " vagrants " or men and women charged with one of the just-mentioned minor offences.

The Central Prisons were instituted with the idea of inflicting a punishment of the severest type. The idea was—there can, I am afraid, be no doubt about it—that you could not take too little trouble with convicts, nor get rid of them too soon. To this end these prisons were provided with such gaolers and keepers— mostly military officers—as were renowned for cruelty; and these ruffians were gifted with full power over their charges, and with full liberty of action, and had orders to be as harsh as possible. The end to which they were appointed has been magnificently attained: the Central Prisons are so many practical hells: the horrors of hard-labour in Siberia have paled before them, and all those who have experience of them are unanimous in declaring that the day a prisoner starts for Siberia is the happiest of his life.

Exploring these prisons as a "distinguished visitor," you will, if you are in search of emotions, be egregiously disappointed. You will see no more than a dirty building, crammed with idle inmates lounging and sprawling on the broad, inclined platforms which run round the walls, and are covered with nothing but a sheet of filth. You may be permitted to visit a number of cells for "secret" or political cases; and if you question the inmates, you will certainly be told by them that they are "quite satisfied with everything." To know the reality, one must oneself have been a prisoner. Records of actual experience are few; but they exist, and to one of the most striking I propose to refer. It was written by an officer who was condemned to hard labour for an assault committed in a moment of excitement, and who was pardoned by the Tsar after a few years' detention. His story was published in a Conservative review (the *Russkaya Ryech*, for January, 1882), at a time, under Loris-Melikoff's administration, when there was much talk of prison reform and some liberty in the press; and there was not a journal that did not recognize the unimpeachable veracity of this tale. The experience of our friends wholly confirms it.

There is nothing uncommon in the account of the material circumstances of life in this Central Prison. They are in some sort invariable all over Russia. If we know that the gaol was built for 250 inmates, and actually contained 400, we do not need to inquire more about sanitary conditions. In like manner, the food was neither better nor worse than elsewhere. Seven kopeks (1¾d.) a day is a very poor allowance per prisoner, and the gaoler and bursar being family men, of course they save as much as they can. A quarter of a pound of black rye bread for breakfast; a soup made of bull's heart and liver, or of seven pounds of meat, twenty pounds of waste oats, twenty pounds of sour cabbage, and plenty of water—many Russian prisoners would consider it as an enviable food. The moral conditions of life are not so satisfying. All day long there is nothing to do—for weeks, and months, and years. There are workshops, it is true; but to these only skilled craftsmen (whose achievements are the prison-keeper's perquisite) are admitted. For the others there is neither work, nor hope of work—unless it is in stormy weather, when the governor may set one half of them to shovel the snow into heaps, and the other half to shovel it flat again. The blank monotony of their lives is only varied by chastisement. In the particular prison of which I am writing, the punishments were varied and ingenious. For smoking, and minor offences of that sort, a prisoner could get two hours of kneeling on the bare flags, in a spot—the thoroughfare of icy winter winds—selected diligently *ad hoc*. The next punishment for the same minor offences was the blackholes—the warm one, and the cold one underground with a temperature at freezing-point. In both, prisoners slept on the stones, and the term of durance depended on the will of the governor.

" Several of us " (says our author) " were kept there for a fortnight; after which some were literally *dragged out* into daylight and then dismissed to the land where pain and suffering are not." Is it any wonder that during the four years over which the writer's experience extended, the average mortality in the prison should have been thirty per cent. per annum? "It must not be thought " (the writer goes on to say) " that those on whom penalties of this sort were inflicted were hardened desperadoes; we incurred them if we saved a morsel of bread from dinner for supper, or if a match was found on a prisoner." The insubordinate were treated after another fashion. One, for instance, was kept for nine months in solitary confinement in a dark cell—originally intended for cases of ophthalmia—and came out all but blind and mad. There is worse to follow.

"In the evening" (he continues) "the governor went his rounds and usually began his favourite occupation—flogging. A very narrow bench was brought out, and soon the place resounded with shrieks, while the governor, smoking a cigar, looked on and counted the lashes. The birch-rods were of exceptional size, and when not in use were kept immersed in water to make them more pliant. After the tenth lash the shrieking ceased, and nothing was heard but groans. Flogging was usually applied in batches, to five, ten men, or more, and when the execution was over, a great pool of blood would remain to mark the spot. Our neighbours without the walls used at these times to pass to the other side of the street, crossing themselves in horror and dread. After every such scene we had two or three days of comparative peace; for the flogging had a soothing influence on the governor's nerves. He soon, however, became himself again. When he was very drunk, and his left moustache was dropping and limp, or when he went out shooting and came home with an empty bag, we knew that that same evening the rods would be set to work." After this it is unnecessary to speak about many other revolting details of life in the same prison. But there is a thing that foreign visitors would do well to lay to heart.

"On one occasion" (the writer says) "we were visited by an inspector of prisons. After casting a look down the scuttle, he asked us if our food was good? or was there anything of which we could complain? Not only did the inmates declare that they were completely satisfied, they even enumerated articles of diet which we had never so much as smelt. This sort of thing" (he adds) "is only natural. If complaints were made, the inspector would lecture the governor a little and go away; while the prisoners who made them would remain behind and be paid for their temerity with the rod or the black-hole."

The prison in question is close by St. Petersburg. What more remote provincial prisons are like, my readers may imagine. I have mentioned above those of Perm and Kharkoff; and, according to the *Golos*, the Central Prison at Simbirsk is a centre of peculation and thievery. In only two of the central prisons, namely at Wilno and Simbirsk, the inmates are occupied with some useful work. At Tobolsk, the authorities, being at their wits' end how to occupy the inmates, discovered a law of March 28th, 1870, which ordered the prisoners to be occupied in the removal of sand, stones, or cannon-balls from one place to another, and from there back again; and they acted accordingly for some time, in order to give some exercise to the inmates, and prevent the spreading of scurvy. As to the other hard-labour prisons, with the exception of some book-binding, or some repairs made by a few prisoners, the great bulk spent their life in absolute idleness. "All these prisoners are in the same abominable state as those of the old time," writes a Russian explorer.[8]

One of the worst of the hard-labour prisons was that of Byelgorod, in the province of Kharkoff, and it was there that the political prisoners condemned to hard-labour were detained in 1874 to 1882, before being sent to Siberia. The first three batches of our friends —those of the Dolgushin and Dmohovsky trial, the trial of the fifty at Moscow, and that of the hundred and ninety-three at St. Petersburg,— were sent to that prison. The most alarming reports were in circulation about this grave,

[8] Mr. Tahlberg, in the St. Petersburg review, the *Vyestnik Evropy*, May, 1879.

where seventy prisoners were buried without being allowed to have any intercourse of any kind with the outer world, and without any occupation. They had mothers, sisters, who, undaunted by repeated refusals, never ceased to apply to all who had any authority at St. Petersburg, to obtain permission to see—were it only for a few minutes—their sons, or their brothers. It was known through the Byelgorod people that the treatment of the prisoners was execrable; from time to time it was reported that somebody had died, or that another had gone mad; but that was all. State secrets, however, cannot be kept *ad infinitum.* The time came when one mother obtained permission to see her son, once a month, for one hour, in the presence of the governor of the prison, and she did not hesitate to live under the walls of the prison for the sake of these short and rare interviews with her son. And then, came the year 1880, when it was discovered at St. Petersburg (after the explosion at the Winter Palace) that it was no longer possible to torture political prisoners at Byelgorod, and to refuse them the right they had acquired to be transported to a hard-labour prison in Siberia. So, in October, 1880, thirty of our comrades were transported from Byelgorod to Mtsensk. It was found that they could not bear the long journey to the Nertchinsk mines, and they were brought to Mtsensk, to recover a little strength. Then the truth came out. Reports about the confinement at Kharkoff were published in the Russian revolutionary papers, and partially penetrated also the press of St. Petersburg; written accounts of the life at Byelgorod were circulated. It then became known that the prisoners had been kept for three to five years in solitary confinement, and in irons, in dark, damp cells that measured only ten feet by six; that they lay there absolutely idle, absolutely isolated from any intercourse with human beings. The daily allowance of the Crown being five farthings a day, they received only bread and water, and thrice or four times a week a small bowl of warm soup, with a few grits mixed with every kind of rubbish. Ten minutes' walk in the yard each second day, was all the time allowed to breathe fresh air. No bed, no sort of pillow, nothing whatever to cover them; for the rest, they slept on the bare floor, with some of their clothes put under their heads, wrapped in the prisoner's grey cloak. Unbearable loneliness, absolute silence; no occupation of any kind! It was only after three whole years of such confinement that they were allowed to have some books.

Knowing by two years and a half of personal experience what solitary confinement is, I do not hesitate to say that, as practised in Russia, it is one of the cruellest tortures man can suffer. The prisoner's health, however robust, is irreparably ruined. Military science teaches that in a beleaguered garrison which has been for several months on short rations, the mortality increases beyond measure. This is still more true of men in solitary confinement. The want of fresh air, the lack of exercise for body and mind, the habit of silence, the absence of those thousand and one impressions, which, when at liberty, we daily and hourly receive, the fact that we are open to no impressions that are not imaginative—all these combine to make solitary confinement a sure and cruel form of murder. If conversation with neighbour prisoners (by means of light knocks on the wall) is possible, it is a relief, the immensity of which can be duly appreciated only by those who have been condemned for one or two years to absolute separation from all humanity. But it is also a new source of suffering, as very often your own moral sufferings are increased by those you experience from witnessing day by day the growing madness of your neighbour, when you perceive in each of his messages the dreadful images that beset and overrun his tormented brain. That is the kind of confinement to which political prisoners are submitted when awaiting trial for three or four years. But it is still worse after the condemnation, when they are brought to the Kharkoff Central Prison. Not only the cells are darker and damper than elsewhere, and the food is worse than common; but, in addition, the prisoners are carefully maintained in absolute idleness. No books, no writing materials, and no implements for manual labour. No means of easing the tortured mind, nor anything on which to concentrate the morbid activity of the brain; and, in proportion as the body droops and sickens, the spirit becomes wilder and more desperate. Physical suffering is seldom or never insupportable; the annals of war, of martyrdom, of sickness abound in instances in proof. But moral torment—after years of infliction—is utterly intolerable. This our friends have found to their cost. Shut up in the fortresses and houses of detention first of all, and afterwards in the central prisons, they go rapidly to decay, and either go calmly to the grave, or become lunatics. They do not go mad as, after being outraged by gendarmes, Miss M——, the promising young painter, went mad. She was bereft of reason instantly; her madness was simultaneous with her shame. Upon them insanity steals gradually and slowly: the mind rots in the body "from hour to hour."

In July, 1878, the life of the prisoners at the Kharkoff prison had become so insupportable, that six of them resolved to starve themselves to death. For a whole week they refused to eat, and when the governor-general ordered them to be fed by injection, such scenes ensued as obliged the prison authorities to abandon the idea. To seduce them back to life, officialism made them certain promises: as, for instance, to allow them walking exercise, and to take the sick out of irons. None of these promises were kept. It was only later on, when several had died, and two went mad (Plotnikoff and Bogoluboff), that the prisoners obtained the privilege of sawing some wood in the yard, in company with two Tartars, who understood not a word of Russian. Only after obstinate demands for work, after weeks spent in black-holes for that obstinacy, they obtained some work in the cells by the end of the third year of their detention.

In October, 1880, a first party of thirty prisoners, condemned mostly in 1874, was sent to the Mtsensk depôt before being despatched to Siberia. They were followed in the course of the winter by forty more of their comrades, from the hundred and ninety-three. All were destinated for the Kara gold-mines in Neztchinsk. They knew well the fate that was reserved for them, and still the day they left the Byelgorod hell was considered as a day of deliverance. After the Central Prison, hard labour in Siberia looks like a paradise.

I have before me an account written by a person who was allowed to visit one of the prisoners at the Mtsensk depôt, and I never saw anything more touching than this plain tale. It was written under the fresh impression of interviews at Mtsensk with a beloved being recovered after many years of disappearance from the world; and with a forgiving heart the writer consecrates but a few lines, a dozen or so, to the horrors that had been suffered at Byelgorod. "I shall not insist on these horrors"—it stands in the account—" because

I am eager to tell what has been a warm ray of light in the great darkness of the prisoners' life," and pages are filled in describing in detail the joy of the short interviews at Mtsensk with those who for so many years had been buried alive.

"Old and young people, parents, wives, sisters and brothers, all were coming to Mtsensk from different parts of Russia, from different classes of society; the common joy of the interviews and the common sorrow of parting had united them into one great family. . . What a dear, precious time it was!"

"What a dear, precious time it was!"— What a depth of sorrow appears in this exclamation coming from the very heart of the writer, when one knows that the interviews were interviews with prisoners who were going to leave Russia for ever, who had a journey of more than four thousand miles before them, who had to be transported for ever to the land of sorrow—Siberia! "What a dear, precious time it was!" And my informant minutely describes the interviews; the supplies of food they brought to the prisoners to invigorate them after a six years' seclusion, the tools to give them some distraction; the tidy preparations for the long journey through Siberia; the padding they were manufacturing to prevent the chains from wounding the ankles of those five who had to perform the whole of the journey in irons; and finally, the sight of a long row of carts, with two prisoners and two gendarmes in each, which took them away to the next railway station, and the sorrow of parting with beloved beings, none of whom have yet returned, while so many have died either on the journey or in Siberian gaols, and so many again have put an end to their lives from sheer despair of ever seeing the day of liberation. . . .

The above fully shows what the common-law prisons in Russia are. More pages could be filled with like descriptions, more separate gaols could be described, it would be a mere repetition. New and old prisons are alike. The whole of our penal institutions is described in one sentence of that record of prison-life on which I have already drawn so much:—

"In conclusion," writes the author, "I must add that the prison now rejoices in another governor. The old one quarrelled with the treasurer on the subject of peculation from the prisoners' allowance, and in the end they were both dismissed. The new governor is not such a ruffian as his predecessor; I understand, however, that with him the prisoners are starved far more than formerly, and that he is in the habit of giving full play to his fists on the countenances of his charges."

This remark sums up the whole "Reform of Prisons" in Russia. One tyrant may be dismissed, but he will be succeeded by some one as bad, or even worse, than himself. It is not by changing a few men, but only by changing completely from top to bottom the whole system, that any amelioration can be made; and such is also the conclusion of a special committee recently appointed by the Government. But it would be mere self-delusion to conceive improvement possible under such a *régime* as we now enjoy. At least half a dozen commissions have already gone forth to inquire, and all have come to the conclusion that unless the Government is prepared to meet extraordinary expenses, our prisons must remain what they are. But honest and capable men are far more needed than money, and these the present Government cannot and will not discover. They exist in Russia, and they exist in great numbers; but their services are not required. There was, for instance, one honest man,

Colonel Kononovitch, chief of the penal settlement at Kara. Without any expense to the Crown, M. Kononovitch had repaired the weatherworn, rotten buildings, and had made them more or less habitable; with the microscopic means at his disposal, he contrived to improve the food. But the praise of an occasional visitor of the Kara colony, together with like praise contained in a letter intercepted on its way from Siberia, were sufficient reasons for rendering M. Kononovitch suspicious to our Government. He was immediately dismissed, and his successor received the order to reintroduce the iron rule of past years. The political convicts, who enjoyed a relative liberty after the legal term of imprisonment had expired, were put in irons once more; not all, however, as two have preferred to kill themselves; and once more affairs are ordered as the Government desires to see them. Another gentleman in Siberia, General Pedashenko, has been dismissed too, for refusing to confirm a sentence of death which had been passed by a military tribunal on the convict Schedrin, found guilty of striking an officer for insulting two of his fellow-sufferers, MM. Bogomolets and Kovalsky.

It is everywhere the same. To devote oneself to any educational work, or to the convict population, is inevitably to incur dismissal and disgrace. Near St. Petersburg we have a reformatory—a penal settlement for children and growing lads. To the cause of these poor creatures a gentleman named Herd—grandson of the famous Scotchman employed by Alexander I. in the reform of our prisons—had devoted himself body and soul. He had an abundance of energy and charm; his whole heart was in the work; he might have rivalled Pestalozzi. Under his ennobling influence boy-thieves and ruffians, penetrated with all the vices of the streets and the lock-ups, learned to be men in the best sense of the word. To send a boy away from the common labour-grounds or from the classes was the greatest punishment admitted in this penal colony, which soon became a real model colony. But men like Herd are not the men our Government is in need of. He was dismissed from his place, and the institution he ruled so wisely has become a genuine Russian prison, complete even to the rod and the black-hole.

These examples are typical both of what we have to suffer and of what we have to expect. It is a fancy to imagine that anything could be reformed in our prisons. Our prisons are the reflection of the whole of our life under the present *régime;* and they will remain what they are now until the whole of our system of government and the whole of our life have undergone a thorough change. Then, but only then, "Russia may show what it *can* realize;" but this, with regard to crime, would be—I hope—something quite different from what is now understood by the name of "a good prison."

CHAPTER III.

THE FORTRESS OF ST. PETER AND ST. PAUL.

No Autocracy can be imagined without its Tower or its Bastille. The St. Petersburg Autocracy is no exception to the rule, and it has its Bastille in the Petropavlovskaya Fortress. This fortress, unlike the Bastille of Paris, has nothing particularly gloomy in its outer aspect, nothing striking. Its low granite bastions facing the Neva have a modern appearance; it contains the Mint, a cathedral where the Emperors and their families are buried, several buildings occupied by engineers and military, extensive arsenals in the new Cronwerk in the north; and the ordinary street traffic passes through it in the day-time.

But a sensation of horror is felt by the inhabitants of St. Petersburg as they perceive on the other side of the Neva, opposite the Imperial palace, the grey bastions of the fortress; and gloomy are their thoughts as the northern wind brings across the river the

The Fortress of St. Peter and St. Paul. 85

discordant sound of the fortress-bells which every hour ring their melancholy tune. Tradition associates the sight and the name of the fortress with suffering and oppressions. Thousands—nay, scores of thousands of people, chiefly Little Russians, died there, as they laid the foundations of the bastions on the low, marshy island of Jäni-saari. No remembrance of glorious defence is associated with it; nothing but memories of suffering inflicted upon the foes of Autocracy.

It was there that Peter I. tortured and mutilated the enemies of the Imperial rule which he tried to force upon Russia. There he ordered the death of his son Alexis—if he did not kill him with his own hands, as some historians say. There, too, during the reign of the Empresses, the omnipotent courtiers sent their personal rivals, leaving it an open question in so many families whether their relatives had been drowned in the Neva or remained buried alive in some stone cellar. There the heroes of the first and only attempt at revolution in St. Petersburg, the Decembrists, were confined—some of them, like Batenkoff, remaining there for twelve whole years. There Karakozoff was tortured and hanged—almost a corpse, hardly showing any signs of life when he was brought to the scaffold. And since that time a whole generation of men and women, inspired with love for their oppressed people, and with ideas of liberty filtrating in from the West, or nursed by old popular traditions, have been detained there, some of them disappearing within the fortress for ever, others ending their life on its glacis, or within its walls, on the gallows; while hundreds have left those mute walls for secret transportation to the confines of the snow-deserts of Siberia—a whole generation in which the hopes of literary and scientific Russia were bound up—suppressed, annihilated, for no purpose! How many are in the fortress still? What is the lonely, disheartening existence they still drag out there? What will become of them? .... Nobody can answer these questions; and a kind of superstitious fear attaches itself to the huge mass of stone-work over which the Imperial banner floats. It is the Bastille—the last stronghold of Autocracy.

The fortress covers more than 300 acres with its six bastions and six courtines, two ravelins, and the wide red-brick cronwerk erected by Nicholas I. on the north. It has,

The Fortress of St. Peter and St. Paul. 87

within its enclosure, plenty of all kinds of accommodation for all kinds of prisoners. Nobody, except the commander of the place, knows all of them.[1]

There is a lofty three-storied building, which

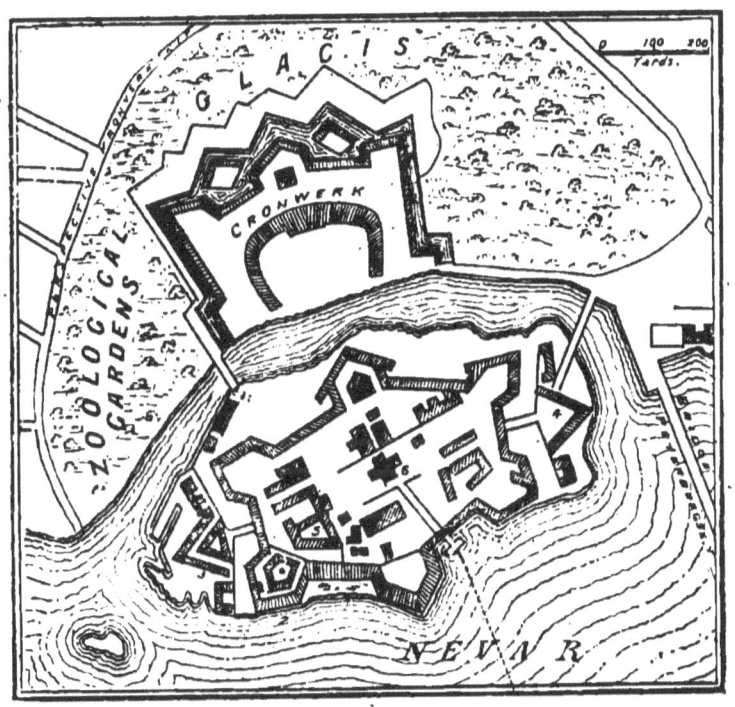

PLAN OF THE FORTRESS OF ST. PETER AND ST. PAUL.

1. Courtine of Catherine.
2. Trubetskoi Bastion.
3. Trubetskoi Ravelin.
4. Alexeyevskiy Ravelin.
5. The Mint.
6. Cathedral.

[1] For those who are unacquainted with fortress terminology the following explanations may be useful. Each fortress has the shape of a polygon. At the protruding angles are *bastions*, that is, pentagonal spaces enclosed

once obtained the nickname of "St. Petersburg Imperial University," because hundreds of students were marched there, between two files of bayonets, after the disorders at the University in 1861. Scores of young men were kept there for months before they were transported to "more or less remote provinces of the Empire," and saw their scientific career destroyed for ever by this "measure of the Emperor's clemency."

There is again the Courtine of Catherine which faces the Neva, under whose wide embrasures graceful flowering bushes grow at the foot of the granite walls, between two bastions. It is there that Tchernyshevsky wrote in 1864 his remarkable novel "What is to be done?" which is just now stirring the hearts of the Socialist youth of America, and in Russia

between two long and two short walls, and having sometimes a second interior building—the *reduct*—this last being a two-storied pentagonal suite of vaulted casemates, intended for the defence of the bastion when its outer wall is already damaged. Each two bastions are connected by a *courtine*. The courtine and the two interior angles of the bastions being the weakest parts of the fortifications, they are often masked by a triangular fortification made outside the fortress proper (but enclosed within the same glacis) – the *ravelin*. The St. Petersburg fortress has but two ravelins; the Trubetskoi in the west, and the Alexeievskiy in the east.

made a revolution in the relations of the students and the women who were striving for their right to knowledge. From the depth of a casemate in the Courtine, Tchernyshevsky taught the young men to see in woman a comrade and a friend—not a domestic slave—and his lesson has borne its fruits.

It was there again that, a few years later, Dmitri Pissareff was imprisoned for having taken up the same noble work. Compelled to abandon it in the fortress, he did not lie idle: he wrote his remarkable analysis of the "Origin of Species," one of the most popular, and surely the most attractive ever penned. Two great talents were thus destroyed precisely as they were reaching their full growth. Tchernyshevsky was sent to Siberia, where he was kept for twenty years, in the mines first, and then, for thirteen years, in Viluisk, a hamlet of a few houses situated on the confines of the Arctic region. A petition for release, signed by an International Literary Congress, produced no effect. The Autocrat was so much afraid of the influence Tchernyshevsky might enjoy in Russia, that he permitted him to return from Siberia and to be settled at Astrakhan, only when he had no more to fear from his noble pen : when the writer was a ruin after a twenty years' life of privation and sufferings among semi-savages. There was a simulacrum of judgment passed upon Tchernyshevsky : his writings, all of which had passed through the hands of the Censorship, his novel written in the fortress, were brought forward as so many proofs of guilt before the Senate. Pissareff was not even brought before a court: he was merely kept in the fortress until reported harmless . . . . He was drowned a few months after his release.

In the years 1870 and 1871 a great number of young men and women were kept in the Courtine in connection with the circles of Netchaieff—the first which dared to say : " Be the people!" and induced the youth of Russia to go and spread Socialism whilst living the life of the people itself. But soon, that is, in 1873, a new, wider and safer prison—the Trubetskoi bastion—was opened within the fortress ; and since that time the Courtine of Catherine has become a military prison for St. Petersburg officers condemned to " detention in fortresses" for breaches of discipline. Its wide and lofty casemates have been rebuilt, decorated and rendered more or less comfortable. Being in connection with the Trubetskoi bastion, where political prisoners are kept whilst awaiting trial, it is there that a few of them are indulged by an occasional interview with kinsfolk. Special Commissions nominated for preliminary inquiries into State affairs, sometimes have their sittings in the same Courtine, extorting information from the prisoners which may guide them in their researches. Political prisoners are no longer lodged there, and Solovioff, who was hanged in 1879, seems to have been the last "political" in the Courtine. Some inmates of the Trubetskoi bastion are, however, still occasionally taken there for a few days, in order to be secluded from their comrades for some unknown purpose. One instance in point within my knowledge, is that of Saburoff. He was secluded in the Courtine, to be stupefied by drugs, that he might be photographed . . . . So he was told, at least, when he returned to consciousness. At any rate, the Courtine of Catherine is no longer a prison for "politicals." The Trubetskoi bastion, close by, was rebuilt for that purpose in 1872, and began to receive inmates from the end of 1873.

There, the "politicals" are kept now for

two, three years, awaiting the decisions of secret Commissions which may send them before a court, or despatch them to Siberia without ever bringing them before any judge.

The Trubetskoi bastion, where I spent more than two years, is no longer enveloped in the mystery which clothed it in 1873, when it was first made use of as a House of Preliminary Detention for political prisoners. The seventy-two cells where the prisoners are kept occupy the two stories of the *reduct*—a pentagonal building with a yard within, one of the five faces of which is occupied by the apartment of the governor of the bastion and the guard-room for the military post. These cells are large enough, each of them being a vaulted casemate, destined to shelter a big fortress gun. They measure eleven paces (about twenty-five feet) on the diagonal, and so I could regularly walk every day seven versts (about five miles) in my cell, until my forces were broken by the long imprisonment.

There is not much light in them. The window, which is an embrasure, is nearly of the same size as the windows in other prisons. But the cells occupy the interior enclosure of the bastion (that is, the *reduct*), and the high wall of the bastion faces the windows of the cells at a distance of fifteen to twenty feet. Besides, the walls of the reduct, which have to resist shells, are nearly five feet thick, and the light is intercepted by a double frame with small apertures, and by an iron grate. Finally, everybody knows that the St. Petersburg sky is anything but bright. Dark they are;[2] still, it was in such a cell—the lightest of the whole building —that I wrote my two volumes on the Glacial Period, and, taking advantage of brighter summer days, I prepared there the maps that accompany the work and made drawings. The lower story is very dark, even in summer. The outer wall intercepts all the light, and I remember that even during bright days writing was very difficult. In fact, it was possible only when the sun's rays were reflected by the upper part of both walls. All the northern face of the reduct is very dark in both stories.

The floor of the cells is covered with a painted felt, and the walls are double, so to say; that is, they are covered also with felt, and, at a

[2] The cells in common prisons—those, for instance, of the prison of Lyons, in France—although having windows of the same size, cannot be compared for brightness with those of the fortress.

distance of five inches from the wall, there is an iron-wire net, covered with rough linen and with yellow painted paper. This arrangement is made to prevent the prisoners from speaking with one another by means of taps on the wall. The silence in these felt-covered cells is that of a grave. I know cells in other prisons. Outer life and the life of the prison reach one by thousands of sounds and words exchanged here and there. Although in a cell, one still feels oneself a part of the world. The fortress is a grave. You never hear a sound, excepting that of a sentry continually creeping like a hunter from one door to another, to look through the "Judas" into the cells. You are never alone, as an eye is continually kept upon you, and still you are always alone. If you address a word to the warder who brings you your dress for walking in the yard, if you ask him what is the weather, he never answers. The only human being with whom I exchanged a few words every morning was the Colonel who came to write down what I had to buy—tobacco or paper. But he never dared to enter into any conversation, as he himself was always watched by some of the warders. The absolute silence is interrupted only by the bells of the clock, which play each quarter of an hour a *Gospodi pomilui*, each hour the canticle *Kol slaven nash Gospod v Sionye*, and each twelve hours *God save the Tsar* in addition to all this. The cacophony of the discordant bells is horrible during rapid changes of temperature, and I do not wonder that nervous persons consider these bells as one of the plagues of the fortress.

The cells are heated from the corridor outside by means of large stoves, and the temperature is kept exceedingly high, in order to prevent moisture from appearing on the walls. To keep up such a temperature, the stoves are very soon shut, whilst the coal is still blazing, so that the prisoner is usually asphyxiated with oxide of carbon. Like all Russians, I was accustomed to keep a high temperature, of 61° to 64° Fahrenheit, in my room. But I could not support the high temperature of the fortress, and still less the asphyxiating gases; and, after a long struggle, I obtained that my stove should not be shut up very hot. I was warned that the walls would be immediately covered with moisture; and, indeed, they soon were dripping in the corners of the vault; even the painted paper of the front wall was as wet as if water were continually poured on it. But, as there was no other choice than between dripping walls and extenuation by a bath-like temperature, I chose the former, not without some inconvenience for the lungs, and not without acquiring rheumatism. Afterwards I learned that several of my friends who were kept in the same bastion expressed the firm conviction that some mephitic gas was sent into their cells. This rumour is widely spread, and has also reached foreigners at St. Petersburg; and it is the more remarkable as nobody has expressed the suspicion of having been poisoned otherwise; for instance, by means of the food. I think that what I have just said explains the origin of the rumour; in order to keep the stoves very hot for twenty-four hours, they are shut up very soon, and so the prisoners are asphyxiated every day, to some extent, by oxide of carbon. Such was, at least, my explanation of the suffocation which I experienced nearly every day, followed by complete prostration and debility. I did not notice it again after I had finally succeeded in preventing the hot-air conduct to my cell from being opened at all.

The food, when General Korsakoff was Commandant of the fortress, was good; not very substantial, but very well cooked; afterwards it became much worse. No provisions from without are allowed, not even fruits—nothing but the *calatchi* (white bread) which compassionate merchants distribute in the prisons at Christmas and Easter—an old Russian custom existing until now. Our kinsfolk could bring us only books. Those who had no relatives were compelled to read over and over again the same books from the fortress library, which contains the odd volumes left there by several generations since 1826. As to breathing fresh air, it is obvious that it could not be allowed to a great amount. During the first six months of my confinement I walked half-an-hour or forty minutes every day; but later on, as we were nearly sixty in the bastion, and as there is but one yard for walking, and the darkness, under the sixtieth degree of latitude, comes at 4 p.m. in the winter, we walked but twenty minutes each two days in the summer, and twenty minutes twice a week during the winter. I must add also that, owing to the heavy white smoke thrown off by the chimney of the Mint which overlooks the yard, this walk was completely poisoned during easterly winds. I could not endure on such occasions the continual coughing of the soldiers, exposed throughout the day to breathe these gases, and asked to be brought back to my cell.

But all these are mere details, and none of us have complained much about them. We know perfectly well that a prison is a prison, and that the Russian Government was never gentle with those who attempted to shake off its iron rule. We know, moreover, that the Trubetskoi bastion is a palace—a true palace—in comparison with those prisons where a hundred thousand of our people are locked up every year, and submitted to the treatment I have described in the foregoing pages.

In short, the material conditions of detention in the Trubetskoi bastion are not exceedingly bad, although very hard, in any case. But half of the prisoners kept there have been arrested on a simple denunciation of a spy, or as acquaintances of revolutionists; and half of them, after having been kept for two or three years, will not even be brought before a court; or, if brought, will be acquitted—as was the case in the trial of the hundred and ninety-three—and thereupon sent to Siberia or to some hamlet on the shores of the Arctic Ocean, by a simple order of the administration. The inquiry is pursued in secrecy, and nobody knows how long it will last; which law will be applied (the common or the martial); what will be the fate of the prisoner;—he may be acquitted, but also he may be hung. No counsel is allowed during the inquiry; no conversation nor correspondence with relatives about the circumstances which led to the arrest. During all this exceedingly long time, no occupation is allowed to prisoners. Pen, ink, and lead-pencils are strictly prohibited in the bastion; only a slate is allowed; and when the Council of the Geographical Society asked for me the permission to finish a scientific work, it had to obtain it from the Emperor himself. As to working-men and peasants, who cannot read throughout the day, to keep them for years without any occupation is merely to bring them to despair. Therefore the great proportion of cases of insanity. In all West-European prisons it is considered that two or three years of cellular confinement is too much, and there is great danger of becoming insane. But in Europe the convict does some manual work in his cell; not only can he read and write, but he receives all necessary implements for carrying on some trade. He is not reduced to live exclusively on the activity of his own imagination;

the body, the muscles, are also occupied. And yet competent persons are compelled, by painful experience, to consider two or three years of cellular confinement as too dangerous. In the Trubetskoi bastion the only occupation allowed is reading; and even this occupation is refused to convicts who are kept in another part of the fortress.

The few liberties given now as to the visits of relatives have been acquired only after a hard struggle. Formerly, the visit of a relation was considered as a great favour, and not as a right. It happened to me once, after the arrest of my brother, to see none of my kinsfolk for three months. I knew that my brother, to whom I was more closely bound than is usually the case between two brothers, was arrested: a letter of a few lines announced to me that for everything concerning the publication of my work I must address myself to another person, and I guessed the cause. But during three months I did not know why he was arrested; of what he was accused; what would be his fate. And I certainly wish nobody in the world to have such a three months in his life as these three which I passed without having any news from the outer world. When I was allowed to see my sister, she was severely admonished that if she said to me anything about my brother, she would be never allowed to see me again. As to my comrades, very many saw nobody during all the two or three years of their detention. Many had no near relations in St. Petersburg, and friends were not admitted; others had kinsfolk, but these last were suspected of having themselves acquaintances with Socialist or Liberal circles, and that was sufficient to deny them the favour of seeing their arrested brother or sister. In 1879 and 1880 the visits of relatives were allowed each fortnight. But it ought to be mentioned how an extension of the right was acquired. It was won, so to say, by fight; that is, by the famous famine strike, during which a number of prisoners in the Trubetskoi bastion refused to take any food for five or six days, and resisted by force all attempts to feed them by means of injections and the blows of the warders by which this operation was accompanied. Of late, these rights have been again taken away; the visits are very scarce, and iron-rule has been re-introduced again.

The worst is, however, the manner in which secret inquiries are conducted,—the most shameful proceedings being resorted to, in order to extort some uncautious avowal from those who have shown a nervous temper. My friend Stepniak has given several instances of such treatment, and the various issues of the *Will of the People* contain many others. Nothing—not even the feeling of a mother—is respected. If a mother has a new-born child—a little creature born in the darkness of a casemate—the baby will be taken away from her, and retained as long as the mother refuses to be " more sincere," that is, refuses to betray her friends. She must refuse food for several days, or attempt suicide, to have her baby back. . . . When such horrible deeds can be perpetrated, what is the use of speaking of minor tortures ? And still, the worst is reserved for those who are abroad at liberty—for those who are guilty of loving their imprisoned daughter, their brother, or their sister ! The basest kinds of intimidation —the most refined and cruel—are used with regard to them by the hirelings of the Autocracy, and I must confess that the educated procureurs in the service of the State Police used to be much worse in this matter than the officers of the gendarmerie or of the Third Section.

Of course, attempts at suicide—sometimes by

means of a piece of glass taken from a broken window, sometimes by means of matches carefully concealed for whole months, or sometimes by means of strangulation with a towel, are the necessary consequences of such a system. Out of the hundred and ninety-three, nine went mad, eleven attempted suicide. I knew one of them after his release. He has made—he said to me— at least half-a-dozen such attempts: he is now dying in a French hospital.

And yet, when I remember the floods of tears shed throughout Russia, in each remotest village, in connection with our prisons; when I remember the horrors of our ostrogs and central prisons; the salt-works of Ust-kut or the gold-mines of Siberia, my pen hesitates to dwell upon the sufferings of a few revolutionists. When I wrote about Russian prisons, I hastened to tell what is the real state of those prisons where thousands of people are groaning every day in the hands of omnipotent wild beasts. I hardly mentioned the state of political prisoners, only alluding to it as far as was necessary to show the development of the struggle that is going on now in Russia. Were it not for the praise bestowed on the Russian Government by its few—very few—admirers,

I even should not write at all about political prisons. But, as the facts have been misrepresented, let them be known as they are.

There is a much harder fate in store for political prisoners in Russia, than that of the inmates of the Trubetskoi bastion. After the "Trial of the Sixteen" (November, 1880), Europe learned with satisfaction that, out of five condemned to death, three had had their sentences commuted by the Tsar. We now know what commutation means. Instead of being sent to Siberia, or to a Central Prison, according to law, they were immured in cells of the Trubetskoi ravelin, in the west of the Petropavlovskaya fortress.[3] These are so dark that candles are burnt in them for twenty-two hours out of the twenty-four. The walls are literally dripping with damp, and "there are pools of water on the floor." "Not only books are disallowed, but everything that might help to occupy the attention. Zubkovsky made geometrical figures with his bread, to repeat geometry; they were immediately taken away, the gaoler saying that hard-labour convicts

---

[3] The authentic record of their imprisonment was published in the *Will of the People*, and reproduced in the publication *Na Rodinye* ("At Home").

were not permitted to amuse themselves." To render solitary confinement still more insupportable, a gendarme and a soldier are stationed within the cells. The gendarme is continually on the watch, and if the prisoner looks at anything or at any point, he goes to see what has attracted his attention. The horrors of solitary confinement are thus aggravated tenfold. The quietest prisoner soon begins to hate the spies set over him, and is moved to frenzy. The slightest disobedience is punished by blows and black holes. All who were subjected to this *régime* fell ill in no time. After less than one year of it, Shiryaeff had become consumptive; Okladsky—a robust and vigorous working man, whose remarkable speech to the Court was reproduced by the London papers, had gone mad; Tikhonoff, a strong man likewise, was down with scurvy, and could not sit up in his bed. By a mere commutation of sentence, the three were brought to death's door in a single year. Of the other five condemned to hard labour, and immured in the same fortress, two —Martynovsky and Tsukermann—went mad, and in that state were constantly black-holed, so that Martynovsky at last attempted suicide.

Others besides were sent to the same ravelin,

and the result was invariably the same: they were brought to the edge of the grave. During the summer of 1883, the Government decided to accord some of them the grace of a hard-labour prison in Siberia. On July 27th (August 8th), 1883, they were brought in cellular waggons to Moscow, and two persons who witnessed their arrival have left a description of it. Voloshenko, covered with scorbutic wounds, could not move. He was brought out of the waggon on a hand-barrow. Pribyleff and Fomin fainted when they were carried into the open air. Paul Orloff, also broken down by scurvy, hardly could walk. "He is all curved, and one leg is quite turned," says the witness. "Tatiana Lebedeva had been condemned to twenty years' hard labour. But she surely will not live so long. Scurvy has destroyed all her gums; the jaws are visible beneath; besides, she is in an advanced stage of consumption. . . . Next came Yakimova with her eighteen months' old baby: every minute it seemed that the baby would die in her arms. As to herself, she did not suffer much, neither physically nor morally. As usual, she was quite calm, notwithstanding her condemnation to hard labour for life. The remainder were strong enough to walk by themselves from one waggon to another. . . . As to Mirsky, the four years' sojourn in the fortress has left no traces on him; he only has reached his maturity."[4] True that he was then only twenty-three years old.

But—how many of those tried at the same time were missing! How many have been buried in the Trubetskoi ravelin? Since direct communication has been interrupted, nothing has transpired of what is happening in the ravelin; and the worst rumours—rumours of a most abominable outrage—circulate at St. Petersburg as to the conditions which brought about the death of Ludmila Terentieva.

Is this all? No! There is something worse still. There are the *oubliettes* of the Alexis ravelin. Four years ago, when Mr. Lansdell, after having been admitted to look into two cells of the Trubetskoi *bastion*, boldly denied the very existence of the half underground cells in the Trubetskoi *ravelin*, described in the *Times*, and triumphantly exclaimed:— "What, then, have become of the *cachots* and *oubliettes* and dismal chambers which have been

[4] *Vyestnik Narodnoi Voli*, No. 3, 1884, p. 180. Stepniak's " Russia under the Tsars," ch. xix.

connected with the 'Peter and Paul' by so many?" I replied then in the following lines:—
" I should not deny the existence of *oubliettes* (in the fortress), as I know that even in our times people disappear in Russia without anybody knowing where they are concealed. I take one instance—Netchaieff. He killed a spy at Moscow, fled to Switzerland, and his extradition was accorded by the Federal Council on the distinct understanding with the Russian Government to treat him as a common-law-prisoner, and not as a political adversary. He was condemned by a jury at Moscow to hard labour, and, after having been ill-treated there in the way I have described elsewhere, he disappeared. According to law he ought to be now at Kara, or at Sakhalin, or at any hard-labour colony in Siberia. But we know that in 1881 he was at none of these places. Where is he then? Last year the rumour was current that he had managed to make his escape from the fortress, but it has not been confirmed since; and I have some reasons to suppose that he was, two years ago, and may be still, in some part of the fortress. I do not say he is ill-treated there: I suppose, on the contrary, that, like all other political prisoners, he won

at last the sympathies of his jailors, and I hope that he is kept in a decent cell. But he has the right to be now in Siberia, and to be enjoying a relative liberty in the Kara village, close by the mines. He has also kinsfolk and friends, who surely would be happy to learn, at least, if he is in life, and where he is. And I ask the author of the report: Is he sufficiently sure of his informants to authorize us to write to Netchaieff's friends that there are no *oubliettes* in the fortress, and that they must search for their friend elsewhere?"[5]

Of course, the above question remained unanswered. But, since that time the Russian Government has itself avowed the existence of *oubliettes* in the fortress, leaving it to its English supporters to explain the contradiction as they like. It has condemned soldiers for carrying letters from these very same *oubliettes* of the Alexis ravelin!

In 1882, eighteen soldiers who used to keep guard in the Alexis ravelin were committed for trial before a Court-martial, together with a medical student, Dubrovin.[6] The soldiers were accused of having carried secret correspondence

[5] *Nineteenth Century*, June, 1883.
[6] Their names and the condemnations are given in Appendix.

between three persons detained in the ravelin and the student Dubrovin. The act of accusation, signed by the military procureur, Colonel Masloff, has been published in full,[7] and the condemnations have been announced in the St. Petersburg press. It appears from the official document brought before the Court-martial, that there were, in 1881, four persons detained in the ravelin. They are not named; the procureur designates them under the names of prisoners occupying the cells No. 1, No. 5, No. 6, and No. 13. Until November, 1879—the accusation states—there were only two state prisoners in the ravelin—in cell No. 5 and in cell No. 6. In November a third prisoner was brought and confined in cell No. 1, and next year (November 19th, 1880), a fourth, who was confined in cell No. 13. This last—it appears from the same document—was Shiryaeff. The soldiers had conversations "of criminal intent" with prisoner No. 5; they carried letters between prisoners Nos. 1, 5, and 13, and since the arrival of this last, they began to carry out letters from the ravelin to the student Dubrovin, and smuggled in, on return, periodical

[7] *Vyestnik Narodnoi Voli*, vol. i., November, 1883.

publications, letters, and money, which they remitted to the three prisoners.

The "conversations of criminal intent" which the soldiers carried on with prisoner No. 5 are related in the accusation exactly as the soldiers described them during the inquiry; and it appears that they had accurately committed them to memory. "There will be a time— No. 5 said—when the peasants will be no longer so oppressed as they are now. The Tsars will govern no more; but instead of them there will be responsible representatives. If the Tsar be good, he may be kept; if not—another will be elected in his place," and so on.

No. 5—we know now—was nobody else but Netchaieff. When publishing this most remarkable document, the *Will of the People* published also some of the letters received by the Executive Committee from Netchaieff. It is, therefore, no secret that, although the Imperial Government when demanding the extradition of Netchaieff had given the formal assurance to the Swiss Republic that he would be treated as a common-law convict, the assurance was a lie. Netchaieff never was treated as a common-law convict. The Moscow Court condemned him to hard-labour, not to detention in the fortress. But he was *not* sent either to Siberia, or to any hard-labour prison. Immediately after the condemnation he was simply immured in the Alexis ravelin, and has remained there since 1874. The official document of accusation directly calls him a state prisoner "*gosudarstvennyi prestupnik.*"

What was the fate of Netchaieff in the ravelin?—It became known that the Government twice made him the proposal "to tell everything,"—once through the medium of Count Levashoff, and another time through General Potapoff. He refused indignantly. The proposal of Potapoff was made in such terms that Netchaieff answered the great Satrap of Alexander II. by a blow in the face. He was dreadfully beaten for that, chained hand and foot, and riveted to the wall of his casemate. By the end of 1881, he had written in his own blood with his nail, a letter to Alexander III.—a most modest letter— merely stating the facts of his imprisonment, and asking the Emperor whether his terrible fate was known by the Monarch and prescribed by his own will? This letter, a copy of which was communicated by Netchaieff to the Executive Committee, and which was printed later on in the *Will of the People*, was entrusted by the captive to some of those persons who walked under his window when repairs were made in the ravelin—the commander of the fortress never coming to see Netchaieff, and he being sure that the governor of the ravelin never would deliver the letter to his superiors.

Since the summer of 1882, no direct news has been received from Netchaieff. A rumour only was afloat that in December, 1882, he lost his temper with the governor of the ravelin, and was dreadfully beaten—" may be flogged,"—and that a few days later he committed suicide, or died. The only thing certain was that on December 5th, or 8th (old style), one of the captives detained in the ravelin died. The Executive Committee considered Netchaieff as dead, and published by the end of 1883 extracts from his letters. But he may be still alive.

As to Shiryaeff, he died on September 28th, 1881. When the captives were deprived of the short walk, formerly allowed; when their windows were shut up with planks (after Netchaieff's letter), and even the hot-air openings of the stoves were shut up, consumption rapidly developed in the poor young man. Netchaieff wrote that he died in a strange state of excitement, and supposed that his death had been accelerated by some exciting drug, in order to obtain avowals.—Why not? They gave drugs to Saburoff to send him to sleep—"in order to photograph him" they said. But, are we sure,—is Saburoff himself sure—that what they gave him contained nothing but chloroform or laudanum? Those who so carefully conceal their deeds *must* do something they dare not to avow publicly.

But—who are the prisoners No. 1 and No. 6? No. 1 must be a Terrorist. As to No. 6, who did not exchange letters with the three others, he is known now through Netchaieff's letters. He is Shevitch, an officer of the Military Academy, reduced to madness, whose insane talk and shrieks are heard in the night by those who pass by the walls of the ravelin. What is his crime? He never was tried in any political trial. He did not belong to any revolutionary organization; he is unknown to revolutionists. What is his crime? The *Will of the People* says that Netchaieff wrote that once, during a military parade, Shevitch left the ranks, addressed Alexander II. in a rough language, reproaching him for his conduct with regard to Shevitch's sister. Is it so? Or, has he committed some other crime to call down upon himself so base a revenge from Alexander II. as to immure him for ever in a cell of the ravelin?—I do not know. But Shevitch's story must be known in St. Petersburg, and surely it will transpire some time. One thing is, however, certain: Shevitch was *not* a political offender, he has not been mixed up with *any* political affair since 1866. He has been brought to madness in the *oubliette* of the Alexis ravelin for some other offence.

Are the *oubliettes* of the Alexis ravelin the only ones in Russia?—Surely not. Who knows how many like *oubliettes* there are in other fortresses? At any rate we know now—it has been openly avowed—that there are other *oubliettes* in the Empire, namely at the Solovetsky monastery, situated on an island of the White Sea.

In 1882, we read with immense pleasure in the St. Petersburg newspapers that one of those who had been kept in such an *oubliette for fifteen years* was at last set at liberty. I mean Pushkin. In 1858 he came to the conclusion that the orthodox religion is not in accordance with truth. He explained his ideas in a book and in schematic drawings, went to St. Petersburg in 1861 and 1863, and asked the Church authorities to publish his work.—" The world," he said, " is rotten in its sins; Christ has not saved it completely, and a new Messiah will come." For these ideas he was arrested in 1866, and sent, between two gendarmes, to the Solovetsky prison—of course without having seen, or heard of, a judge. There he was put in a dark and damp cell, and kept therein for fifteen years. He has a wife; she was not admitted to see him during fourteen years, that is, until 1881. Loris-Melikoff—when nominated Dictator after the explosion of the Winter Palace—granted her the permission. Until then Pushkin was kept as a state prisoner in the greatest secrecy. Nobody was allowed to enter his cell during all this time, excepting the archimandrite of the monastery, and Mr. H. Dixon. M. Prougavin, who is an official of the staff of the Governor of Arkhangelsk, visited him in 1881. Pushkin was fifty-five years old when M. Prougavin saw him, and he said, " I do not know what are my faults; how can I exculpate myself? They say to me: 'Go to church, abandon your heresy, and you will be free.' But how can I do it? I have sacrificed everything for my convictions—my fortune, the happiness of my own family, my own life. Can I abjure my convictions? Time will show if I am right, and I hope so. But if I am wrong, if it only seems to me to be the truth, then let this prison be my grave!" In 1881 his wife was admitted to see him, and thence she went directly to St. Petersburg to ask for his release. By this time M. Prougavin had published all this awful story in a review, and in newspapers. The press called for clemency, and Pushkin was pardoned; but he had been kept for fifteen years in an *oubliette*.[8]

Is Pushkin the sole person who has been so tortured? I do not think so. Some fifteen years ago a German geologist, a friend of mine, discovered an artillery officer in the same condition as Pushkin. We made all kinds of applications at St. Petersburg to influential persons, in order to obtain his release. A Grand Duchess was interested in the fate of this ex-officer. We obtained nothing, and

---

[8] Let those who will not fail to express "a doubt" about this story, read M. Prougavin's paper in the November number of the Panslavist review *Russkaya Mysl* for 1881, his papers in the *Golos* of the same epoch, the *Moscow Telegraph* of November 15, 1881, and so on.

probably he is still in an *oubliette*, if the prison has not been his grave.

A strange fate, however, has attached itself of late to the *oubliettes* of the Russian Government. In times past, when somebody had entered the vaulted archway of the fortress in company with two gendarmes, he disappeared. Ten, twenty years would pass before anything was heard of him, except such news as circulated in great secrecy among a few kinsfolk. As to those who had the misfortune of being sent to the Alexis ravelin, the Autocrats were sure that nothing would ever oose through its walls as to their fate. Things have changed now; and the change is perhaps one of the best illustrations of how the *prestige* of Autocracy fades away. As the numbers of foes of the existing *régime* grew, people were sent to the fortress in such great numbers that it became materially impossible to bury them alive there, like their predecessors. Autocracy itself was compelled to make concessions to public opinion, and found it impossible to execute, or to transport for ever to Siberia all those who had been imprisoned in the fortress. Some of them, at least, were transported to "less remote parts of the Empire"—the peninsula of Kola, for instance—and thence they managed to escape. One of these has told in the European press the story of his imprisonment.[9] Moreover, the fortress itself ceased to keep it secret. The suite of cells in the Trubetskoi bastion had been built in 1873. I was among the first who inaugurated its occupation early in 1874. Then, the bastion was a grave. Nothing but rigorously supervised letters could be brought out of it. There were only six of us occupying thirty-six cells in the upper story, and four or five empty cells separated us from each other. Five soldiers mounted guard in the corridor, so that nearly each one of us had a soldier at his door, and each soldier was closely watched by freshly nominated subalterns, who kept an eye upon the soldiers with all the zeal of novices. No communication whatever was possible between us; still less with the outer world. The system was just introduced, and worked admirably: mutual spying was as perfect as in a Jesuit monastery.

But two years had hardly elapsed, before the system disintegrated. In some unknown ways, the revolutionists were found informed

[9] Pavlovsky, in a series of articles published by the Paris *Temps*, with a preface of Turgueneff.

about what was going on in the Trubetskoi bastion. The fortress kept no more secrets. The severest measures were taken with regard to the few interviews granted. By the end of 1875, we were prevented from approaching our kinsfolk who came to see us : the colonel in command of the bastion, and a gendarme officer placed between us. Later on, I was told that iron-gratings and other "last words of civilization" were introduced. But it was all useless, and my friend Stepniak says that piles of clandestine letters have been received since from the bastion.

A new suite of cells which had received no inmates for many years, was opened then,—the *ispytatelnyia kamery* of the Trubetskoi ravelin. There—the Government supposed—its enemies might be buried alive, and nobody would learn their fate. But letters managed to penetrate the thick walls of the ravelin: they were published. One of the most secure parts of the fortress thus yielded its secrets. And later on, some of those who had been imprisoned there, finally saw the daylight. It is most probable that the first idea of the Government was to keep them immured in the ravelin throughout the twelve or twenty years they were condemned to—perhaps for life. But again, so many people were sent to the terrible ravelin, and there they died, or went mad, so rapidly, that the original scheme was abandoned, and after having been brought to the edge of the grave, some of them were sent to Siberia.

But there were still in the fortress a series of *oubliettes* which had remained sealed, whence no news of any kind had ever transpired since they were erected. I speak, of course, of the Alexis ravelin,—the State prison *par excellence*, —the mute witness of so many abominations. Everybody at St. Petersburg knows this terrible name. It was considered as the safest burial-place, and only two men were kept there. But, we have seen that as soon as they were four, instead of two, the ravelin, too, began to betray its secrets. The soldiers who kept the guard in the ravelin were condemned. But— who would swear that new soldiers nominated in their place would not also carry letters from the ravelin?

Then, the Government of Alexander III. reverted to another tradition of the reign of Paul I. Paul I.'s palace at Gatchina, with its secret doors, traps, concealed flights of steps leading up to watch-towers and down to subterranean corridors, had once more become the favourite residence of the Emperor. Why, then, not revert also to Paul I.'s favourite prison at Schlüsselburg?

It is forty miles distant from St. Petersburg, at the head of the Neva, where it issues from Lake Ladoga—a bare fortress on a lonely island. It is surrounded but by a small and desolate town, all the inhabitants of which can be easily watched, and years may pass before the revolutionists find a way to force the fortress and to penetrate with their propaganda into the place. So we learned that the Russian Government—so poor that it cannot spare some odd ten thousand roubles for the repair of the foul and dilapidated prisons of Kara—has spent a hundred and fifty thousand roubles in arranging a new State prison at Schlüsselburg, and that the most energetic revolutionists condemned to hard-labour will be sent there. The new prison ought to be a palace; but certainly the money has been spent less in accommodations for prisoners than in arrangements for closely watching them, and preventing any communication with the outer world.

Who has been sent there? We know a dozen names, but how many more are there

—nobody knows. What will be their fate there?—nobody knows. Will they be drowned there? Maybe! Will they be shot one after the other "for breaches of discipline," like Minakoff, or like Colonel Aschenbrenner who was "pardoned" and sent to Schlüsselburg, and there—shot in secrecy! Or, will they be left quietly to die from scurvy or consumption? Maybe also. But nobody knows as yet what is the fate of the Schlüsselburg prisoners. Concealed by the thick walls of the fortress, the courtiers can do there what their masters order—until a Russian Fourteenth of July comes to sweep away all the rottenness of a decaying institution.[1]

[1] Reprinted from the *Nineteenth Century*, by permission.

CHAPTER IV.

OUTCAST RUSSIA.

The Journey to Siberia.[1]

SIBERIA—the land of exile—has always appeared in the conceptions of the Europeans as a land of horrors, as a land of the chains and *knoot*, where convicts are flogged to death by cruel officials, or killed by overwork in mines; as a land of unutterable sufferings of the masses and of horrible prosecutions of the foes of the Russian Government. Surely nobody, Russian or foreigner, has crossed the Ural Mountains and stopped on their water-divide, at the border-pillar that bears the inscription "Europe" on one side, and "Asia" on the other, without shuddering at the idea that he is entering the land of woes. Many a traveller has certainly said to himself that the inscription of Dante's

[1] Reprinted from the *Nineteenth Century*, by permission.

Inferno would be more appropriate to the boundary-pillar of Siberia than these two words which pretend to delineate two continents.

As the traveller descends, however, towards the rich prairies of Western Siberia; as he notices there the relative welfare and the spirit of independence of the Siberian peasant, and compares them with the wretchedness and subjection of the Russian peasant; as he makes acquaintance with the hospitality of the supposed ex-convicts—the " Siberyaks "—and with the intelligent society of the Siberian towns, and perceives nothing of the exiles, and hears nothing of them in conversations going on about everything but this subject; as he hears the boasting reply of the Eastern Yankee who drily says to the stranger that in Siberia the exiles are far better off than peasants in Russia—he feels inclined to admit that his former conceptions about the great penal colony of the North were rather exaggerated, and that, on the whole, the exiles may be not so unfortunate in Siberia, as they were represented to be by sentimental writers.

Very many visitors to Siberia, and not foreigners alone, have made this mistake. Some occasional circumstance—something like a convoy of exiles met with on the muddy road during an autumn storm, or a Polish insurrection on the shores of Lake Baikal, or, at least, such a rencontre with an exile in the forests of Yakutsk, as Adolf Erman made and so warmly described in his *Travels*—some occasional striking fact, in short, must fall under the notice of the traveller, to give him the necessary impulse for discovering the truth amidst the official misrepresentation and the non-official indifference : to open his eyes and to display before them the abyss of sufferings that are concealed behind those three words : Exile to Siberia. Then he perceives that besides the official story of Siberia there is another sad story, through which the shrieks of the exiles have been going on as a black thread from the remotest times of the conquest until now. Then he learns that, however dark, the plain popular conception of Siberia is still brighter than the horrible naked truth ; and that the horrible tales he has heard long ago, in his childhood, and has supposed since to be tales of a remote past, in reality are tales of what is going on now, in our century which writes so much, and cares so little, about humanitarian principles.

This story already lasts for three centuries.

As soon as the Tsars of Moscow learned that their rebel Cossacks had conquered a new country "beyond the Stone" (the Ural), they sent there batches of exiles; and they ordered them to settle along the rivers and footpaths that connected together the blockhouses erected, in the space of seventy years, from the sources of the Kama to the Sea of Okhotsk. Where no free settlers would settle, the chained colonizers had to undertake a desperate struggle against the wilderness. As to those individuals whom the rising powers of the Tsars considered most dangerous, we find them with the most advanced parties of Cossacks who were sent "across the mountains, in search for new lands." No distance, however immense, no wilderness, however unpracticable, seemed sufficient to the suspicious rule of the *boyars* to be put between such exiles and the capital of the Tsardom. And, as soon as a blockhouse was built, or a convent erected, at the very confines of the Tsar's dominions—beyond the Arctic circle, in the *toundras* of the Obi, or beyond the mountains of Daouria—the exiles were there, building themselves the cells that had to be their graves.

Even now, Siberia is, on account of its steep mountains, its thick forests, wild streams, and rough climate, one of the most difficult countries to explore. It is easy to conceive what it was three centuries ago. Even now it is that part of the Russian Empire where the arbitrariness and brutality of officers are the most unlimited. What was it, then, during the seventeenth century? "The river is shallow; the rafts are heavy; the chiefs are wicked, and their sticks are big; their whips cut through the skin, and their tortures are cruel; fire and strappado; but the men are hungry, and they die, poor creatures, at once after the torture,"—wrote the *protopope* Avvakum, the fanatic priest of the "old religion" whom we met with the first parties going to take possession of the Amor.—"How long, my master, will these tortures last?" asks his wife, as she falls unable to move farther on the ice of the river, after a journey that already has lasted for five years. —"Until our death, my dear; until our death," replies this precursor of the steel-characters of our own times; and both, man and wife, continue their march towards the place where the *protopope* will be chained to the walls of an icy cellar. digged out by his own hands.

Since the beginning of the seventeenth century, the flow of exiles poured into Siberia has never ceased. During the first years of the century, we see the inhabitants of Uglitch exiled to Pelym, together with their bell which rang the alarm when it became known that the young Demetrius had been assassinated by order of the regent Boris Godunoff. Men and bell alike have tongues and ears torn away, and are confined in a hamlet on the borders of the *toundra*. Later on they are followed by the *raskolniks* (nonconformists) who revolt against the aristocratic innovations of Nikon in Church matters. Those who escape the massacres, like that " of the Three Thousand," go to people the Siberian wildernesses. They are soon followed by the serfs who make desperate attempts at overthrowing the yoke freshly imposed on them; by the leaders of the Moscow mob revolted against the rule of the *boyars*; by the militia of the *streltsy* who revolt against the all-crushing despotism of Peter I.; by the Little Russians who fight for their autonomy and old institutions; by all those populations who will not submit to the yoke of the rising empire; by the Poles—by three great and several smaller batches of Poles—who are despatched to Siberia by thousands at once, after each attempt at recovering their independence. . .

Later on, all those whom Russia fears to keep in her towns and villages—murderers and simple vagrants, nonconformists and rebels; thieves and paupers who are unable to pay for a passport; serfs who have incurred the displeasure of their proprietors; and still later on, "free peasants," who have incurred the disgrace of an *ispravnik*, or are unable to pay the ever-increasing taxes—all these are going to die in the marshy lowlands, in the thick forests, in the dark mines. This current flows until our own days, steadily increasing in an alarming proportion. Seven to eight thousand were exiled every year at the beginning of this century; 19,000 to 20,000 are exiled now—not to speak of the years when this figure was doubled, as was the case after the last Polish insurrection—making thus a total of more than 700,000 people who have crossed the Ural Mountains since 1823, when the first records of exile were taken.

Few of those who have endured the horrors of hard labour and exile in Siberia have committed to paper their sad experience. The *protopope* Avvakum did, and his letters still feed the fanaticism of the *raskolniks*. The melancholy story of the Menshikoff, the Dolgorouky, the Biron, and other exiles of high rank have been transmitted to posterity by their sympathizers. Our young republican poet Ryléeff, before being hung in 1827, told in a beautiful poem, " Voinarovsky," the sufferings of a Little Russian patriot. Several memoirs of the "Decembrists" (exiled for the insurrection of December 26th, 1825), and the poem of Nekrasoff, " The Russian Women," are still inspiring the young Russian hearts with love for the prosecuted and hate to the prosecutors. Dostoevsky has told in a remarkable psychological study of prison-life his experience at the fortress of Omsk after 1848; and several Poles have described the martyrdom of their friends after the revolutions of 1831 and 1848. . . But, what are all these pains in comparison with the sufferings endured by half a million of people, from the day when, chained to iron rods, they started from Moscow for a two or three years' walk towards the mines of Transbaikalia until the day when, broken down by hard labour and privations, they died at a distance of 5000 miles from their native villages, in a country whose scenery and customs were as strange to them as its inhabitants—a strong, intelligent but egotistic race!

What are the sufferings of the few, in comparison with those of the thousands under the cat-o'-nine-tails of the legendary monster Rozghildéeff, whose name is still the horror of the Transbaikalian villages; with the pains of those who, like the Polish doctor Szokalsky and his companions, died under the *seventh thousand* of rod strokes for an attempt to escape; with the sufferings of those thousands of women who followed their husbands and for whom death was a release from a life of hunger, of sorrow and of humiliation ; with the sufferings of those thousands who yearly undertake to make their escape from Siberia and walk through the virgin forests, living on mushrooms and berries, inspired with the hope of at least seeing again their native village and their kinsfolk ?

Who has told the less striking, but not less dramatic pains of those thousands who spin out an aimless life in the hamlets of the far north and put an end to their wearisome existence by drowning in the clear waters of the Yenisei? M. Maximoff has tried, in his work on "Hard Labour and Siberia," to raise a corner of the veil that conceals these sufferings; but he has shown only a small corner of the dark picture.

The whole remains, and probably will remain, unknown; its very features are obliterated day by day, leaving but a faint trace in the folklore and in the songs of the exiles; and each decade brings its new features, its new forms of misery for the ever-increasing number of exiles.

It is obvious that I shall not venture to draw the whole of this picture in the narrow limits of these chapters. I must necessarily limit my task to the description of the exile as it is now —say, during the last ten years. No less than 165,000 human beings have been transported to Siberia during this short space of time; a very high figure of criminality, indeed, for a population numbering 80,000,000, if all exiles were "criminals." Less than one half of them, however, crossed the Urals in accordance with sentences of the courts. The others were thrown into Siberia without having seen any judges, by simple order of the Administrative, or in accordance with resolutions taken by their communes—nearly always under the pressure of the omnipotent local authorities. Out of the 151,184 exiles who crossed the Ural during the years 1867 to 1876, no less than 78,676 belonged to this last category. The remaining were condemned by courts: 18,582 to hard labour, and 54,316 to be settled in Siberia, mostly for life, with or without loss of all their civil rights.[2]

[2] Our criminal statistics are so imperfect that a thorough classification of exiles is very difficult. We have but one good work on this subject, by M. Anuchin, published a few years ago by the Russian Geographical Society and crowned with its great gold medal; it gives the criminal statistics for the years 1827 to 1846. However old, these statistics still give an approximate idea of the present conditions, as recent partial statistics has shown that since that time all figures have doubled, but the relative proportions of different categories of exiles have remained nearly the same. Thus, to quote but one instance, out of the 159,755 exiled during the years 1827 to 1846, no less than 79,909, or 50 per cent., were exiled by simple orders of the Administrative; and thirty years later we find again nearly the same rate—slightly increased—of arbitrary exile (78,871 out of 151,184 in 1867 to 1876). The same is approximately true with regard to other categories. It appears from M. Anuchin's researches that out of the 79,846 condemned by courts, 14,531 (725 per year) were condemned as assassins; 14,248 for heavier crimes, such as incendiarism, robbery, and forgery; 40,666 for stealing, and 1426 for smuggling, making thus a total of 70,871 cases (about 3545 per year), which would have been condemned by the Codes—although not always by a jury— of all countries in Europe. The remainder, however (that is, nearly 89,000), were exiled for offences which depended chiefly, if not entirely, upon the political institutions of Russia; their crimes were: rebellion against any serf-proprietors and authorities (16,456 cases); nonconformist fanaticism (2138 cases); desertion from a twenty-five years' military

Outcast Russia. 135

Twenty years ago, the exiles traversed on foot all the distance between Moscow and the place to which they were despatched. They had thus to walk something like 4700 miles in order to reach the hard-labour colonies of Transbaikalia, and 5200 miles to reach Yakutsk. Nearly a two years' walk for the former, and two years' and a half for the second. Some

service (1651 cases); and escape from Siberia, mostly from Administrative exile (18,328 cases). Finally, we find among them the enormous figure of 48,466 " vagrants," of whom the laureate of the Geographical Society says :—" Vagrancy mostly means simply going to a neighbouring province without a passport"—out of 48,466 "vagrants," 40,000 at least, "being merely people who have not complied with passport regulations "—(that is, their wife and children being brought to starvation, they had not the necessary five or ten roubles for taking a passport, and walked from Kalouga, or Tula, to Odessa, or Astrakhan, in search of labour). And he adds :—" Considering these 80,000 exiled by order of the Administrative, we not only doubt their criminality, we simply doubt the very existence of such crimes as those imputed to them." The number of such "criminals" has not diminished since. It has nearly doubled, like other figures. Russia continues to send every year to Siberia, for life, four to five thousand men and women, who in other States would be simply condemned to a fine of a few shillings. To these "criminals" we must add no less than 1500 women and 2000 to 2500 children who follow every year their husbands or parents, enduring all the horrors of a march through Siberia and of the exile.

amelioration has been introduced since. After having been gathered from all parts of Russia at Moscow, or at Nijniy-Novgorod, they are transported now by steamer to Perm, by rail to Ekaterinburg, in carriages to Tumen,[3] and again by steamer to Tomsk. Thus, according to a recent English book on exile to Siberia, they have to walk " only the distance beyond Tomsk." In plain figures, this trifling distance means 2065 miles to Kara, something like a nine months' foot journey. If the prisoner be sent to Yakutsk he has "only" 2940 miles to walk; and, as the Russian Government, having discovered that Yakutsk is a place still too near to St. Petersburg to keep political exiles there, are sending them now to Verkhoyansk and Nijne-Kolymsk (in the neighbourhood of Nordenskjöld's wintering-station), a distance of some fifteen hundred miles must be added to the former "trifling" distance, and we have again the magic figure of 4500 miles—or two years' walk reconstituted in full.

However, for the great mass of exiles, the foot journey has been reduced by one-half, and they begin their peregrinations in Siberia

[3] The railway across the Urals having been opened for traffic, they will be transported by rail.

in special carriages. M. Maximoff has very vividly described how the convicts at Irkutsk, to whose judgment such a moving machine was submitted, declared at once that it was the most stupid vehicle that could be invented for the torment of both horses and convicts. Such carriages, which have no accommodation for deadening the shocks, move slowly on the rugged, jolting road, ploughed over and over by thousands of heavily loaded cars. In Western Siberia, amidst the marshes on the eastern slope of the Ural, the journey becomes a true torture, as the highway is covered with loose beams of wood, which recall the sensation experienced when a finger is dragged across the keys of a piano, the black keys included. The journey is hard, even for the traveller who is lying on a thick felt mattress in a comfortable *tarantass*, and it is easy to conceive what the convict experiences, who is bound to sit motionless for eight or ten hours on the bench of the famous vehicle, having but a few rags to shelter him from snow and rain.

Happily enough this journey lasts but a few days, as at Tumen the exiles are embarked on special barges, or floating prisons, taken in tow by steamers, and in the space of eight or ten days are brought to Tomsk. I hardly need say that, however excellent the idea of thus reducing by one-half the long journey through Siberia, its partial realization has been most imperfect. The convict barges are usually so overcrowded, and are usually kept in such a state of filthiness, that they have become real nests of infection. "Each barge has been built for the transport of 800 convicts and the convoy," wrote the Tomsk correspondent of the *Moscow Telegraph*, on November 15, 1881; "the calculation of the size of the barges has not been made, however, according to the necessary cubical space, but according to the interests of the owners of the steamers, MM. Kurbatoff and Ignatoff. These gentlemen occupy for their own purposes two compartments for a hundred men each, and thus eight hundred must take the room destined for six hundred. The ventilation is very bad, there being no accommodation at all for that purpose, and the cabinets are of an unimaginable nastiness." He adds that "the mortality on these barges is very great, especially among the children," and his information is fully confirmed by official figures published last year in all newspapers. It appears from these figures that eight to ten per cent. of the convict passengers died during their ten days' journey on board these barges; that is, something like sixty to eighty out of eight hundred.

"Here you see," wrote friends of ours who have made this passage, "the reign of death. Diphtheria and typhus pitilessly cut down the lives of adults and children, especially of these last. Corpses of children are thrown out nearly at each station. The hospital, placed under the supervision of an ignorant soldier, is always overcrowded."

At Tomsk the convicts stop for a few days. One part of them—especially the common-law exiles, transported by order of the Administrative—are sent to some district of the province of Tomsk which extends from the spurs of the Altay mountains on the south to the Arctic Ocean on the north. The others are despatched farther towards the east. It is easy to conceive what a hell the Tomsk prison becomes when the convicts arriving every week cannot be sent on to Irkutsk with the same speed, on account of inundations, or obstacles on the rivers. The prison was built to contain 960 souls, but it never holds less than 1300 to 1400, and very often 2200, or more.

One-quarter of the prisoners are sick, but the infirmary can shelter only one-third, or so, of those who are in need of it; and so the sick remain in the same rooms, upon or beneath the same platforms where the remainder are crammed to the amount of three men for each free place. The shrieks of the sick, the cries of the fever-stricken patients, and the rattle of the dying mix together with the jokes and laughter of the prisoners, with the curses of the warders. The exhalations of this human heap mix with those of their wet and filthy clothes and with the emanations of the horrible *Parasha*. "You are suffocated as you enter the room, you are fainting and must run back to breathe some fresh air; you must accustom yourself by-and-by to the horrible emanations which float like a fog on the river" —such is the testimony of all those who have entered unexpectedly a Siberian prison. The "families room" is still more horrible. "Here you see," says a Siberian official in charge of the prisons—M. Mishlo—"hundreds of women and children closely packed together, in such a state of misery as no imagination could picture." The families of the convicts receive no cloth from the State. Mostly peasant women, who, as a rule, never have more than one dress at once; mostly reduced to starvation as soon as their husbands were taken into custody, they have buckled on their sole cloth when starting from Arkhangelsk or Astrakhan, and, after their long peregrinations from one lock-up to another, after the long years of preliminary detention and months of journey, only rags have remained on their shoulders from their weather-worn clothes. The naked emaciated body and the wounded feet appear from beneath the tattered clothes as they are sitting on the nasty floor, eating the hard black bread received from compassionate peasants.

Amidst this moving heap of human beings who cover each square foot of the platforms and beneath them, you perceive the dying child on the knees of his mother, and close by, the new-born baby. The baby is the delight of, the consolation to, these women, each of whom surely has more human feelings than any of the chiefs and warders. It is passed from hand to hand; the best rags are parted with to cover its shivering limbs, the tenderest caresses are for it. . . . How many have grown up in this way! One of them stands by my side as I write these lines, and repeats to me the stories she has heard so many times from her mother about the humanity of the "scelerates" and the infamy of their "chiefs." She describes to me the toys that the convicts made for her during the interminable journey—plain toys inspired by a good-hearted humour, and side by side, the miserable proceedings, the exactions of money, the curses and blows, the whistling of the whips of the chiefs.

The prison, however, is cleared by-and by, as the parties of convicts start to continue their journey. When the season and the state of the rivers permit it, parties of 500 convicts each, with women and children, leave the Tomsk prison every week, and begin their foot journey to Irkutsk and Transbaïkalia. Those who have seen such a party on march will never forget it. A Russian painter, M. Jacoby, has tried to represent it on canvas; his picture is sickening, but the reality is still worse.

You see a marshy plain where the icy wind blows freely, driving before it the snow that begins to cover the frozen soil. Morasses with small shrubs, or crumpled trees, bent down by wind and snow, spread as far as the eye can reach; the next village is twenty miles distant. Low mountains, covered with thick pine forests, mingling with the grey snow-clouds, rise in the dust on the horizon. A track, marked all along by poles to distinguish it from the surrounding plain, ploughed and rugged by the passage of thousands of cars, covered with ruts that break down the hardest wheels, runs through the naked plain. The party slowly moves along this road. In front, a row of soldiers opens the march. Behind them, heavily advance the hard-labour convicts, with half-shaved heads, wearing grey clothes, with a yellow diamond on the back, and open shoes worn out by the long journey and exhibiting the tatters in which the wounded feet are wrapped. Each convict wears a chain, riveted to his ankles, its rings being twisted into rags—if the convict has collected enough of alms during his journey to pay the blacksmith for riveting it looser on his feet. The chain goes up each leg and is suspended to a girdle. Another chain closely ties both hands, and a third chain binds together six or eight convicts. Every false movement of any of the pack is felt by all his chain-companions; the feebler is dragged forward by the stronger, and he must not stop:

the way—the *étape*—is long, and the autumn day is short.

Behind the hard-labour convicts march the *poselentsy* (condemned to be settled in Siberia) wearing the same grey cloth and the same kind of shoes. Soldiers accompany the party on both sides, meditating perhaps the order given at the departure :—" If one of them runs away, shoot him down. If he is killed, five roubles of reward for you, and a dog's death to the dog !" In the rear you discover a few cars that are drawn by the small, attenuated, cat-like, peasant's horses. They are loaded with the bags of the convicts, with the sick or dying, who are fastened by ropes on the top of the load.

Behind the cars hasten the wives of the convicts; a few have found a free corner on a loaded car, and crouch there when unable to move further; whilst the great number march behind the cars, leading their children by the hands, or bearing them on their arms. Dressed in rags, freezing under the gusts of the cold wind, cutting their almost naked feet on the frozen ruts, how many of them repeat the words of Avvakum's wife :—" These tortures, how long will they last ? " In the rear comes a second detachment of soldiers, who drive with the butt-ends of their rifles those women who stop exhausted in the freezing mud of the road. The procession is closed by the car of the commander of the party.[4]

As the party enters some great village, it begins to sing the *Miloserdnaya*—the "charity song." They call it a song, but it hardly is that. It is a succession of woes escaping from hundreds of breasts at once, a recital in very plain words expressing with a childish simplicity the sad fate of the convict—a horrible lamentation by means of which the Russian exile appeals to the mercy of other miserables like himself. Centuries of sufferings, of pains and misery, of persecutions that crush down the most vital forces, of our nation, are heard in these recitals and shrieks. These tones of deep

[4] According to law the families of the convicts must not be submitted to the control of the convoy. In reality they are submitted to the same treatment as the convicts. To quote but one instance. The Tomsk correspondent of the *Moscow Telegraph* wrote on the 3rd of November, 1881:—" We have seen on the march the party which left Tomsk on the 14th of September. The exhausted women and children literally stuck in the mud, and the soldiers dealt them blows to make them advance and to keep pace with the party."

sorrow recall the tortures of the last century, the stifled cries under the sticks and whips of our own time, the darkness of the cellars, the wildness of the woods, the tears of the starving wife. The peasants of the villages on the Siberian highway understand these tones; they know their true meaning from their own experience, and the appeal of the *Neschastnyie* —of the "sufferers," as our people call all prisoners—is answered by the poor; the most destitute widow, signing herself with the cross, brings her coppers, or her piece of bread, and deeply bows before the chained "sufferer," grateful to him for not disdaining her small offering.

Late in the afternoon, after having covered some fifteen or twenty miles, the party reaches the *étape* where it spends the night and takes one day's rest each three days. It accelerates its pace as soon as the paling that incloses the old log-wood building is perceived, and the strongest run to take possession by force of the best places on the platforms. The *étapes* were mostly built fifty years ago, and after having resisted the inclemencies of the climate, and the passage of a hundred thousand of convicts, they have become now rotten and foul from top to bottom. The old log-wood house refuses shelter to the chained travellers brought under its roof, and wind and snow freely enter the interstices between its rotten beams; heaps of snow are accumulated in the corners of the rooms. The *étape* was built to shelter 150 convicts; that being the average size of parties fifty years ago. At present the parties consist of 450 to 500 human beings, and the 500 must lodge on the space parsimoniously calculated for 150.[5]

The stronger ones, or the aristocracy among the convicts—the elder vagrants and the great murderers — cover each square inch of the platforms; the remainder, that is, double the number of the former, lie down on the rotten floor, covered with an inch of sticky filth,

---

[5] The Russian law, which mostly has been written without any knowledge of the real conditions it deals with, forbids to send out such numerous parties. But, in reality, the normal party numbers now 480 persons. In 1881, according to the *Golos*, 6607 convicts were sent in sixteen parties, making thus an average of 406 convicts per party. Some of them numbered 420 men. Besides, 954 women, with 895 children, followed these sixteen parties, raising thus the average number in each party to 521 persons. In 1884, the average size of parties was about 400 (300 men and 100 women and children).

beneath and between the platforms. What becomes of the rooms when the doors are closed, and the whole space filled with human beings who lie naked on their nasty clothes impregnated with water, will be easily imagined.

The *étapes*, however, are palaces when compared with the *half-étapes*, where the parties spend only the nights. These buildings are still smaller, and, as a rule, still more dilapidated, still more rotten and foul. Sometimes they are in such a state as to compel the party to spend the cold Siberian nights in light barracks erected in the yard, and without fire. As a rule, the *half-étape* has no special compartment for the women, and they must lodge in the room of the soldiers (*see* Maximoff's *Siberia*). With the resignation of our " all-enduring " Russian mothers, they squat down with their babies wrapped in rags, in some corner of the room below the platforms or close by the door, among the rifles of the escort.

No wonder that, according to official statistics, out of the 2561 children less than fifteen years old who were sent in 1881 to Siberia with their parents, " *a very small part survived.*" " The majority," the *Golos* says, " could not support the very bad conditions of the journey, and died before, or immediately after, having reached their destination in Siberia." In sober truth, the transportation to Siberia, as practised now, is a real "Massacre of Innocents."[6]

Shall I add that there is no accommodation for the sick, and that one must have exceptionally robust health to survive an illness during the journey? There are but five small hospitals, with a total of a hundred beds, on the whole stretch between Tomsk and Irkutsk, that is, on a distance which represents at least a four months' journey. As for those who cannot hold out until a hospital is reached, it was written to the *Golos*, on January 5th, 1881 : —" They are left at the *étapes* without any medical help. The sick-room has no bedsteads, no beds, no cushions, no coverings, and of course nothing like linen. The forty-eight and a half *kopecks* per day that are allowed for the sick, remain mostly in full in the hands of the authorities."

[6] The number of children with the convict-parties reaches now from 5000 to 8000. Many of them must make a two years' journey before reaching their destination. According to the *Yuriditcheskiy Vyestnik* ("Law Messenger") of 1883, no girl of fourteen or less reaches the end of the journey without having been submitted to a gross offence.

Shall I dwell upon the exactions to which the convicts are submitted, notwithstanding their dreadful misery, by the warders of the *étapes?* Is it not sufficient to say that the warders of these buildings are paid by the Crown, besides the allowance of corn flour for black bread, only with three roubles, or 6s. per year? "The stove is out of order, you cannot light the fire," says one of them, when the party arrives quite wet or frozen; and the party pays its tribute for permission to light the fire. "The windows are under repair," and the party pays for having some rags to fill up the openings through which freely blows the icy wind. "Wash up the *étape* before leaving, or pay so much," and the party pays again, and so on, and so on. And shall I mention, too, the manner in which the convicts and their families are treated during the journey? Even the political exiles once revolted, in 1881, against an officer who had permitted himself to assault in the dark corridor a lady marched to Siberia for a political offence. The common-law exiles surely are not treated better than the political ones.

All these are not tales of the past. They are real pictures of what is going on now, at the

very moment when I write these lines. A
Russian friend, who made the same journey
a few years ago, and to whom I have shown
these pages, fully confirms all the above statements, and adds much more which I do not
mention only for economy of space. What really
is a tale of the past—of a very recent past—is
the chaining together of eight or ten convicts.
This horrible measure, however, was abolished
only in January, 1881. At present, each convict
has his hands chained separately from his comrades. But still the chain, being very short,
gives such a posture to the arms as renders the
ten and twelve hours' march very difficult, not
to speak of the insupportable rheumatic pain
occasioned in the bones by the contact of the
iron rings during the hard Siberian frosts.
This pain, I am told and readily believe it,
soon becomes a real torture.

I hardly need add that, contrary to the statements of a recent English traveller through
Siberia, the political convicts perform the
journey to Kara, or to the places where they
are to be settled as *poselentsy*, under the same
conditions as, and together with, the commonlaw convicts. The very fact of Izbitskiy and
Debagorio-Mokrievitch having exchanged names

with two common-law convicts, and having thus escaped from hard labour, proves that the English traveller's information was false. It is true that a great number of Polish exiles of 1864, and notably all noblemen and chief convicts, condemned to hard labour, were transported in carriages, on posting horses. But, since 1866, the political convicts (condemned by courts to hard labour or exile) have mostly made the journey on foot, together with common-law convicts. An exception was made in 1877—1879 for the few who were transported to Eastern Siberia during those three years. They were transported in cars, but following the line of the *étapes*. Since 1879, however, all political convicts—men and women alike—have made the journey precisely in the way I have described, very many of them chained, contrary to the law of 1827. The only change was, that the "politicals" were sent in separate parties, and had a few cars for occasional relief of the sick. As to those exiled by simple order of the Administrative, they were, and are now, transported in cars, following the same lines of the *étapes*, and stopping at the *étapes* and prisons with common-law prisoners.

When writing his remarkable book on hard

labour,⁷ M. Maximoff concluded it with the wish that the horrors of the foot-journey he had described might become as soon as possible matter of history. But M. Maximoff's wish has not been realized. The Liberal movement of 1861 was crushed down by the Government; the attempts at reform were considered as "dangerous tendencies," and the transport of exiles to Siberia has remained what it was twenty years ago—a source of unutterable sufferings for nearly 20,000 people.

The shameful system, branded at that time by all those who had studied it, has maintained itself in full; and, whilst the rotten buildings on the highway are falling to pieces, and the whole system disintegrates more and more, new thousands of men and women transported for such crimes as those, "the very existence of which" was doubted twenty years ago, are added annually to the thousands already transported to Siberia, and their number is increasing every year in an awful proportion.

⁷ *Sibir i Katorga* (" Siberia and hard labour"), 3 vols., St. Petersburg, 1871.

CHAPTER V.

THE EXILE IN SIBERIA.

IT is not in vain that the word *katorga* (hard labour) has received so horrible a meaning in the Russian language, and has become synonymous with the most awful pains and sufferings. "I cannot bear any longer this *katorjnaya* life," this life of moral and physical sufferings, of infamous insults and pitiless persecutions, of pains beyond man's strength, say those who are brought to despair before attempting to put an end to their life by suicide. It is not in vain that the word *katorga* has received this meaning, and all those who have seriously inquired into the aspects of hard labour in Siberia have come to the conclusion that it really corresponds to the popular conception. I have described the journey which leads to the *katorga*. Let us see now what are the conditions of the con-

The Exile in Siberia. 155

victs in the hard-labour colonies and prisons of Siberia.

Some fifteen years ago, nearly all those 1500 people who were condemned every year to hard labour were sent to Eastern Siberia. One part of them was employed at the silver, lead, and gold mines of the Nertchinsk district, or at the iron-works of Petrovsk (not far from Kiakhta) and Irkutsk, or at the salt-works of Usolie and Ust-Kut; a few were employed at a drapery in the neighbourhood of Irkutsk, and the remainder were sent to the gold-mines, or rather gold-washings, of Kara, where they were bound to dig out the traditional "hundred poods" (3200 lbs.) of gold for the "Cabinet of his Majesty," that is, for the personal purse of the Emperor. The horrible tales of subterranean work in the silver and lead-mines, under the most abominable conditions, under the whips of overseers who compelled each ten men to accomplish a work that would be hard even for double this number; of convicts working in the darkness, charged with heavy chains and riveted to barrows; of people dying from the poisonous emanations of the mines; of prisoners flogged to death, or dying under five and six thousand strokes of the rod, by order of traditional monsters like Rozghildéeff—all these tales, well known everywhere, are not tales due to the fancy of imaginative writers, they are true historical records of a sad reality.[1]

And they are not tales of a remote past, for such were the conditions of hard labour in the Nertchinsk mining district no farther back than twenty-five years ago. They might be told by men still in life.

More than that; many, very many, features of this horrible past have been maintained until our own times. Every one in Eastern Siberia knows of the terrible scurvy epidemics which broke out at the Kara gold-mines in 1857, when

[1] The Kutomara and Alexandrovsk silver-mines have always been renowned for their insalubrity, on account of the arsenical emanations from the ore; not only men, but also cattle, suffered from them, and it is well known that the inhabitants of these villages were compelled, for this reason, to raise their young cattle in neighbouring villages. As to the quicksilver emanations, every one who has consulted any serious work on the Nertchinsk mining district knows that the silver-ore of these mines is usually accompanied with cinnabar—especially in the mines of Shakhtama and Kultuma, both worked out by convicts who were poisoned by mercurial emanations—and that attempts to get mercury from these mines have been made several times by the Government. The Akatui silver-mines of the same district have always had the most dreadful reputation for their unhealthiness.

—according to official reports perused by M. Maximoff—no less than a thousand convicts died in the course of one single summer, and the cause of the epidemics is a secret to nobody; it is well known that the authorities, having perceived that they would be unable to dig out the traditional hundred *poods* of gold, caused the convicts to work without rest, above their strength, until many fell dead in the very mines. And later on, in 1873, have we not seen again a similar epidemic, due to similar causes, breaking out in the Yeniseisk district, and sweeping away hundreds of lives at once? The places of torture, the proceedings were slowly modified, but the very essence of hard labour has remained the same, and the word *katorga* has still maintained its horrible meaning.

During the last twenty years the system of hard labour has undergone some modification. The richer silver-mines of the Nertchinsk mining district have been worked out; instead of enriching every year the Cabinet of the Emperor with 220 to 280 *poods* of silver (7000 to 9000 lbs.), as it was before, they yielded but five to seven *poods* (150 to 210 lbs.) in 1860 to 1863, and they were abandoned. As to the gold-washings, the mining authorities succeeded about the same time in convincing the Cabinet that there were no more goldwashings worth being worked in the district; and the Cabinet abandoned the district to private enterprise, reserving for the Crown only the mines on the Kara river, a tributary of the Shilka (of course, rich mines, well known before, were ": discovered " by private persons immediately after the promulgation of the law). The Government was thus compelled to find some other kind of employment for the convicts, and to modify to a certain extent the whole system of hard labour. The central prisons in Russia, of which I have given a description in a preceding chapter, were invented; and, before being sent to Siberia, the hard-labour convicts remain now in these prisons for about one-third of the duration of their sentence. The number of these sufferers, for whom even the horrible *katorga* in Siberia appears as a relief, together with those who are kept in the hard-labour prisons of Siberia, is about 7000. Besides, an attempt was made to colonize the Sakhalin island with hard-labour convicts.

As to the eighteen to nineteen hundred hardlabour convicts who are transported every year

to Siberia, they are submitted to different kinds
of treatment. A certain number of them
(2700 to 3000) are locked up in the hard-
labour prisons of Western and Eastern Siberia;
whilst the remainder are transported, either to
the Kara gold-washings, or to the salt-works
of Usolic and Ust-Kut. The few mines and
works of the Crown in Siberia being, however,
unable to employ the nearly 10,000 convicts
condemned to hard labour who ought to be
kept in Siberia, a novel expedient was invented, in renting the convicts to private
owners of gold-washings. It is easy to perceive that the punishment of convicts belonging to the same hard-labour category can be
thus varied to an immense degree, depending
on the caprice of the authorities, and a good
deal on the length of the purse of the
convict. He may be killed under the *plètes*
at Kara or Ust-Kut, as also he may comfort-
ably live at the private gold-mine of some
friend, as "overseer of works," and be aware
of his removal to Siberia only by the long
delay in receiving news from his Russian
friends.

Leaving aside, however, these exceptional
favours and a variety of subdivisions of less

importance, the hard-labour convicts in Siberia can be classified under three great categories: those who are kept in prison; those who are employed at the gold-mines of the Imperial Cabinet or of private persons; and those who are employed at the salt-works.

The fate of the first is very much like the fate of those who are locked up in central prisons in Russia. The Siberian gaoler may smoke a pipe, instead of a cigar, when flogging his inmates; he may make use of lashes, instead of birch rods, and flog the convicts when his soup is spoiled, whilst the Russian gaoler's bad temper depends upon an unsuccessful hunting: the results for the convicts are the same. In Siberia, as in Russia, a gaoler "who pitilessly flogs" is substituted by a gaoler "who gives free play to his own fists and steals the last coppers of the prisoners;" and an honest man, if he is occasionally nominated as the head of a hard-labour prison, will soon be dismissed, or expelled from an administration where honest men are a nuisance.

The fate of those 2000 convicts who are employed at the Kara gold-mines is not better. Twenty years ago the official reports represented the prison at Upper Kara as an old, weather-worn log-wood building, erected on a swampy ground, and impregnated with the filthiness accumulated by long generations of overcrowded convicts. They concluded that it ought to be pulled down at once; but the same foul and rotten building continues to shelter the convicts until now; and, even during M. Kononovitch's reasonable rule, it was said to be whitewashed only four times each year. It is always filled up to double its cubical capacity, and the inmates sleep on two stories of platforms, as also on the floor that is covered with a thick sheet of sticky filth, their wet and nasty clothes being mattresses and coverings at once. So it was twenty years ago; so it is now. The chief prison of the Kara gold-washings, the Lower Kara, was described by M. Maximoff in 1863, and by the official documents I perused, as a rotten nasty building where wind and snow freely penetrate. So it is described again by my friends. The Middle Kara prison was restored a few years ago, but it soon became as filthy as the two others. For six to eight months, out of twelve, the convicts remain in these prisons without any occupation; and it is quite sufficient, I imagine, to

M

mention this circumstance to suggest what are the results of this confinement, and what influence it exercises. Let those who wish to know the real influence of Russian lock-ups and prisons on their inmates peruse the remarkable psychological studies by Dostoevsky, MM. Maximoff, Lvoff, and so many others.

The work at the gold-washings is altogether very hard. True, it is carried on above ground; deep excavations being made in the aluvium of the valley, to extract the gold-bearing mud and sands, which are transported in cars to the gold-washing machine. But it is most unhealthy and difficult work. The bottom of the excavation is always below the level of the river, which flows at a certain height in an artificial channel to the machine; and therefore it is always covered to a certain depth with the water which is leaking through its walls, not to speak of the icy water which flows everywhere down the walls, as the frozen mud thaws under the hot rays of the sun. The pumps are usually insufficient, and so (I write from my own experience) people are working throughout the day in an icy water that covers their feet to the knees, and sometimes to the stomach; and, when returned to the prison,

The Exile in Siberia. 163

the convict obviously has nothing to change his wet dress for: he sleeps on it. It is true that the same work is done under the same conditions, by thousands of free working-men, on the private gold-washings. But it is well known that the owners of gold-washings in Siberia would have no hands for their mines if the enlistment of workmen were not practised in the same way as were the enlistments for the armies in the seventeenth century. The engagements are always made in a drunken state and in exchange for large sums of hand-money, which passes immediately to the pockets of the publicans. As to the settled exiles—the *poselentsy*—whose starving army furnishes the largest contingent of workmen for the private gold-washings, they are mostly merely rented by the village authorities, who seize the hand-money for the taxes, always in arrear. The intervention of the district authorities, and very often a military convoy, are therefore necessary to send the "free hands" to the gold-washings.

It is obvious that the conditions of work at the Kara mines are still harder for the convicts. The day's task which each of them must accomplish is greater and harder than on the private mines, and many of them are loaded with chains; at Kara, they have moreover to walk five miles from the prison to the excavation, adding thus a nearly three hours' march to the day's task. Sometimes, when the auriferous gravel and clay are poorer than was expected, and the quantity of gold calculated on could not be extracted, the convicts are literally exhausted by overwork; they are compelled to work until very late in the nights, and then the mortality, which is always high, becomes really horrible. In short, it is considered as a rule, by all those who have seriously studied the Siberian hard-labour institutions, that the convict who has remained for several years at Kara, or at the salt-works, comes away quite broken in health, and unfit for ulterior work, and that he remains thenceforth a burden on the country.

The food—however less substantial than at the private gold-washings—might be considered as nearly sufficient when the convicts receive the rations allowed to the men when at work; the daily allowance being in such cases $3\frac{9}{10}$ English pounds of rye bread, and the amount of meat, cabbage, buckwheat, &c., that can be supplied for one rouble per month. A good manager could give for that price nearly half a pound of meat every day. But, owing to the want of any real control, the convicts mostly are pitilessly robbed of their poor allowance. If, at the St. Petersburg House of Detention, under the eyes of scores of inspectors, robbery was carried on for years on a colossal scale, how could it be otherwise in the wildernesses of the Transbaikalian mountains? Honest managers, who supply the convicts with all due to them, are rare exceptions. Besides, the above allowance is given only during the short period of gold-washing, which lasts for less than four months in the year. During the winter, when the frozen ground is as hard as steel, there is no work at all. And as soon as the washing of gold—the year's crop of the mines—is finished, the food is reduced to an amount hardly sufficient to keep muscles and bones together. As to the payment for work, it is quite ludicrous, being something like three to four shillings per month, out of which the convict mostly purchases some cloth to supply the quite insufficient dress given by the Crown. No wonder that scurvy—that terror of all Siberian gold-washings—is always mowing down the lives of the convicts, and that the mortality at Kara is from 90 to 287, out of less than 2000, every year; that is, one out of eleven to one out of seven, a very high figure indeed for a population of adults. These official figures, however, are still below the truth, as the desperately sick are usually sent away, to die in some *bogadelnya* or invalid house.

The situation of the convicts would be still worse if the overcrowding of the prisons and the interests of the owners of the gold-mines had not compelled the Government to shorten the time of imprisonment. As a rule, the hard-labour convict must be kept in prison, at the mines, only for about one-third of the time to which he has been condemned. Beyond this time, he must be settled in the village close by the mine, in a separate house, with his family, if his wife has followed him; he is bound to go to work like other convicts, but without chains, and he has his own house and hearth. It is obvious that this law might be an immense benefit for the convicts, but its provisions are marred by the manner in which it is applied. The liberation of the convict depends entirely upon the caprice of the superintendent of the mine. Moreover, with the absurd payment for his labour, which hardly reaches a few shillings per month in addition to the ration of flour, the liberated convict falls, with but few exceptions, into the most dreadful misery. All investigators of the subject are agreed in representing under the darkest aspects the misery of this class of convicts, and in saying that the immense number of runaways from this category of exile is chiefly due to their wretchedness.

The punishments depend also entirely upon the fancy of the superintendent of the works, and mostly they are atrocious. The privation of food and the blackhole—and I have told on the preceding pages what blackhole means in Siberia—are considered as merely childish punishments. Only the *plète*, the cat-o'-nine-tails, distributed at will, for the slightest delinquency, and to the amount dictated by the good or bad temper of the manager, is considered as a punishment.

It is so usual a thing in the minds of the overseers, that "hundred *plètes*," a hundred lashes with the cat-o'-nine-tails, are ordered with the same easiness as one week's incarceration would be ordered in European prisons; but there are other heavier punishments in store: for instance, the chaining for several years to the wall of an underground blackhole, especially at the Akatui prison; the riveting for five or six years to the barrow, which is, perhaps, the worst imaginable moral torture; and finally, the *leessa* (the fox)—that is, a beam of wood, or a piece of iron, weighing forty-eight pounds, attached to the chain for several years. The horrible punishment by the *leessa* is becoming rare, but the chaining for several years to a barrow is quite usual. Quite recently, the political convicts, Popko, Fomicheff, and Bereznuk were condemned, for an attempt at escape from the Irkutsk prison, to be riveted to barrows for two years.

I hardly need to add that the superintendent of the mines is a king in his dominions, and that to complain about him is quite useless. He may rob his inmates of their last coppers, he may submit them to the most horrible punishments, he may torture the children of convicts—no complaints will reach the authorities; and the convict who would be bold enough to dare a complaint would be simply starved in blackholes, or killed under the *plètes*. All those who write about exile in Siberia ought to bear constantly in mind that there is no serious control over the managers of the

The Exile in Siberia. 169

penal colonies, and that an honest man will never remain for long at the head of a penal colony in Siberia. If he is merely humane with the convicts, he will be dismissed for what will be described at St. Petersburg as dangerous sentimentalism. If not, he will be expelled by the association of robbers who gather around so lucrative a business as the management of a gold-mine of the Crown. The Russian proverb says: "Let him nourish a Crown's sparrow, he will nourish all his family;" but a gold-mine is something much more attractive than a Crown's sparrow. There are thousands of convicts to supply with food and tools; there are the machines to repair; and there is the most lucrative clandestine trade in stolen gold. There is at these mines a whole tradition and a solid organization of robbery, established and grown up long ago, an organization which even the despotic and almighty Mouravieff could not break down. An honest man cast amidst these organized gangs of robbers is considered by his comrades as a troublesome individual, and, if not recalled by the Government, he will be compelled to leave himself, weary of warfare. Therefore, the Kara gold-mines have seldom seen at their head honest men like Barbot de

Marny or Kononovitch, but nearly always such people as Rozghildéoff.

And so it goes on until our own times. Not only the abominable cruelty of the managers of Kara has become proverbial, but we need not go further back than 1871 to discover the mediæval torture flourishing there in full. Even so cautious a writer as M. Yadrintseff relates a case of torture applied by the manager of the mines, Demidoff, to a free woman and to her daughter, eleven years old.

"In 1871," he says, "the chief of the Kara gold-mines, Demidoff, was informed of a murder committed by a convict. The better to discover the details of the crime, Demidoff submitted to torture, through the executioner, the wife of the murderer—a free woman, who went to Siberia to follow her husband—and her daughter, eleven years old. The girl was suspended in the air, and the executioner flogged her from the head to the soles of her feet. She had already received several lashes with the cat-o'-nine-tails when she asked to drink. A salted herring was presented to her. The torture would have been prosecuted if the executioner had not refused to continue." [2]

[2] "Siberia as a Colony," p. 207. St. Petersburg, 1882.

Man does not become so ferocious at once, and every intelligent thinker will discover behind this single case a whole training in cruelty of the Demidoffs; a whole horrible story of barbarities carried on with the conviction of impunity. As the woman in this case was not a convict, her complaints reached the authorities; but, for one case brought to publicity, how many hundreds of like cases never come, and never will come, to the knowledge of public opinion!

I have but little to say about those hard-labour convicts who are rented of the Crown by private owners of gold-washings. This innovation was not yet introduced when I was sojourning in Siberia, and little has transpired about it since it has been practised. I know that the experiment has been recognized a failure. The best proprietors did not care to employ convicts, as they soon learned how expensive every contact with the authorities is in Siberia; and only the worst owners continued to take them to their mines. At such mines the convicts had perhaps less to suffer from their managers, but still more from want of food, from overwork, and bad lodgings, not to speak of the hardness of long journeys to and from the gold-mines, on footpaths crossing the wild Siberian forests.

As to the salt-works, where a number of convicts are still employed, they imply the worst kind of hard labour, and I shall never forget the Polish exiles I saw at the Ust-Kut salt works. The water of the salt springs is usually pumped by means of the most primitive machines; and the work, which is pursued even during the winter, is unanimously considered as one of the most exhausting. But the condition of those men who are employed at the large pans, where the salt solution is concentrated by an immense fire blazing under the pans, is still worse. They stay for hours quite naked, stirring up the salt in the pan; the perspiration is literally streaming on their bodies, whilst they are exposed to a strong current of cold air blowing through the building in order to accelerate the evaporation. With the exception of the few who are employed at some privileged work at the mine, I have seen but livid phantoms, among whom consumption and scurvy find an abundant harvest.

I shall not touch in this chapter the recent innovation—the hard labour and settlement of convicts in a new and remoter Siberia—the

The Exile in Siberia. 173

island of Sakhalin. The fate of the convicts on this island, where nobody would settle freely, and their struggles against an inhospitable soil and climate, deserve a separate study. Nor shall I touch on these pages the condition of the Polish exiles of 1864. This subject deserves more than a short notice; and I have not yet spoken of the immense class of exiles transported to Siberia to be settled there as agricultural and industrial labourers.

Those who are condemned to hard labour, not only lose all their civil and personal rights, they are separated for ever from their motherland. After their release from hard labour they are embodied in the great category of the *ssylno-poselentsy*, and they remain in Siberia for life. No possible return, under any circumstances, to Russia. The category of settled exiles is the most numerous in Siberia. It comprises not only the released hard-labour convicts, but also the nearly 3000 men and women (28,382 in the space of ten years, 1867 to 1876) transported every year under the head of *ssylno-poselentsy*—that is, to be settled in Siberia, also for life, and with a total or partial loss of their civil and personal rights. To these *ssylno-poselentsy*—or, simply *poselentsy* in the current language—must be added the 23,383 exiled during the same ten years *na vodvorenie*, that is, to be settled with a partial loss of their civil rights; 2551 exiled *na jitie* ("to live in Siberia") without loss of their personal rights; and the 76,686 exiled during the same time by simple orders of the Administrative, making thus a total of nearly 130,000 exiles for ten years. During the last five years this figure has still increased, reaching from 16,000 to 17,000 exiles every year.

I have already said what are the "crimes" of this mass of human beings cast out from Russia. As to their situation in the land of exile, it proved so bad that a whole literature on this subject, full of the most terrible revelations, has grown up during the last ten years. Official inquiries have been made, and scores of papers have been published on the consequences of the transportation to Siberia, all being agreed as to the following conclusion :—Leaving aside some isolated cases, such as the excellent influence of the Polish and Russian political exiles on the development of skilled labour in Siberia, as well as that of the Nonconformists and Little Russians (who have been transported by whole communes at once) on agriculture—leaving aside these few exceptions, the great mass of exiles, far from supplying Siberia with useful colonists and skilled working-men, supplies it with a floating population, mostly starving and quite unable to do any useful work (see the works and papers by MM. Maximoff, Lvoff, Zavalishin, Rovinsky, Yadrintseff, Peysen, Dr. Sperch, and many others, and the extracts from official inquiries they have published).

It appears from these investigations that, whilst more than half a million of people have been transported to Siberia during the last sixty years, only 200,000 are now on the lists of the local Administration; the remainder have died without leaving any posterity, or have disappeared. Even of these 200,000 who figure on the official lists, no less than one-third, that is, 70,000 (or even much more, according to other valuations), have disappeared during the last few years without anybody knowing what has become of them. They have vanished like a cloud in the sky on a hot summer day. Part of them have run away and have joined the human current, 20,000 men strong, that silently flows through the forest-lands of Siberia, from east to west, towards the Urals. Others—and these are the great number—already have dotted with their bones the "runaway paths" of the forests and marshes, as also the paths that lead to and from the gold-mines. And the remainder constitute the floating population of the larger towns, trying to escape an obnoxious supervision by assuming false names.

As to the 130,000 (or much less, according to other statisticians) who have remained under the control of the Administration, the unanimous testimony of all inquiries, official or private, is that they are in such a wretched state of misery as to be a real burden on the country. Even in the most fertile provinces of Siberia—Tomsk and the southern part of Tobolsk—only one-quarter of them have their own houses, and only one out of nine have become agriculturists. In the eastern provinces the proportion is still less favourable. Those who are not agriculturists—and they are some hundred thousand men and women throughout Siberia—are wandering from town to town without any permanent occupation, or going to and from the gold-washings, or living in villages from hand to mouth, in the worst imaginable misery, with all the vices that never fail to follow misery.[3]

[3] See Appendix B.

Several causes contribute to the achievement of this result. The chief one—all agree in that—is the demoralization the convicts undergo in the prisons, and during their peregrinations on the *étapes*. Long before having reached their destination in Siberia, they are demoralized. The laziness enforced for years on the inmates of the lock-ups; the development of the passion for games of hazard; the systematic suppression of the will of the prisoner, and the development of passive qualities, quite opposite to the moral strength required for colonizing a young country; the prostration of the strength of character and the development of low passions, of shallow and futile desires, and of anti-social conceptions generated by the prison—all this ought to be kept in mind to realize the depth of moral corruption that is spread by our gaols, and to understand how an inmate of these institutions never can be the man to endure the hard struggle for life in the sub-arctic Russian colony.

But not only is the moral force of the convict broken by the prison; his physical force, too, is mostly broken for ever by the journey and the sojourn at the hard-labour colonies. Many contract incurable diseases; all are weak. As

N

to those who have spent some twenty years in hard-labour (an attempt at escape easily brings the seclusion to this length), they are for the most part absolutely unable to perform any work. Even put in the best circumstances, they would still be a burden on the community. But the conditions imposed on the *poselentsy* are very hard. He is sent to some remote village commune, where he receives several acres of land—the least fertile in the commune, and he must become a farmer. In reality he knows nothing of the practice of agriculture in Siberia, and, after three or four years' detention, he has lost the taste for it, even if he formerly was an agriculturist. The village commune receives him with hostility and scorn. He is "a Russian"—a term of contempt with the Siberyak—and, moreover, a convict! He is also one of those whose transport and accommodation cost the Siberian peasant so heavily. For the most part he is not married and cannot marry, the proportion of exiled women being as one to six men, and the Siberyak will not allow him to marry his daughter, notwithstanding the fifty roubles allowed in this case by the State, but usually melted away on their long journey through the hands of numerous officials. There was no lack in Siberia of official scheme-inventors who ordered the peasants to build houses for the exiles, and who settled the *poselentsy*, five or six together, dreaming of pastoral exile-communities. The practical result was invariably the same. The five *poselentsy* thus associated in their miseries invariably ran away after a useless struggle against starvation, and went under false names to the towns, or to the gold-mines, in search of labour. Whole villages with empty houses on the Siberian highway still remind the traveller of the sterility of official Utopias introduced with the help of birch rods.

Those who find some employment on the farms of the Siberian peasants are not happier. The whole system of engaging workmen in Siberia is based on giving them large sums of hand-money in advance, in order to put them permanently in debt, and to reduce them to a kind of perpetual serfdom; and the Siberian peasants largely use this custom. As to those exiles—and they are the great proportion—who earn their livelihood by work on the gold-washings, they are deprived of all their savings as soon as they have reached the first village and public-house, after the four or five months of labour—of hard labour, in fact, with all its privations—at the mines. The villages on the Lena, the Yenissei, the Kan, &c., where the parties of gold-miners arrive in the autumn, are widely famed for this peculiarity. And who does not know in Siberia the two wretched, miserable hamlets on the Lena, which have received the names of Paris and London, from the admirable skill of their inhabitants in depriving the miners of their very last copper? When the miner has left in the public-house his last hat and shirt, he is immediately re-engaged by the agents of the gold-mining company for the next summer, and receives in exchange for his passport, some hand-money for returning home. He comes to his village with empty hands, and the long winter months he will spend —perhaps, in the next lock-up ! In short, the final conclusion of all official inquiries which have been made up to this time is, that the few housekeepers among the exiles are in a wretched state of misery ; and that the paupers are either serfs to the farmers and mine-proprietors, or—to use the words of an official report—" are dying from hunger and cold."

The *taiga*—the forest-land which covers thousands of square miles in Siberia—is thickly peopled with runaways, who slowly advance, like a continuous human stream, towards the west, moved by the hope of finally reaching their native villages on the other slope of the Urals. As soon as the cuckoo cries, announcing to the prisoners that the woods are free from their snow covering, that they can shelter a man without the risk of his becoming during the night a motionless block of ice, and that they will soon provide the wanderer with mushrooms and berries, thousands of convicts make their escape from the gold-mines and salt-works, from the villages where they starved, and from the towns where they concealed themselves. Guided by the polar star, or by the mosses on the trees, or by old runaways who have acquired in the prisons the precious knowledge of the "runaway paths" and "runaway stations," they undertake the long and perilous backward journey. They pass around Lake Baikal, climbing the high and wild mountains on its shores, or they cross it on a raft, or even—as the popular song says—in a fish-cask. They avoid the highways, the towns, and the settlements of the Buryates, but freely camp in the woods around the towns; and each spring you see at Tchita the fires of the *chaldons* (runaways) lighted all around the little capital of Transbaikalia, on the woody slopes of the surrounding mountains. They freely enter also the Russian villages, where they find, up to the present day, bread and milk exposed on the windows of the peasants' houses " for the poor runaways."

As long as nothing is stolen by the ramblers, they may be sure of not being disturbed in their journey by the peasants. But as soon as any of them breaks this tacit mutual engagement, the Siberyaks become pitiless. The hunters—and each Siberian village has its trappers—spread through the forests, and pitilessly exterminate the runaways, sometimes with an abominable refinement of cruelty. Some thirty years ago, "to hunt the *chaldons*" was a trade, and the human chase has still remained a trade with a few individuals, especially with the *karyms* or half-breeds. "The antelope gives but one skin," these hunters say, "whilst the *chaldon* gives two at least, his shirt and his coat." A few runaways find employment on the farms of the peasants, which are spread at great distances from the villages, but these are not very numerous, as the summer is the best season for marching towards the west: the forests feed and conceal the wanderers during the warm season. True, they are filled then with clouds of small mosquitos (the terrible *moshka*), and the *brodyagha* (runaway) you meet with in the summer is horrible to see : his face is but one swollen wound ; his eyes are inflamed and hardly seen from beneath the burning and swollen eyelids ; his swollen nostrils and mouth are covered with sores. Men and cattle alike grow mad from this plague, which continues to pursue them even among the clouds of smoke that are spread around the villages. But still the *brodyagha* pursues his march towards the border-chain of Siberia, and his heart beats stronger as he perceives its bluish hills on the horizon. Twenty, perhaps thirty thousand men are continually living this life, and surely no less than one hundred thousand people have tried to make their escape in this way during these last fifty years. How many have succeded in entering the Russian provinces ? Nobody could tell, even approximately. Thousands have found their graves in the *taiga*, and happy were they whose eyes were closed by a devoted fellow-traveller. Other thousands have returned of their own accord to the lock-ups when the mercury was freezing and the frost stopped the circulation of the last drop of blood in an emaciated body. They submitted themselves to the unavoidable hundred *plètes*, returned again to Transbaikalia, and next spring tried again the same journey, with more experience. Other thousands have been hunted down, seized, or shot by the Buryates, the Karyms, or some Siberian trapper. Others again were seized a few days after having reached the soil of their " mother-Russia," after having thrown themselves at the feet of their old parents, in the village they had left many years ago, to satisfy the caprice of the *ispravnik* or the jealousy of the local usurer. . . . What an abyss of suffering is concealed behind those three words : " Escape from Siberia " !

* * * *

I have now to examine the situation of political exiles in Siberia. Of course I shall not venture to tell here the story of political exile since the year 1607, when one of the forefathers of the now reigning dynasty, Vassiliy Nikitich Romanoff, opened the long list of proscriptions, and terminated his life in an underground cell at Nyrdob, loaded with sixty-four pounds' weight of heavy chains. I shall not try to revive the horrible story of the Bar confederates arriving in Siberia with their noses and ears torn away, and—so says, at least, the tradition—rolled down the hill of the Kreml at Tobolsk tied to big trees; I shall not tell the infamies of the madman Treskiñ and his *ispravnik* Loskutoff; nor dwell upon the execution of March 7th, 1837, when the Poles Szokalski, Sieroczynski, and four others were killed under the strokes of the rods; nor will I describe the sufferings of the "Decembrists" and of the exiles of the first days of Alexander II.'s reign; neither give here the list of our poets and publicists exiled to Siberia since the times of Radischeff until those of Odoevsky, and later on, of Tchernyshevsky and Mikhailoff. I shall speak only of those political exiles who are now in Siberia.

Kara is the place where those condemned to hard labour were imprisoned, to the number of 150 men and women, during the autumn of 1882. After having been kept from two to four years in preliminary detention at the St. Petersburg fortress, at the famous Litovskiy Zamok, at the St. Petersburg House of Detention, and in provincial prisons, they were sent, after their condemnation to the Kharkoff

Central Prison. There they remained for three to five years, again in solitary confinement, without any occupation. Then they were transferred, for a few months to the Mtsensk depôt —where they were treated much better—and thence they were sent to Transbaikalia. Most of them performed the journey to Kara in the manner I have already described—on foot beyond Tomsk, and chained. A few were favoured with the use of cars, for slowly moving from one *étape* to another. Even these last describe this journey as a real torture, and say: —" People become mad from the moral and physical tortures endured during such a journey. The wife of Dr. Bielyi, who accompanied her husband, and two or three others, have had this fate."

The prison where they are kept at Middle Kara is one of those rotten buildings I have already mentioned. It was overcrowded when ninety-one men were confined in it, and it is still more overcrowded since the arrival of sixty more prisoners; wind and snow freely enter the interstices between the rotten pieces of logwood of the walls, and from beneath the rotten planks of the floor. The chief food of the prisoners is rye-bread and some buckwheat; meat is distributed only when they are at work in the gold-mine, that is, during three months out of twelve, and only to fifty men out of 150. Contrary to the law and custom, all were chained in 1881, and went to work loaded with chains.

There is no hospital for "the politicals," and the sick, who are numerous, remain on the platforms, side by side with all others, in the same cold rooms, in the same suffocating atmosphere. Even the insane Madame Kovalevskaya is still kept in prison. Happily enough, there are surgeons among them. As to the surgeon of the prison, it is sufficient to say of him that the insane Madame Kovalevskaya was kicked down and beaten under his eyes during an attack of madness. The wives of the prisoners were allowed to stay at Lower Kara, and to visit their husbands twice a week, as also to bring them books. The greater number are slowly dying from consumption, and the list of deaths rapidly increases.

But the most horrible curse of hard labour at Kara is the absolute arbitrariness of the gaolers; the prisoners are completely at the mercy of the caprices of men who were nominated by the Government with the special purpose of "keeping them in urchin-gloves." The chief of the garrison openly says he would be happy if some "political" offended him, as the offender would be hanged; the surgeon doctors by means of his fists; and the adjutant of the Governor-General, a Captain Zagarin, loudly said, "I am your Governor, your Minister, your Tsar," when the prisoners threatened him with making a complaint to the Ministry of Justice. One must read the story of the "insurrection" at the Krasnoyarsk prison, provoked by this Captain Zagarin, to be convinced that the right place for such an individual would be a lunatic asylum. Even ladies did not escape his mad brutality, and were submitted by him to a treatment which revolted the simplest feelings of decency; and, when the prisoner Schedrin, in defence of his bride, gave him a blow on his face, the military Court condemned Schedrin to death. General Pedashenko acted in accordance with the loudly expressed public feeling at Irkutsk, when he commuted *the sentence of death into a sentence of incarceration for a fortnight*, but few officials have the courage of the then provisional Governor-General of Eastern Siberia. The blackholes, the chains, the riveting to barrows, are usual punishments, and they are accompanied sometimes with the regulation " hundred *plètes.*" " I shall kill you under the rods, you will rot in the blackholes," such is the language that continually sounds in the ears of the prisoners. But, happily enough, corporal punishment has not been used with political prisoners. A fifty years' experience has taught the officials that the day it was applied " would be a day of great bloodshed," as the publishers of the *Will of the People* said when describing the life of their friends in Siberia.

As to the prescriptions of the law with regard to exiles, they are openly trampled upon by the higher and lower authorities. Thus, Uspenskiy, Tcharoushin, Semenovskiy, Shishko were liberated from the prison and settled in the Kara village after having reached the term of "probation" established by the law. But in 1881, a ministerial decision, taken at St. Petersburg without any reasonable cause, ordered them to be again locked up.

The law being thus trampled under foot, and the last hopes of amelioration of the fate of the prisoners having thus vanished, two of them committed suicide. Uspenskiy, who endured horrible sufferings in hard labour since 1867, and whose character could not be broken by these pains, was unable to live more of this hopeless life, and followed the example of his two comrades. If the political convicts at Kara were common murderers, they would still have the hope that, after having performed their seven, ten, or twelve years of hard labour for having spread Socialist pamphlets among workmen, they would finally be set at liberty and transferred to some province of Southern Siberia, thus becoming settlers, according to the prescriptions of our penal system. But there is no law for political exiles. Tchernyshevsky, the translator of J. S. Mill's "Political Economy," terminated in 1871 his seven years of hard labour. If he had murdered his father and mother, and burned a house with a dozen children, he would be settled at once in some village of the government of Irkutsk. But he had written economical papers; he had published them with the authorization of the Censorship; the Government considered him as a possible leader of the Constitutional Party in Russia,—and he was buried in the hamlet of Viluisk, amidst marshes and forests, 500 miles beyond Yakutsk. There, isolated from all the outside world, closely watched by two *gendarmes* who lodged in his house, he was kept for ten years, and neither the entreaties of the Russian press nor the resolutions of an International Literary Congress could save him from the hands of a suspicious Government. Such will be, too, without doubt, the fate of those who are now kept at Kara. The day they become *poselentsy* will not be for them a day of liberation: it will be a day of transportation from the milder regions of Transbaikalia to the *tundras* within the Arctic Circle.

However bitter the condition of the hard-labour convicts in Siberia, the Government has succeeded in punishing as hardly, and perhaps even more so, those of its political foes whom it could not condemn to hard labour or exile, even by means of packed courts, nominated *ad hoc*. This result has been achieved by means of the "Administrative exile," or transportation to "more or less remote provinces of the Empire" without judgment, without any kind or even phantom of trial, on a single order of the omnipotent Chief of the Third Section.

Every year some five or six hundred young men and women are arrested under suspicion of revolutionary agitation. The inquiry lasts for six months, two years, or more, according to the number of persons arrested in connection with, and the importance of, "the affair." One-tenth of them are committed for trial. As to the remainder, all those against whom there is no specific charge, but who were represented as "dangerous" by the spies; all those who, on account of their intelligence, energy, and "radical opinions," are supposed to be able to become dangerous; and especially those who have shown during the imprisonment a "spirit of irreverence"—are exiled to some more or less remote spot, between the peninsula of Kola and that of Kamchatka. The open and frank despotism of Nicholas I. could not accommodate itself to such hypocritical means of prosecution; and during the reign of the 'iron despot' the Administrative exile was rare. But throughout the reign of Alexander II., since 1862, it has been used on so immense a scale, that you hardly will find now a hamlet, or borough, beyond the fifty-fifth degree of latitude, from the boundary of Norway to the coasts of the Sea of Okhotsk, not containing five, ten, twenty Administrative exiles. In January, 1881, there were 29 at Pinega, a hamlet which has but 750 inhabitants, 55 at

Mezen (1800 inhabitants), 11 at Kola (740 inhabitants), 47 at Kholmogory—a village having but 90 houses, 160 at Zaraisk (5000 inhabitants), 19 at Yeniseisk, and so on.

The causes of exile were always the same; students and girls suspected of subversive ideas; writers whom it was impossible to prosecute for their writings, but who were known to be imbued with "a dangerous spirit;" workmen who have spoken "against the authorities;" persons who have been "irreverent" to some governor of province, or *ispravnik*, and so on, were transported by hundreds every year to people the hamlets of the "more or less remote provinces of the Empire." As to Radical people suspected of "dangerous tendencies," the barest denunciation and the most futile suspicions were sufficient for serving as a motive to exile. When girls (like Miss Bardine, Soubbotine, Lubatovich, and so many others) were condemned to six or eight years of hard labour for having given one Socialistic pamphlet to one workman; when others (like Miss Goukovskaya, fourteen years old) were condemned to exile as *poselentsy* for having shouted in the crowd that it is a shame to condemn people to death for nothing; when hard labour

o

and exile were so easily distributed by the courts, it is obvious that only those were exiled by the Administrative, against whom no palpable charge at all could be produced.[4] In short, the Administrative exile became so scandalously extended during the reign of Alexander II. that, as soon as the Provincial Assemblies received some liberty of speech during the dictatorship of Loris-Melikoff, a long series of representations were addressed by the Assemblies to the Emperor, asking for the immediate abolition of this kind of exile, and stigmatizing in vigorous expressions this monstrous practice.[5]

[4] One of the most characteristic cases out of those which became known by scores in 1881, is the following:—In 1872, the Kursk nobility treated the Governor of the province to a dinner. A big proprietor, M. Annenkoff, was entrusted with proposing a toast for the Governor. He proposed it, but added in conclusion :—" Your Excellence, I drink your health, but I heartily wish that you would devote some more time to the affairs of your province."

Next week a post-car with two *gendarmes* stopped at the door of his house ; and without allowing him to see his friends, or even to bid a farewell to his wife, he was transported to Vyatka. It took six months of the most active applications to powerful persons at St. Petersburg, on behalf of his wife and the marshals of the Fatesh and Kursk nobility, to liberate him from this exile (*Golos, Poryadok*, &c. for February 20th and 21st, 1881).

[5] Extracts from the speech of M. Shakéeff at the sittings of

The Exile in Siberia. 195

It is known that nothing has been done, and after having loudly announced its intention of pardoning the exiles, the Government has merely nominated a commission which examined the cases, pardoned a few—very few—and appointed for the greater number a term of five to six years, when each case was to be re-examined.[6] They have been re-examined indeed, and for very many the detention was prolonged for three years, after which term their cases will be re-examined again. A great many did not wait for the new re-examination, and last year there was a real epidemic of suicides in Siberia.

One will easily realize the conditions of these exiles if he imagines a student, or a girl from a well-to-do family, or a skilled workman, taken by two *gendarmes* to a borough numbering a hundred houses and inhabited by a few Laponians or Russian hunters, by one or two fur-traders, by the priest, and by the police official. Bread is at famine prices; each manufactured

---

the representatives of the St. Petersburg nobility are given in the Appendix C.

[6] In the course of 1881, 2837 cases of "politicals," exiled by order of Administration, were examined; out of them 1950 were in Siberia (*Poryadok*, September 17th, 1881).

o 2

article costs its weight in silver, and, of course, there is absolutely no means of earning even a shilling. The Government gives to such exiles only four to eight roubles (eight to ten shillings) per month, and immediately refuses this poor pittance if the exile receives from his parents or friends the smallest sum of money, be it even ten roubles (1*l*.) during twelve months. To give lessons is strictly forbidden, even if there were lessons to give, for instance to the *stanovoy's* children. Most of the exiles do not know manual trades. As to finding employment in some private office—in those boroughs where there are offices—it is quite impossible :—

" We are afraid of giving them employment " (wrote the Yeniseisk correspondent of the *Russkiy Kurier*), " as we are afraid of being ourselves submitted to the supervision of the police. . . . It is sufficient to meet with an Administrative exile, or to exchange a few words with him, to be inscribed under the head of suspects. . . . The chief of a commercial undertaking has recently compelled his clerks to sign an engagement stating that they will not be acquainted with 'politicals,' nor greet them in the streets."

More than that, we read in 1880 in our

papers that the Ministry of Finance brought forward a scheme for a law "to allow the common-law and political Administrative exiles to carry on all kinds of trades, with the permission of the Governor-General, which permission is to be asked in each special case." I do not know if this scheme has become law, but I know that formerly nearly all kinds of trade were prohibited to exiles, not to speak of the circumstance that to carry on many trades was quite impossible, the exiles being severely prohibited from leaving the town even for a few hours. Shall I describe, after this, the horrible, unimaginable misery of the exiles?— " Without dress, without shoes, living in the nastiest huts, without any occupation, they are mostly dying from consumption," was written to the *Golos* of February 2nd, 1881. " Our Administrative exiles are absolutely starving. Several of them, having no lodgings, were discovered living in an excavation under the bell tower," wrote another correspondent. " Administrative exile simply means killing people by starvation "—such was the cry of our press when it was permitted to discuss this subject. " It is a slow, but sure execution," wrote the *Golos*.

And yet, misery is not the worst of the condition of the exiles. They are as a rule submitted to the most disgraceful treatment by the local authorities. For the smallest complaint addressed to newspapers, they are transferred to the remotest parts of Eastern Siberia. Young girls, confined at Kargopol, are compelled to receive during the night the visits of drunken officials, who enter their rooms by violence, under the pretext of having the right of visiting the exiles at any time. At another place, the police-officer compels the exiles to come every week to the police-station, and "submits them to a visitation, together with street-girls."[7] And so on, and so on!

Such being the situation of the exiles in the less remote parts of Russia and Siberia, it is easy to conceive what it is in such places as Olekminsk, Verkhoyansk, or Nijne-kolymsk, in a hamlet situated at the mouth of the Kolyma, beyond the 68th degree of latitude, and having but 190 inhabitants. For, all these hamlets

[7] *Golos*, February 12th, 1881. Since April, 1881, the editors of newspapers were severely prohibited from publishing anything about the Administrative exiles; and all newspapers having the slightest pretension to be independent were suppressed.

consisting of a few houses each, have their exiles, their sufferers, buried there for ever for the simple reason that there was no charge brought against them sufficient to procure a condemnation, even from a packed court. After having walked for months and months across snow-covered mountains, on the ice of the rivers, and in the *toundras*, they are now confined in these hamlets where but a few hunters are vegetating, always under the apprehension of dying from starvation. And not only in the hamlets—it will be hardly believed, but it is so—a number of them have been confined to the *ulusses*, or encampments of the Yakuts, and they are living there under felt tents, with the Yakuts, side by side with people covered with the most disgusting skin diseases. "We live in the darkness," wrote one of them to his friends, taking advantage of some hunter going to Verkhoyansk, whence his letter took *ten months* to reach Olekminsk; "we live in the darkness, and burn candles only for one hour and a half every day; they cost too dear. We have no bread, and eat only fish. Meat can be had at no price." Another says: "I write to you in a violent pain, due to periostosis. . . . I have asked to be transferred to a hospital, but without success. I do not know how long this torture will last; my only wish is to be freed from this pain. We are not allowed to see one another, although we are separated only by the distance of three miles. The Crown allows us four roubles and fifty kopeks—nine shillings—per month." A third exile wrote about the same time : " Thank you, dear friends, for the papers; but I cannot read them : I have no candles, and there are none to buy. My scurvy is rapidly progressing, and having no hope of being transferred, I hope to die in the course of this winter."

" I hope to die in the course of this winter ! " That is the only hope that an exile confined to a Yakut encampment under the 68th degree of latitude can cherish !

When reading these lines we are transported back at once to the seventeenth century, and seem to hear again the words of the protopope Avvakum :—" And I remained there, in the cold block-house, and afterwards with the dirty Tunguses, as a good dog lying on the straw; sometimes they nourished me, sometimes they forgot." And, like the wife of Avvakum, we ask now again : " Ah, dear, how long, then, will these sufferings go on ? " Centuries have elapsed since, and a whole hundred years of pathetic declamations about progress and humanitarian principles, all to bring us back to the same point where we were when the Tsars of Moscow sent their adversaries to die in the *toundras* on the simple denunciation of a favourite.

And to the question of Avvakum's wife, repeated now again throughout Siberia, we have but one possible reply: No partial reform, no change of men can ameliorate this horrible state of things; nothing short of a complete transformation of the fundamental conditions of Russian life.

CHAPTER VI.

THE EXILE ON SAKHALIN.

THERE is in the Northern Pacific, close by the coasts of Russian Mandchuria, a wide island—one of the largest in the world,—but so out of the way of seafarers, so wild and barren, and so difficult of access, that until the last century it was quite ignored and considered as a mere appendix to the continent. Few places in the Russian Empire are worse than this island; therefore, it is to Sakhalin that the Russian Government sends now its hard-labour common-law exiles.

A treble aim has always been prosecuted by exile to Siberia: to get rid of criminals in Russia at the lowest expense to the Central Government; to provide the mines which were the private property of the Emperors with cheap labour; and to colonize Siberia. For many years it was supposed that this treble aim was achieved; as long as the Siberians could not make their voice heard otherwise than through the medium of governors nominated by Russia, the illusion could be maintained. But during the last twenty years it has become more and more difficult to stifle the voices both of the Siberians and of those who know the conditions of exile, and a whole literature has grown up of late which has destroyed all the above illusions. The St. Petersburg Government was compelled to order inquiries into the present condition and results of exile; and the inquiries fully confirmed the opinions expressed by private explorers.

It appeared, first, that if the Imperial Cabinet really gets cheap labourers in the hard-labour convicts, who extract silver and gold from its mines, it gets them at too heavy a sacrifice of human life. The scandalous manslaughter which was going on at these mines revolted the public conscience. If hundreds of men could be slaughtered twenty years ago at Kara, in order to raise gold to the amount prescribed from St. Petersburg; if they could be overworked and underfed so as to die by hundreds in the course of one summer, and nobody dared to utter a word about it, it became impossible to do the same when the facts were brought to public knowledge. After the opening of the navigation on the Amur, the Imperial gold-mines at Kara and the Imperial silver-works on the Gasimur were no longer at the end of the world. As to the supposed cheapness of labour, it appeared that, while the Imperial Cabinet really had the convicts for a few pence a day, their transport from Russia, their terrible mortality, and the maintenance of a large administration, as also of soldiers and Cossacks, and the incredible number of runaways—all this implied so heavy a charge on Russia and Siberia, that the country would certainly be able to present the Imperial family with twice the amount of gold and silver extracted by the convicts at a much lower cost.

As to the benefits derived by Siberia from colonization by exiles, this fallacy could not be easily got rid of. There stood the figures showing that from 1754 to 1885 nearly 1,200,000 exiles had been transported to Siberia, and, whatever the number of runaways and premature deaths, still many hundred thousands had been added in this way to the population of the country. It was even argued that if Siberia has now a population of 4,100,000 souls, it has been chiefly indebted for this population to the exiles.

The figures given in the preceding chapter, and many others of the same kind, have weakened, however, this fallacy too. The official inquiries made in 1875 have shown that, although there is a notable percentage of descendants from exiles in the 4,000,000 inhabitants of Siberia, nevertheless the free immigration has contributed much more towards the colonization of the country, and introduced much better elements, than the batches of exiles, demoralized by protracted detention in prisons, emasculated by hard labour, and settled without having the slightest intention of beginning a new life in Siberia. If statistics do not entirely support the extreme view of some Siberians, who are inclined to deny that almost any part has been played by exiles in the increase of the population of their country, it must be recognized, at least, that this increase is achieved by too great an amount of human suffering, because far less than one-half of those who cross the Urals in convict-parties become permanent settlers. With regard to the other half, it is a mere burden upon the colony.[1]

[1] See *Yadrintseff's Siberia*, and *Vostochnoye Obozrenie*.

The poor results obtained in Siberia from colonization by exiles would certainly not have been accepted as an inducement to extend the practice if the lives of the convicts had been taken into any account. Nevertheless, the desire of having a settled Russian population on Sakhalin—backed by the desire of the Governor-Generals of Siberia, anxious to get rid of the yearly increasing numbers of hard-labour convicts brought to the Nertchinsk mines—inclined the Government to make a new experiment in the hard-labour colonization of this wild island. Such being the views held at St. Petersburg, the Governor-General of Siberia found no lack of complacent officials to represent the island as a most appropriate place for such experiments, and to describe its coal-mines as so many hidden treasures. The voices of honest explorers—scientific people, mining engineers, and officers who represented the island for what it was worth—were stifled; and since 1869 the stream of hard-labour convicts has been directed thither.

For several years nothing was heard about this foolish attempt. But finally the truth began to leak out, and we now know sufficient to have, at least, a broad idea of the experiment.

The Exile on Sakhalin. 207

Although its superficial area entitles it to occupy the first rank amidst the islands of the globe, Sakhalin ranks amidst the last in suitability for habitation. Novaya Zemlya and New Siberia certainly lay behind it; but not many islands besides. It is, properly speaking, a link between the Japanese archipelago and the Kurilians, and Japan considered it as a part of its territory until the Russians established there, in 1853, their first military post in the southern part of the island. Three years later another post was settled at the Due coal-mines, opposite the mouth of the Amur. Russia thus took possession of the island, and it was explored by a series of scientific expeditions in the course of 1860 to 1867. The military stations were reinforced ; some attempts were made to raise coal from the Jurassic coal-layers at Due, and in 1875 Japan, which continued to consider South Sakhalin as its own territory, abandoned it to Russia in exchange for the Kurilian islands.

In fact, there is nothing attractive on the island, and although it is 670 miles in length, and from 20 to 150 miles in width, its population hardly numbers 5000 inhabitants. Some 2000 Ghilaks carry on a wretched existence

by hunting in the north; some 2500 Ainos—
a bearded people akin to the Kurilians—are
scattered in a few settlements in the south; and
a few hundred of Oroks, i.e. Tunguses, lead a
nomadic life in the mountains. The Ainos are
real serfs to a few Japanese merchants who
supply them with corn, salt, and other necessaries, and in exchange make this wretched
people work hard for them: they take all the
fish they can catch in the gulfs and at the
mouths of a few rivers, and leave the Ainos
just what is strictly necessary to maintain their
poor existence. Throughout its history, that
is, under the Chinese dominion, and later on,
under the Japanese, nobody except poverty-
stricken hunters and fishers would settle on
Sakhalin.

In fact, only hunters and fishermen could
find there the means of living. Not that the
island is situated in very uncongenial latitudes.
Its southern extremity reaches the 46th degree, and its northern point does not extend
farther than the 54th degree. But the warm
sea-current, which might bring it some of the
warmth of the Chinese waters, does not reach it;
while the ice-bound cold current issuing from
the 'great cellar' of the Pacific—the sea of

The Exile on Sakhalin.

Okhotsk—washes its eastern coast. In the midst of the summer Russian explorers found the east coast bound with ice-fields and heaps of floating ice which were brought by north-east winds. And to the west, the narrow elongated island has that immense refrigerator —the cold and high mountain tracts of Siberia— separated from it only by a narrow and shallow channel. The rays of the sun are concealed by heavy clouds and dense fogs. When M. Polyakoff landed at Due (in Middle Sakhalin), at the end of June, he found the neighbouring hills covered with patches of snow, and the soil was frozen at a depth of twenty-one inches. The summer crops were hardly germinating, and vegetables could not be bedded out before June 20th. June was drawing to a close, and still the thermometer had never risen above 64° Fahr. Nor had there yet been a single fine day, while thick fogs enveloped coast and hills for eight days in the course of the month.

Several chains of mountains, from 2000 to 5000 feet high, intersect the island. Their damp or stony slopes are covered from top to bottom with thick forests—poor forests, con-sisting of species characteristic of the sub-arctic region; and between the hills one finds but

P

narrow, damp, marshy valleys, quite unfit, as a whole, for agriculture. The steep slopes of the mountains run down to the waters of the channel, so that no road could be laid out along the sea-coast, unless by piercing the stony crags; and, in fact, there are but two larger valleys which intersect the mountains: that of the Due river, continued to the north-east by the Tym; and that of the Poronai in the south of the island.

It is to the former, close by the spot where coal-layers are found, that the hard-labour convicts have been directed. M. Polyakoff, who visited Sakhalin in 1881-2, on a scientific mission from the St. Petersburg Academy of Sciences, describes thus the valley which in the fallacies of the Russian rulers was to become a centre for Russian civilization on the island. The hills which enclose the narrow valley are mostly barren, and their slopes are too steep to be adorned with corn-fields. As to the bottom of the valley, it is covered with a thick layer of heavy clay, coated but with a thin sheet of arable soil. The whole is exceedingly marshy. " One can walk on it without sinking very deeply in the mud; but it is intersected by peat-moors and deep marshes... Nowhere is the ground fit for agriculture.... It mostly resembles that of the worst parts of Olonets, with this difference, that it is often covered with pools of water, even in the forests, and that even the kind of cultivation which is carried on in Olonets by means of clearing and burning the forests is rendered impossible by the marshy ground of the forests themselves." " These conditions render both agriculture and gardening impossible in the vicinity of Due." Only a very few patches higher up the valley, and on the upper Tym can be utilized for agricultural and gardening purposes. But these few patches which are met with sporadically, are already mostly under cultivation.[2]

It is, however, precisely there, that is, in the vicinity of the Due coal-mines, that the hard-labour convicts are settled after having finished their terms of imprisonment at the hard-labour prison of Alexandrovsk. The settlement around this prison is exceedingly gloomy. There are two big barracks which bear the name of prisons; a few houses are scattered

---

[2] I. Polyakoff, *Reise nach der Insel Sakhalin in den Jahren* 1881-82. A us dem Russischen übersetzt von Dr. Arzruni. Berlin, 1884.—Russian original in the *Izveztia* of the Russian Geographical Society, 1883.

round about; and beyond them begins the wilderness. Only Little Alexandrovsk, higher up the valley, and the few houses of Korsakova have the aspect of a more prosperous settlement; but there again all land available for gardening is already under cultivation. It was, however, precisely with the aim of having permanent agricultural settlements that the convicts were sent to Sakhalin. It was supposed that after having passed one part of their terms at work in the coal-mines they would be settled around the mines, and raise corn sufficient to support themselves and to provide the penal colony with supplies of food.

Further up the valley which—according to the concocted reports of the Administration—was to become a granary for Sakhalin, the soil is the same; and the small settlements of Rykovo and Malo-Tymovskaya—" the most appropriate spot for agriculture on all the island"—have to support the same struggle against Nature. Oats do not ripen there, and only barley can be grown. As to the roads which connect these settlements, they are simply impassable. Tracks have been cut through the forests, but horses sink in the marshes. Much hope had been placed also in the valley of the

Tym, which continues the Alexandrovsk valley to the north-east, and reaches the Sea of Okhotsk. But its marshy soil, and still more the cold and fogs of the Sea of Okhotsk, render agriculture quite impossible in this valley, except at its top. Its vegetation is sub-polar; and on the sea-coast it has all the characters of the *tundra*. "If latter on," M. Polyakoff writes in an official report, " a few spots available for orchards and corn-fields can be found in the valley of the Tym, after a careful search, it would be advisable to await the results obtained in the already existing settlements before creating new ones; and all the more as great difficulty is already experienced in supplying these settlements with food, and as there is already now a serious lack of provisions in the colony. As to the hope entertained of creating villages at the mouth of the Tym, it would be a delusion to entertain it, the region being a region of tundras and polar-birch.".

These conclusions, most cautiously expressed —too cautiously perhaps—are fully supported by those arrived at by Dr. Petri in 1883, with the difference that the Italian Doctor is less cautious than the Russian scientist. The whole "colonization of Sakhalin," he wrote to the *Jahresbericht* of the Bern Geographical Society for 1883-84, is a big lie circulated by the authorities. While the local authorities show on paper that there are already 2700 acres under cultivation, the survey of M. Karaulovski has shown that only 1375 are cultivated; the 700 families of hard-labour convicts who were promised to have twenty acres of arable soil per male soul, have succeeded in clearing less than two acres per family.[3] Dr. Petri's conclusion is that the island is quite unfit for agriculture, and that the Government has been induced to take this false step by the false reports of people interested in the undertaking.

As far as we can now judge, experience has fully confirmed the views held by M. Polyakoff and Dr. Petri. The raising of corn is subject to such difficulties and uncertainty, that the new settlers have had to be maintained until now on food brought from Russia, and there is no hope of improvement. Food is transported from the valley of the Due to that of the Tym (Derbinskoye), across a chain of mountains, on

---

[3] "*Jahresbericht der Geographischen Gesellschaft von Bern,*" 1883-84, pp. 129 and 39. See also *St. Petersburg's Herold*, NN. 353—356. 1884.

foot, on the backs of the convicts, for a distance of sixty miles;[4] and one can easily guess what M. Polyakoff's words about a "lack of provisions" really mean. As to the few free settlers who were induced by false promises to leave their homes in Tobolsk and to settle at Takoy, starting there a village of twenty-five houses, they were compelled to leave Sakhalin after a three years' desperate struggle against the inhospitable climate and soil. No subsidies of the Crown would help them. They were compelled to migrate again and to settle on the continent, on the Pacific coast.

Surely, Sakhalin will never become an agricultural colony. If settlers are maintained there as they are in the lower Amur, they will remain a burden upon the State; the Government will be compelled, sooner or later, to permit most of them to emigrate elsewhere, or to provide them for years and years with food. Cattle-breeding might be more successful. But all that could be expected would be that a few colonists, living by means of their cattle and a little fishing, would remain there.

Much ado was made in Russia about the Sakhalin coal-mines. But in this direction,

[4] Dr. Petri, l.c.

too, there was much exaggeration. The Sakhalin coal is reputed in the East as preferable to the Australian; but it is considered as much inferior to the Newcastle or Cardiff coal.[5]

The extraction of coal on Sakhalin was already begun in 1858, and during the first ten years 30,000 tons were extracted. But mixed as it was with stone, it was of a bad quality, while the extraction (which was carried on by the light of stearine candles)[6] cost in reality fabulous prices. But the coal in stock rapidly accumulated, while batches upon batches of convicts were sent every year; so that now they are occupied in laying down roads on the shore to bring Due into easy communication with Alexandrovsk. A tunnel is therefore pierced in the rocks; but this famous tunnel which was to add to the fame of Sakhalin when its completion was announced in the Russian Press, was not yet terminated at all in 1886: it was a loop-hole through which men could pass only creeping.

[5] According to Dr. Petri the Sakhalin coal costs from seven to seven and a half dollars per ton, while the Japanese and Australian are paid only five dollars.

[6] Köppen's "Sakhalin; its Coal Mines and Coal Industry," St. Petersburg, 1875. A most reliable work.

The worst is, however, that on the whole circumference of Sakhalin there is not a single harbour, and that the approach to its coasts is always difficult owing to the fogs, the late arrival of summer, and the want of beacons in the Tartarian Strait. At Due, the roadstead is open to all winds. The great bay of Patience is too shallow, the depth being only four fathoms at a distance of half a mile from the coast. The best bay—the Aniva—which freezes only for a few weeks, is also open to all winds and has no harbours. Only the Mordvinoff Bay has a good anchorage.

Decades and decades must elapse before the Sakhalin coal could compete with European coal in the Chinese ports; and in the meantime, a hundred and twenty men would fully supply the Siberian flotilla of the Russian navy with the 5000 tons which represent its annual consumption. Thousands of convicts have thus nothing to do on Sakhalin, and the coal they could raise would be years and years without finding any use.

The first batch of eight hundred convicts was sent to Sakhalin seventeen years ago, in 1869. Following the established traditions, the Administration could invent nothing better than to send them across Siberia ; that is, those who were shipped from the Kara goldmines had to make a journey of 2000 miles down the Amur, and those who were brought from Russia had a journey of no less than 4700 miles to be done, before reaching Nikolaevsk at the mouth of the Amur.

The results of such a journey were really terrific. When the first party of 250 men reached Nikolaevsk, *all*, 250, except the dead, were suffering from scurvy ; fifty were entirely laid up with the same disease;[7] and these were the men who were to begin the colonization of Sakhalin ! No wonder that during the first years the mortality was 117 in the thousand, and that each man was taken to the hospital on an average of three times a year.[8]

It was only after a series of like blunders which were loudly denounced even in the gagged Press, that the transport of convicts to Sakhalin *via* Siberia was abandoned, and they were sent *via* Odessa and the canal of Suez. It must be fresh in the memories of Englishmen in what conditions the transport was made on

[7] Tahlberg, "Exile to Sakhalin," in *Vyestnik Evropy*, May, 1879.

[8] Köppen, *l.c.*

this new route, and what a cry of indignation was raised in the English Press. Things are a little better during the last few years, and we have before us reports of medical officers which state that the transport of convicts on ships from Odessa has latterly been made under reasonable conditions. But again, last month, the news came that the last transport sent out in 1886 was overtaken by an epidemic of small pox, and that the mortality was once more dreadful. The customary official denial will surely appear, but whom will it convince?

Little is known about the condition of convicts on Sakhalin itself. In 1879, a report appeared in the Russian Press, signed by a Russian merchant, stating that the arbitrary conduct of the chief commander at Sakhalin knew no limits. The Prison Administration was accused of stealing the last coppers of the convicts. A doctor, Mr. A. A., wrote in October, 1880, from Alexandrovsk: "I am ordered to the Korsakoff hospital (on the south coast), but I cannot reach it before next June. My colleague abandons his post . . . he can no longer bear all that is going on there!" Significant words, which permit a Russian reader to guess the truth, especially when they are followed by these: "The chief of the settlement seldom visits the barracks; he does not appear otherwise than surrounded by armed warders. The governor of the prison dare not appear amongst the convicts."[9] Later on, we saw in the *Strana* (a St. Petersburg newspaper),[1] an account of the disorders discovered on Sakhalin by the Chief Commander of the Russian Pacific squadron. It appeared that while the poorer convicts were compelled to heaviest labour, in chains, rich scoundrels and thieves were kept in a quite privileged position; they lived free on the island, squandered money, and made festivals to the authorities.

The above-mentioned revelations provoked an official inquiry. The newspapers announced it with great rejoicing, but what became of it nobody knows; and no news have penetrated since in the press, except those brought in by Dr. Petri. The overcrowding in the Alexandrovsk prison must be terrible. It has been built for 600 inmates, but it had 1103 men in 1881, and 2230 in 1882. Some pro-

[9] The *Poryadok*, published by Professor Stasulevitch (suppressed since), September 8 (20), 1881.
[1] January 31, 1882. Dr. Petri, *l.c.*

visional barracks must have been erected, I suppose. But I imagine what "provisional barracks" must be in Sakhalin!

It is evident from what was said above that the greatest difficulty for the Sakhalin administration is to lodge the convicts, and to invent an occupation for those who are liberated. There being no place, either in Russia or in Siberia, where hard-labour convicts can be kept, more and more of them are sent every year to Sakhalin. In Siberia, after their liberation, they receive an allotment of land and agricultural implements, and then, after two years, the Government troubles no more about them. But, what is to be done for them on Sakhalin? Agriculture being almost impossible, people are literally starving in the new settlements, and food for them must be brought from Russia, subject to accidents of all kinds. So for instance, last summer, it appeared in the (semi-official) paper, published at Vladivostok, that the shipment of flour destinated for Sakhalin arrived all damaged, and full of worms and beetles. An inquiry had been ordered; of course, it will be made, but people on Sakhalin will remain in the meantime without food.

Sakhalin is merely a new edition of what

I saw twenty years ago on the Amur and the Usuri, but in still worse conditions. As to buying food, they have to pay twenty roubles for a sack of five puds of rye flour of the worst quality (fifty shillings the 160 lbs.), and certainly double that price as soon as some accident has happened to the Crown stores. The agriculturists, who were supposed soon to supply the prison with all necessaries, and who surely would have done so in reasonable circumstances, must themselves be saved from starvation. It is not on two acres per family, cleared from beneath the marshy forests, that they can possibly subsist.

One of the great inducements of Sakhalin in the eyes of the Administration was that escapes will be exceedingly difficult. This inducement surely exists. Not that escapes are impossible. In 1870, no less than sixteen per cent. of the prisoners escaped nevertheless. But most of them are taken by the indigenes, and either killed by them when they have been captured far away from the military posts, or returned to the post, if the natives find it worth while to make the journey. Each prisoner captured in Siberia by indigenes is valued at ten roubles when brought back alive, and five roubles when killed. Three roubles in the latter case and six roubles in the former do serve on Sakhalin to induce the Ghiliaks to hunt the runaways. They do so in the most barbarous way, especially since the Sakhalin authorities have distributed rifles among them. Dr. Petri writes that once they came across a party of nonconformists belonging to the sect of *byeguny* (runners), whom their religious beliefs prescribe to break completely with the present world—given up to the Anti-Christ— and to live a life of restless wanderers, who never have a house or any kind of property. They were twelve, they had infants in arms. All were killed by the Ghiliaks. The most remarkable thing is that these wretched creatures have no hatred against the runaway convicts: they keep on the best terms if the convict can give them something worth the three roubles. But if he cannot pay the redemption, they kill him pitilessly, in order to receive the three roubles from the prison administration. As soon as the premium was temporarily abolished, they were the first to help the escapes. "What will you"—our runaways say—"they are starving themselves, and three roubles and our cloth are a great temptation for a starving people."

And still escapes are numerous. The runaways make their way to the south-east with the greatest difficulties, across hills and forests, and wait till they sight from the coast an American whaler. Some of them cross the Tartarian Strait, six miles in width at Cape Pogobi, when an ice-bridge connects Sakhalin with the continent; whilst others, again, make a raft of three or four trees, and entrust themselves to the rough sea. The schooner "Vostok" recently met with such a raft in the channel. A black point having been sighted from the schooner, she approached it, and found two men on a raft of four logs. They had with them a pail of soft water, some black bread biscuits, two pieces of brick-tea, and so they floated along without having any idea where the current would land them. When asked where they were going—"There, to Russia!" they answered, pointing towards the West. Most of them perish from the squalls, others during the dreadful snowstorms—Amur snowstorms, which sometimes bury Nikolaevsk for several days under the snow. And when on the continent, they endure the most terrible sufferings before reaching the inhabited parts of the Amur. Cannibalism has been spoken of.

And yet some runaways succeed to return to Russia. A few years ago, one of them, Kamoloff, who had reached his native village, but was betrayed by some personal enemy, was brought before a Court; and his simple speech moved the hearts through Russia. He had wandered for two years across lakes and rivers, through the forests and over the Steppes, before reaching his house. He found his wife awaiting for his return. He was happy for a few weeks. "The streams, the stormy Baikal, the terrible snowstorms did me no harm," he said; "beasts pitied me. Men—my own villagers—were pitiless; they betrayed me!"

"There, to Russia!" that is the idea which haunts every exile. They may send him to Sakhalin—his thoughts will always draw him westward, and even from Sakhalin he will try to return to his native village, to find out his abandoned house. The system of exile has served its time if the exiles must be sent to the lonely island in order to prevent escapes.

We hope the days are not far distant when it will be definitely done away with. The sooner the better; because Siberia is large, and administrative fancies have no bounds. Who knows if to-morrow the whim will not seize them to create new agricultural colonies in the Land of the Tchuktchis, or on Novaya Zemlya, and sacrifice new hecatombs of sufferers for no other purpose than to provide a few officials with lucrative appointments?

At any rate, the ignoramuses of St. Petersburg seem to have abandoned their fantastical schemes of making a penal colony of Sakhalin. The last news is that they are planning to enlarge the Kara prisons, and to send there one thousand more convicts; while the abandoned silver-mines of Nertchinsk are to be reopened. In the matter of exile, as in so many others, we are reverting to the very same point where we were thirty-five years ago, on the eve of the Crimean war.

CHAPTER VII.

A FOREIGNER ON RUSSIAN PRISONS.

THE foreigners who have visited Russia, and have been sufficiently keen observers, have often noticed a characteristic feature of the Russian Administration. People who belong to it know well its deficiencies, its worst features; very well indeed, because they themselves are not the last in contributing to its bad repute. They not only know it: they frankly acknowledge it when in company with their Russian friends. Even in official reports to the heads of the ministries, they do not conceal the bad organization of their respective departments.

But let a foreigner enter a drawing-room where, a few minutes before, the Administration was sharply criticized, and the critics will be unanimous in repeating to the foreigner that "surely there are some minor deficiencies in the

Administration; but the sun itself has its black spots, and His Excellency So and So is just now taking the most energetic measures for removing the very last remains of the disorder which unhappily crept into the Administration under his predecessor, General So and So." And if the foreigner is a man who writes for some newspaper in his own country, and shows an inclination to trumpet through the world what he hears, those very same people who thought everything worse than ever a few minutes before, will be happy to show the foreigner everything in its best light, and thus to confound all "vindictive writers" who "divulge to foreigners" the reports written for home-use by those very same officials. I have remarked the same feature in the Mantchurian Administration, and I often noticed it both at Irkutsk and St. Petersburg. Surely I never saw a more disheartening picture of wholesale robbery in the higher Administration of Russia than that drawn in the reports of the Comptroller-General to Alexander II. as the Comptrol was first introduced in Russia, and nothing more characteristic than the open recognizance of the truth of these Comptroller-General's views, which was written by the Tsar on one of the reports. Everybody in the upper circles of the Russian society knew the contents of the reports and the answer of the Tsar. But what a chorus of maledictions would greet the Russian who should translate these reports, and circulate them in the foreign press! *Soru iz izby ne vynosi!* "Do not take the dirt out of the house!" would be the unanimous outcry.

One can easily understand how difficult it is for a foreigner to ascertain the truth under such circumstances, especially if he moves only in the Administrative circles, if he does not know Russian, and does not take the trouble to look through the Russian literature bearing on the subject. Even if he were inspired with the most sincere desire to know the truth, and not to be a puppet in the hands of Administrators, who are only too glad to find docile instruments in the foreign press, his way would be beset with difficulties.

This simple truth has not been understood by an Englishman, Mr. Lansdell, who has crossed Siberia a few years ago, and, after having hastily cast a glance on a few Siberian prisons, published a book, in which he tried to represent Russian and Siberian prisons under a smiling aspect. No wonder that his description did not agree with mine. It was quite natural also that he should try to explain the contradiction, and so he did, in an article contributed to the English press in February, 1883. The following from my rejoinder will complete the above picture of Russian prisons:[1]—

Mr. Lansdell does not contradict my statements. He even seems not to notice the facts which I have divulged, and which represent the Russian prisons in quite another light than his own account of them. When I say, for instance, that the St. Petersburg House of Detention—which is quoted by Mr. Lansdell as a sample of "what Russia *can* do"—was recognized by the Commission under State-Secretary Groth as a building that must be built anew to be rendered inhabitable, notwithstanding the fabulous sums of money it has cost (see the summary of the official report given in the *Golos* for the 24th of January, 1881); when I mention the wholesale stealing which was discovered in the same prison in 1881; when I call to mind the disgraceful treatment of political prisoners in this "model-prison" by General Trepoff, which

[1] The following pages are reprinted, by permission, from the *Nineteenth Century*, June, 1883.

treatment was condemned, so to say, even by a Russian Court, during the trial of Vera Zassoulitch; Mr. Lansdell turns a deaf ear to all this, and does not say if, in spite of all this, the St. Petersburg House of Detention still "may be supposed to represent the very beau-ideal of what a House of Detention ought to be." When I produce, further, the narrative of an inmate of a central prison, published in Russia (under the responsibility of a Conservative editor, M. Eug. Markoff), and the reliability of which was recognized at once by all St. Petersburg newspapers; when I describe how the jailor of this central prison flogs his inmates, and how his successor gives free play to his own fists, Mr. Lansdell does not say if he still believes that in Russian prisons "justice and mercy go hand-in-hand"—he likes better not to touch these subjects—but he asks me several questions about other things.

Mr. Lansdell asks me first, what I meant when I wrote: "In the space of fourteen hours, indeed, he breakfasted, he dined, he travelled over forty miles, and he visited the three chief jails of Siberia: at Tobolsk, at Alexandrovsky Zavod, and at Kara." I simply meant to say that, whilst crossing the continent at the speed of a Siberian courier who outstrips the post, Mr. Lansdell has devoted less than fourteen hours to the study of the three chief penal establishments of Siberia. In fact, it appears from his own book (chapters v. ix. xxi. xxxvi. and xxxvii.), that he has spent a couple of hours in visiting the Tobolsk prison, two hours at Alexandrovsky Zavod, and less than ten hours in visiting the prisons of Kara, as in the space of one day he had not only to visit the jails, but also to travel between the different prisons scattered over a space of nearly twenty miles, and to experience the well-known Siberian hospitality in the shape of breakfasts and dinners (fully described in his book). As to the second day of his stay at Kara, during which day he had to visit the prisons of Lower Kara, it proved to be the name-day of the Superintendent of the works, Colonel Kononovitch, and in the evening Mr. Lansdell was bound to take the steamer at Ust-Kara, so that "when we came to the first prison," he writes, "where the officer was standing ready to receive us, I was afraid we should not have time, and that our staying might involve the missing of our steamer. I therefore begged that we might push on, which we did, to Ust-Kara."

In fact, I even would not have mentioned this "less than fourteen hours' knowledge" of the chief centres of penal servitude in Siberia, if it were not necessary to reduce to its true value the following affirmation of Mr. Lansdell (vol. ii. page 5): "I think it only right to say that I have visited Russian Houses of Detention from the White Sea in the north to the Black Sea and Persian frontier in the south, and from Warsaw in the west to the Pacific in the east." The truth is that Mr. Lansdell has cast a hasty glance on what the authorities were willing to show him; that he has not seen a single central prison; and that had he visited every prison in Russia in the way he visited some of them, he still would remain as ignorant as he is now about the real conditions of prison-life of Russia.

Still—if Mr. Lansdell were able to appreciate the relative value of the information he obtained in the course of his official scamper through the Siberian prisons, and especially if he had taken notice of existing Russian literature on the subject, his book might have been a valuable one. This he did not, and so he is absolutely ignorant of what has been written in Russia on the subject. Himself does not partake of this opinion, and he writes:—

"Yet there is a fair sprinkling on my list of 120 works 'consulted or referred to,' of Russian authors, and of those whom I have called the 'vindictive class of writers' (some of them escaped or released convicts), who, trading upon the credulity and ignorance of the public, have retailed and garnished accounts of horrible severities, which they never profess to have witnessed, nor attempt to support by adequate testimony. One of these was Alexander Herzen, who wrote *My Exile to Siberia*, though he never went there, but only as far as Perm, where one of the prisons is situated of which Prince Kropotkin complains so bitterly."

It is true that at the end of Mr. Lansdell's book there is a list of 120 works "consulted or *referred to*" (that is, quoted by the authors whose works he has consulted). I find even in this list Daniel Defoe's *Life and Adventures of Robinson Crusoe*. But the "fair sprinkling of Russian names" (if we exclude the authors who deal with Church matters, or merely with geography, as MM. Venukoff and Prjevalsky) must be reduced to the following:—(1) M. Andreoli's paper on Polish Exiles in 1863–1867, appeared in *Revue Moderne*, and which Mr. Lansdell contradicts without knowing anything

A Foreigner on Russian Prisons. 235

about the sad story of Polish exile but what he has learned from occasional conversations during his hasty travel. (2) Dostoevsky's *Buried Alive*, dealing with seclusion in the Omsk fortress, *thirty-five years ago;* (3) Piotrovsky's romantic *Escape from Siberia*, *thirty-eight years ago;* (4) Baron Rozen's *Memoirs*, dealing with the Decembrists, *fifty-five years ago;* and (5) Herzen's *My Exile to Siberia*, telling his sojourn in exile at Perm, nearly *forty years ago*. But, of course, I do not find in this list either M. Maximoff's *Siberia and Hard Labour*, which is the result of serious studies made in Siberia, with the authorization of Government; nor the results of M. Nikitin's many years' official inquiry into the state of our prisons; nor the Siberian *stryapchiy* (or Procureur) M. Mishlo's papers on the Prisons submitted to his own control in Siberia; nor M. Yadrintseff's *Siberia as a Colony;* nor any of the official reports; not even M. Mouravioff's papers on prisons, published by M. Katkoff in his arch-conservative review. Shortly, *none* of the works which contain any information about the present state of Russian prisons. This ignorance of works which contain reliable information about our prisons is the more remarkable, as none of the just-mentioned authors belong to the "vindictive class of writers who villify the land of their punishment," but they all were, and several are, officials in the service of the Government.

Let us see now if these authors are not more in accordance with the "vindictive writers" than with Mr. Lansdell's testimony. The chief lock-up for prisoners waiting for trial at St. Petersburg, the so-called Litovskiy Zamok, appears as follows under the pen of M. Nikitin :—

"It contains 103 rooms for 801 inmates. . . . The rooms are dreadfully dirty; even on the staircase you feel the smell which suffocates you. The black holes produce a dreadful impression (*potryasayushcheie vpechatlenie*); they are almost absolutely deprived of light; the way to them leads through dark labyrinths, and in the holes themselves all is wet: there is nothing but the rotten floor and the wet walls. A man coming from the open air rushes away asphyxiated. . . . Specialists say that the *most healthy man* will surely die, if he be kept there for three or four weeks. The prisoners who were kept there for some time went out quite exhausted; several could hardly stand on their feet. Only a few prisoners of the less important categories are allowed to work. The others remain with crossed hands for months and years." When M. Nikitin asked for accounts of the money brought to prisoners by their kinsfolk, or earned by themselves, he met with an absolute refusal from the authorities high and low.—*Nikitin, on the St. Petersburg Prisons.*

The same author writes about the prisons at the police-stations of the capital :—

" In the rooms for common people the dirt is dreadful; they sleep on bare wooden platforms, and half of them sleep *beneath the platforms on the floor*. Each prison has its black holes; they are very small holes, where rain and snow enter freely. There is nothing but the floor to sleep upon; the walls and the floor are quite wet. The privileged prisoners who are kept in cells fall soon into melancholy; several are very near to insanity. . . . No books are given in the common rooms, excepting religious ones, which are taken for making cigarettes."—*Police Prisons at St Petersburg.*

The Official Report of the St. Petersburg Committee of the Society for Prisons, published at St. Petersburg in 1880, described the prisons of the Russian capital as follows:—

"The prison (Litovskiy Zamok) is built for 700 inmates, and the depôt-prison for 200 men; but they often contain, the former from 900 to 1000 persons, and the depôt-prison from 350 to 400, and even more. Besides, long since, these buildings correspond no more, neither to the hygienic conditions, nor to those of a prison altogether."

M. Katkoff's review, the *Russkiy Vyestnik*, does not give a better idea of Russian prisons. After having given a description of the police-stations, the author, M. Mouravioff, says that the *ostrog* is not better; it is usually an old, dirty building, or a collection of such buildings enclosed by a wall. It is not better inside: moisture, dirt, overcrowding, and stench, such is the type of all *ostrogs* in the capitals and in provincial towns.

"The dress is of two different kinds; the old and insufficient dress which is usually worn by the prisoners, and another which is distributed when the prison is to be shown to some visitor; but usually it is kept in the store-house. . . . No schools, no libraries. . . . The depôts for convicts are still worse. . . .

Let us stop before one of the rooms. It is a spacious room with platforms along the walls and narrow passages between. Hundreds of women and children are collected here. It is the so-called family-room, for the families of the convicts. In this dreadful atmosphere you see children of all ages in the greatest misery. No Crown dress is allowed them, and therefore their bodies are covered with rags— with dirty strips of cloth torn to pieces, which can shelter neither from cold nor from wet; and with these rags they will be sent on their journey to Siberia."—*Russkiy Vyestnik*, 1878.

M. Yadrintseff—the same whom Mr. Lansdell condescends now to quote—writes as follows about the Siberian prisons which Mr. Lansdell imagines he knows after the hasty visits he has paid to them. I condense the description:—

"*Almost in every ostrog* there is a nearly underground corridor, moist and fetid, a grave; in this corridor are the cells for the more important prisoners *waiting for their trial*. These cells are half underground. The floor is always wet and rotten. Mould and fungoid growths cover the walls. Water is continually oozing from beneath the floor. A small painted window makes the cell always completely dark. The men are kept there in irons. There is no bedstead, no bed; the prisoners are lying on the floor which is covered with worms and myriads of fleas; and for bed they have rotten straw, for covering their poor cloak, torn to pieces. The moist and cold air makes you shiver even in the summer. The sentry runs away to breathe fresh air. And in such cells the prisoners spend several years, waiting for their trial! These prisoners, even the most healthy of them, become insane. 'I remember to have heard once in the night horrible cries,' says one of the prisoners in his memoirs; 'it was a giant who was becoming insane.'"

And so on, and so on. I could fill pages with like descriptions. Was Mr. Lansdell shown all this? If not, was I not right to say that he ought to notice the existing Russian literature on the subject? And will Mr. Lansdell still maintain that he has noticed it?

As to Herzen's work, Mr. Lansdell's reply deserves a few words more. I have quoted, in my paper on Russian Prisons, a description of the Perm prison, which was written two years ago, that is, in 1881, by an inmate of the prison. It was published by Professor Stasulevitch in so scrupulously managed a paper as was the *Poryadok;* it was reproduced by all the newspapers, and was contradicted by nobody; even the usual official denial did not appear. What does Mr. Lansdell oppose to this recent testimony? He writes that he has consulted the memoirs of Alexander Herzen, who was at Perm, 'where one of the prisons is situated of which Prince Kropotkin complains so bitterly.' But Herzen was settled at Perm *forty years ago;* he never was there in a prison, and, as far as I remember, he does not even speak about the prisons at Perm. Shall I suppose that Mr. Lansdell knows of Herzen's work but its title?

As to the title, Mr. Lansdell accuses Herzen again and again of having published a book on his exile to Siberia without having been there. In the preface to his book, *Through Siberia,* he writes :—

" My speciality in Siberia was the visitation of its prisons and penal institutions, considered, however, not so much from an economic or administrative, as from a philanthropic and religious point of view. *Much has been written about them that is unsatisfactory, and some* things that are absolutely false. One author has published 'My Exile to Siberia' who never went there."

The truth is that Herzen has never written about the prisons and penal institutions of Siberia, in fact, nothing about Siberia at all. He has written his memoirs under the title *Past and Thoughts* (Byloye i Dumy), one chapter of which, dealing with his incarceration at St. Petersburg and exile to Perm, was entitled "Prison and Exile" ("Tyurma i Ssylka.") It is probably this chapter which was translated into English; and if the English publisher has thought it necessary to give it the title of *My Exile to Siberia*, I suppose that Herzen had nothing to do with that. The French, German, and Italian translations of the same work are simply entitled *Prison and Exile*.[2]

[2] Mr. Lansdell repeats this accusation against Herzen with such a persistence, in different parts of his book, and in the *Contemporary Review*, that, in order to be certain about this subject I wrote to the son of Herzen, the distinguished Professor of Physiology, A. A. Herzen. Here is a translation of his reply, dated Lausanne, February 26, 1881:—

"SIR,—You are quite right; it is merely the part of the memoirs of my father which deals with his arrest and exile; there is not a word about Siberia. It is the English publisher who has added to the title the words 'to Siberia,'

In any case, Herzen's Memoirs, forty years old, have nothing to do with Siberia, and still less with the Perm prisons of our time; and that is precisely the subject which interests us.

I wrote further that the chief prison of St. Petersburg, the Litovskiy Zamok (of which I just have given an idea by quoting a few lines from M. Nikitin's description), is an "old-fashioned, damp, and dark building, which should be simply levelled to the ground." "To this proceeding," Mr. Lansdell says, "I would not utter a word of protest." He admits, too, that I, "perhaps justly," "find a good deal of fault with this prison." Well, I am glad to hear that Mr. Lansdell finds a good deal of fault with one Russian prison; but I regret that, though having visited the Litovskiy Zamok, he did not describe in his book the *chief prison of the Russian capital;* his readers would know what they have to expect from provincial prisons.

As to the overcrowding of Russian prisons,

without the knowledge of my father, and my father has publicly protested at once against this 'humbug' (à l'insu de mon père, et mon père a dès alors protesté publiquement contre ce 'humbug.') . . .

"Believe me, &c., (Signed) A. HERZEN."

Mr. Lansdell doubts they were so overcrowded as I said. I cannot answer better than by producing a few quotations from the materials I have at hand :—

"The Tomsk depôt" (writes the correspondent of the *Siberian Gazette*) is overcrowded. To the 1520 people we had, 700 new ones are added, and so the prison which was built for 900 people contains 2220 inmates. There are 207 on the sick-list. (*Siberian Gazette* and *Moscow Telegraph*, August 28, 1881.)

At Samara :—" The *average* number of inmates in our prisons, on the first of each month for this year, was 1147; the aggregate cubic capacity of all our prisons being for 552 inmates." (*Golos*, May 13, 1882.)

At Nijniy-Novgorod :—" The prison, built for 300 men, contains, while the rivers are open for navigation, as many as 700, sometimes 800 prisoners." (Official report mentioned by the *Golos*, March, 1882.)

In Poland :—" Each place in the prisons of Poland is occupied by four prisoners instead of one. It is proposed to build a number of new prisons" (they are not yet built). (*Moscow Telegraph*, November, 1881.)

Shall I fill one page or more with like

quotations, or, rather, see what is said by official persons entrusted with the supervision of prisons:—

M. Mouravioff, a contributor to M. Katoff's review, in an elaborate paper on Russian prisons (written precisely in the spirit that the admirers of the Russian Government like), says:—"*Almost all our prisons* contain one and a half to twice the number of prisoners for which they were built." ("Prisons and the Prison Question," *Russkiy Vyestnik*, 1878.)

The Siberian *stryapchiy*, M. Mishlo, writes about *Siberian* prisons which were under his own control:—" The jailor brought me to the rooms. Everywhere dirt, overcrowding, wet, want of air and light. After having visited the rooms, I entered the hospital. As soon as I entered the first room I involuntarily shrank back before the unutterable stench. . . . The cabinets were luxurious apartments in comparison with the hospital. . . . *Everywhere the number of prisoners is thrice the number admitted by the law.* At V. (Verkhneudinsk), for instance, the *ostrog* is built for 240 inmates, and usually contains 800." (*Otechestvennyia Zapiski*, 1881.)

It was precisely to such overcrowding,

together with a phenomenal amount of dirt, that the famous typhus epidemic at the Kieff prison was due. It may have been imported by Turkish prisoners, as the authorities said, but its dreadful ravages were owing to overcrowding and filth. "Buildings erected for 550 inmates contained twice this number," says the *Golos* correspondent, in a letter dated the 30th of October, 1880; and he adds:— "The professors of the University who have visited the prison, arrived, as known, at the conclusion that overcrowding was the chief cause of the epidemic." The circular of the Chief Director of Prisons (mentioned in chapter II.) confirms, in its first paragraphs, the exactitude of this conclusion. No wonder that, after a partial evacuation of the prison, there were still 200 laid up with typhus out of 750 inmates. No wonder also that the mortality at Kharkoff has assumed the proportion (200 out of 500) described by the priest of the prison, in a sermon which was reproduced by the local *Eparchial Gazette*—a paper appearing under the supervision of the Archbishop.

I come now to the fortress of St. Peter and St. Paul, where Mr. Lansdell was admitted to look through inspecting holes into the cells of the Troubetskoi bastion and to enter an empty cell, and where I was kept for nearly two years in the same building.

The system of Mr. Lansdell in dealing with this subject is really very strange. He mentions first what a friend of his (a person of high "intelligence and probity," who " moves in high circles at St. Petersburg") said about prisoners in the fortress. They were fed, he said, " with salt herrings and given no water to drink, so that they became half mad with thirst;" this " business was only stopped by Count Schouvaloff;" but his friend " still thinks that drugs are sometimes given to prisoners to make them frantic, in the hope that during their excitement they may be led to confess." Then he describes his own visit to the fortress, and how he " peeped breathlessly," after having " duly prepared his nerves to see how this arch-offender is treated." And as he is shown nothing but a man lying at this moment on his bed, or a lady reading at her table, he discharges his bad temper against the " exaggerated and vindictive expressions of released prisoners" who " vilify the land of their punishment," &c. I really do not see how the "vindictive" writers could be held responsible for the opinions of Mr. Lansdell's friends, who probably gather their information from the high circles where they move, and have sufficient intelligence to discriminate between mere fables and reality.

As to "vindictive writers" who are accused of exaggerations, there is only one who has written about the Troubetskoi bastion, and this one seems to be quite unknown to Mr. Lansdell—I mean Pavlovsky, who has published in the Paris *Temps* (in 1878, I think) a description of his imprisonment in the fortress, with a preface by Tourgueneff, whose name is a sufficient guarantee of the *absolute* trustworthiness of Pavlovsky's description. Mr. Lansdell's diatribes against "exaggerated and vindictive expressions" of released prisoners, are, therefore, mere flowers of polemics.

If Mr. Lansdell had limited himself to the description of what he saw, and had added that those prisoners whom he saw in the bastion were waiting for trial, or for exile without trial, for two, three years, or more, he would have merely done what he ought to do. But he goes on to deny the descriptions of such parts of the fortress which he has not seen, and of which he has not the slightest idea.

I had brought to the knowledge of public

opinion in England, in order to show the hypocrisy of our Government, the treatment to which were submitted, the *condemned* revolutionists, who, instead of being sent to Siberia, according to law, were kept in the fortress, in dark cells, without any occupation, and were brought to madness, or on the edge of the grave, in the proportion of five to ten in less than one year. This I had written, according to a description published in the *Will of the People* and in the pamphlet *Na Rodinye*, as I knew that each word of this description is absolutely exact.

This part of the fortress (where Shiryaeff, Okladsky, Tikhonoff, Martynovsky, Tsukerman, &c., were kept in 1881, that is, the Trubetskoi ravelin, *not* the bastion) was not shown to Mr. Lansdell, and he knows absolutely nothing about it ; so that the only account which, in my opinion, he was entitled to give was the following :—

" Although Count Tolstoy had promised me that I *should see everything* (he might say), but I was shown only that building where prisoners are kept when waiting for trial, and the Courtine, where I found no political prisoners. I was not shown any building where condemned Terrorists were kept, and I do not remember any of the names mentioned in the

Times being named to me in the Trubetskoi bastion. So I can say nothing about the fate of Shiryaeff, Okladsky, and their comrades. In fact, I have visited only one bastion out of six, and have no idea about what the ravelins and the remainder of the fortress may contain."

That would have been, I think, the only correct way to give an account of his visit to the fortress, and this the more as, out of two informants of Mr. Lansdell—both belonging to the State secret police—one (who belonged to the third section), said that he has visited once a building with cells underground which were "lighted from the corridor above, hardly enough," he said, "to read," which cells are probably the same that I have mentioned, where lamps are lighted for twenty-two hours out of twenty-four; and the other informant ("a chief of the gendarmerie") mentioned a more comfortable building, three stories high, in the Alexis Ravelin, where prisoners were kept too. There are thus at least two prisons, or two suites of cells, which were not shown to Mr. Lansdell. But notwithstanding that, Mr. Lansdell tries to cast a doubt upon the just-mentioned description of the shameful treatment to which Shiryaeff, Okladsky, and their comrades were submitted, and, in order to show its inaccuracy, tells us a long story about a Russian, Mr. Robinson, who was kept, some twenty years ago, for three years (without being brought before a court) in the Alexis Ravelin, and was treated there as in a good hotel. Everybody will understand, however, that Mr. Robinson's case has absolutely nothing to do with that of Shiryaeff and Okladsky, and that the well-lighted room where he was kept (like hundreds of students and young men arrested at the same epoch) has nothing to do with the suite of dark cells mentioned not only by " vindictive writers," but even by a third section informant of Mr. Lansdell. The fortress covers several hundred acres, and contains all kinds of buildings, from the palace of the Commandant to the cells where people are brought to death, or madness, in the course of a few months.

There is, however, one point upon which Mr. Lansdell's doubts are justifiable. It is when he doubts that physical torture has been applied to Ryssakoff. We doubted also. But, who will be convinced of the contrary by such arguments of Mr. Lansdell as these:—Nobody was tortured in his presence, and Mr. Jones, a British subject, who was arrested once, and set at liberty after an examination which lasted for a quarter of an hour, was not put to torture![3] Everybody understands that torture would not be applied in the fortress under the eyes of Mr. Lansdell, and still less to Mr. Jones.

But Mr. Lansdell has made up his mind that after having seen a corner of the fortress, one would know everything about it; and he goes still further, he victoriously exclaims—" What, then, have become of the *cachots, oubliettes*, and dismal chambers which have been connected with the Peter and Paul by so many?" Well, I also know the Troubetskoi bastion; I know also the rooms of the Courtine; still I should never permit myself, on the ground of this limited knowledge, either to affirm or to deny the existence of *oubliettes* in the fortress. I should not affirm their existence, as I know that *oubliettes* are usually discovered only after a 14th of July; and I should not deny it, as I know that the Troubetskoi bastion does not embody even a tenth part of the fortifications of the fortress. The facts given in a foregoing chapter amply prove that there are *oubliettes*, with men therein, and that Mr. Lansdell, in

[3] *Contemporary Review*, p. 285.

denying their existence, has pushed too far his zeal in whitewashing the Russian Government.

And now let me add a few words about the difficulties which beset the way of those who earnestly wish to know the real state of Russian prisons. I shall not follow Mr. Lansdell's example, and accuse him of a want of good faith for his holding different views on Russian prisons from our Russian explorers and myself. I am fully aware of the difficulties one meets with in this way. I know them from my own experience, and still more from the written experience of those who attempted to make on a larger scale an inquiry into the state of our prisons. Even officials, to whom their official position opened the doors of the prisons at any time, and who had plenty of time before them to pursue their inquiry, openly acknowledge these difficulties. All serious explorers of our penal institutions are unanimous in saying that one learns nothing from a mere inspection of a prison. "Each prison undergoes a magical change when a visitor is expected," says one of them. "I did not recognize the lock-up which I had visited *incognito*, when I went afterwards to the same lock-up in my official quality," says another. "The prisoners never unveil to an inspector the horrors committed in the prison, as they know that the inspector goes away and the jailer remains," says a third explorer. One must know the prisons beforehand to discover the horrible blackholes, like those described by MM. Nikitin and Yadrintseff, as they obviously will never be shown to a visitor who knows nothing about them ; and so on.

Such being the difficulties for Russian officials, they are still greater for a foreigner. He is in the worst imaginable position, on account of the continuous fear of Russian administrators of being treated by the foreign press as barbarians. He has before him this dilemma. Either he will thoroughly inquire into the state of the prisons, he will go to the bottom, and he will discover the bestialities of the Makaroffs, the Trepoffs, and their acolytes ; and then he will not receive permission to visit prisons. Or, he will make only an official scamper through a few prisons ; he will know nothing but what the Government is willing to let him know; and, being unable to test for himself what is reported to him by officials, he will become the vehicle for bringing to public knowledge what his official acquaintances desire to be published. Such is the case of Mr. Lansdell.

But the greater the difficulties, the greater must be the efforts of those who really are desirous to know the truth; and we have seen foreigners who have vanquished these difficulties. One may differ with Mr. Mackenzie Wallace on many points, perhaps himself would change now his opinion on several subjects; but still his book, though not received with congratulations by MM. Katkoff and Tolstoy, was recognized unanimously by the independent Russian press as a serious and conscious work. And as to our prisons, several Russian officials, by displaying much patience and by spending much time, have come to learn the true state of our penal institutions. The English prisons are not Russian *ostrogs*. But if a foreigner went to England, without knowing a word of English, without taking the pains to study what was written in England about her penal institutions, and, after having paid a hasty visit to some prisons, should write that all those who hold different views on prisons from himself are merely inspired with a feeling of vindictiveness, surely he would be accused of great levity and presumption. But Russia is not England, and to know the truth in Russia is far more difficult.

Levity is always regrettable, but it is the

more regrettable in questions like this, and in a country like Russia. For twenty years all honest men in our country have been loudly crying against our prisons, and loudly asking for an immediate reform. For twenty years public opinion vainly asks for a thorough renovation of the prison administration, for more light, for more supervision in the whole system. And the Government, which refuses that, will be only too glad if it can answer them : " You see, there is a foreigner who knows everything about prisons throughout the world, and who thinks that all you say is mere exaggeration; that our prisons are not at all bad in comparison with those of other countries."

When thousands, nay, a hundred thousand, of men, women, and children are groaning under the abominable *régime* of prisons which we see in Russia, one ought to proceed with the greatest cautiousness; and I earnestly invite the foreigners who may be tempted to study this question, never to forget that each attempt to extenuate the dark features of our prisons will be a stone brought to consolidate the abominable *régime* we have now.

CHAPTER VIII.

IN FRENCH PRISONS.[1]

THE St. Paul prison at Lyons, where I spent the first three months of my incarceration, is not one of those old, dilapidated, and damp dungeons which are still resorted to in many French provincial towns for lodging prisoners. It is a modern prison, and pretends to rank among the best *prisons départementales*. It covers a wide area enclosed by a double girdle of high walls; its buildings are spacious, of modern architecture, and clean in aspect; and in its general arrangement the modern ideas in penitentiary matters have been taken into account, as well as all necessary precautions for making it a stronghold in the case of a revolt. Like other departmental prisons, its destination is to receive those prisoners who are awaiting their trial, as also those of the

[1] Reprinted from the *Nineteenth Century*, by permission.

condemned whose penalty does not exceed one year of imprisonment. A subterraneous gallery connects it with another spacious prison for women—the St. Joseph.

It was on a December night that I arrived there from Thonon, accompanied by three gendarmes. After the usual questions, I was introduced into a *pistole* which had been cleaned and heated for receiving me, and this *pistole* became my abode until the following March. On a payment of six francs per month and three francs to the waiter, each prisoner incarcerated for the first time may hire a *pistole* during his preventive incarceration, and thus avoid living in the cells. The *pistole* is also a cell, but it is somewhat wider and much cleaner than the cells proper. A deep window under the ceiling gives enough of light, and six or seven paces may be measured on its stone pavement, from one corner to the opposite one. It has a clean bed and a small iron stove heated with coke, and for one who is occupied and is accustomed to solitude it is a tolerably comfortable dwelling-place—provided the incarceration does not last too long.

Not so the cells, which occupy a separate wing of the prison. Their arrangement is the same as everywhere now in Europe: you enter a broad and high gallery, on both sides of which you see two or three stories of iron balconies; all along these balconies are the doors of the cells, each of which is ten feet long and six or seven feet wide, and has an iron bed, a small table, and a small bench—all three made fast to the walls. These cells are very dirty at Lyons, full of bugs, and never heated, notwithstanding the wetness of the climate and the fogs, which rival in density, if not in colour, those of London. The gas-burner is never lighted, and so the prisoner remains in an absolute obscurity and idleness from five, or even four on a winter night, until the next morning. Each prisoner himself cleans his cell; that is, he descends every morning to the yard to empty and wash his bucket with dirty water, and he enjoys its exhalations during the day. Even the simplest accommodation for avoiding this inconvenience, which we found later on at Clairvaux, has not been introduced at Lyons. Of course, no occupation is given to the prisoners during the preventive incarceration, and they mostly remain in perfect idleness throughout the day. The prison begins to exercise its demoralizing influence as soon as the prisoner has entered within its walls.

Happily enough, the imprisonment before the trial is not so dreadfully protracted as in my own mother-country. If the affair is not too complicated, it is brought before the next assizes, which sit every three months, or before the following ones; and cases where the preventive incarceration lasts for more than ten or twelve months are exceptional. As to those affairs which are disposed of by the *Police Correctionnelle* Courts, they are usually terminated—always by a condemnation—in the course of one month, or even a fortnight. A few prisoners, already condemned, are also kept in the cells—there being a recent law which permits the prisoners to make their time in cellular imprisonment, three months of which are counted as four months of the penalty. This category, however, is not numerous, a special permission of the Ministry being necessary in each separate case.

Small yards, paved with asphalte, and one of them subdivided into three narrow compartments for the inmates of the cellular department, occupy the spaces between the high wings of the prison. There the prisoners take some exercise, or spend several hours in such work as may be done out-doors. Every morning I could see from my window some fifty men descending into the yard; there, taking seats on the asphalte pavement, they were beating the wound-off cocoons from which the floss silk is obtained. Through my window, or while occasionally passing by, I sometimes saw also swarms of boys invading one of the yards; and at a three years' distance I cannot remember these boys without a sad feeling and heartburn.

The condemnations pronounced against children by the always condemning *Police Correctionnelle* Courts are, in fact, much more ferocious than those pronounced against adults. The adult may be condemned to a few months or a few years of imprisonment; the boy is invariably sent for the same crime to a "House of Correction," to be kept there until his eighteenth or twenty-first year. When the prosecutions against the Anarchists at Lyons had reached their culminating-point, a boy of fifteen, Cirier, was condemned by the Lyons Court of Appeal to be kept in prison until the age of twenty-one, for having abused the police in a speech pronounced at a public meeting.

The president of the same meeting, for exactly the same offence, was condemned to one year of imprisonment, and he is long since at liberty, while the boy Cirier will remain for several years more in prison. Similar condemnations are quite usual in French Courts.

I do not exactly know what the French penitentiary colonies and reformatories for children may be, the opinions which I have heard being very contradictory. Thus I was told that in the colonies the children are treated not very badly, especially since improvements have been introduced of late;[2] but I was told also, on the other side, that a few years ago, in a penitentiary colony in the environs of Clairvaux, the children were unscrupulously overworked by a person to whom they were intrusted, or rather rented by the State, and that they were abused. At any rate, we saw at Lyons numbers of boys—mostly runaways and " incorrigible ones " from the penitentiary colonies; and to see the education given to these poor boys was really awful. Brutalized as they are by the warders, and left without any honest and moralizing influence, they are foredoomed to

[2] See Appendix D.

become permanent inmates of prisons, and to die in a central prison, or in New Caledonia. The warders and the priest of the St. Paul prison were unanimous in saying that the only desire which day and night haunts these young people is that of satisfying the most abject passions. In the dormitories, in the church, in the yards, they are always perpetrating the same shameful deeds. When we see the formidable numbers of the *attentats à la pudeur* brought before the Courts every year, let us always remember that the State itself maintains, at Lyons and in fact in all its prisons, special nurseries for preparing people for those crimes. I seriously invite, therefore, those who elaborate schemes for the legal extermination of recondemned convicts in New Guinea, to hire, for a fortnight or so, a *pistole* at Lyons, and to re-examine there their foolish schemes. They would perceive that they begin their reforms from the wrong end, and that the real cause of the *récidive* lies in the perversion due to such infection-nests as the Lyons prison is. As for myself, I suppose that to lock up hundreds of boys in such infection-nests is surely to commit a crime much worse than any of those committed by any of the convicts themselves.

On the whole, the prisons are not places for teaching much honesty, and the St. Paul prison makes no exception to the rule. The lessons in honesty given from above are not much better than those imparted from below, as will be seen from what follows. Two different systems are in use in French prisons for supplying the inmates with food, dress, and other necessaries. In some of them the State is the undertaker who supplies both food and dress, as also the few other things which the prisoner can purchase at the canteen with his own money (bread, cheese, some meat; wine and tobacco for those who are not yet condemned; prison-knives, combs, brushes, paper, and so on). In this case, it is the State which raises a certain percentage, varying from three to nine-tenths on the payment due to the prisoner for the work he has done in prison, either for the State, or for private undertakers; three-tenths of the wages are retained if the prisoner is under preventive incarceration; five-tenths if he is condemned for the first time; and six, seven, eight, or nine-tenths if he has had one, two, three, four, or more previous condemnations; one-tenth of the salary always remaining for the prisoner, whatever the number of condemnations. In other prisons the whole is rented to a private undertaker, who is bound to supply everything due in accordance with regulations. The undertaker in this case raises the just-named tenths on the salaries of the prisoner, and he is paid, moreover, by the State a few centimes per day for each prisoner. As to those inmates who find it more advantageous to labour for the trade outside (skilled shoemakers, tailors, and scribes are often in this case), they are bound to pay to the undertaker a certain redemption money—mostly 10*d*. per day—and then they are dispensed from compulsory labour. Now, the St. Paul prison is established on the second system ; everything is supplied by a private undertaker, and I must confess that everything is of the worst quality. The undertaker unscrupulously robs the prisoners. Of course the food is far from being as bad as it is in Russian prisons, but still it is very bad, especially if compared with what it is at Clairvaux. The bread is of a low quality, and the soup and *ratin* of boiled rice, or kidney-beans, are ofter execrable. As to the canteen, everything is dear and of the lowest kind ; while the Clairvaux administration supplied us for threepence a piece of good steak with potatoes, we paid at Lyons sixpence for a slice of very bad boiled meat, and in the same proportion for everything.

How the works are conducted and paid at Lyons I cannot judge from my own experience, but the above account does not inspire much confidence in the honesty of the enterprise. As to the dress, it is of the worst kind, and also much inferior to what we saw at Clairvaux, where also it leaves very much to desire. When taking my daily walk in one of the yards at Lyons, I often saw the recently condemned people going to change their own dress for that of the prisoners, supplied by the undertakers. They were mostly workmen, poorly but still decently dressed—as French workmen, even the poorest, usually are. When they had, however, put on the uniform of the prison—the brown jacket, all covered with multicoloured rags roughly sewn to cover the holes, and the patched-up trousers six inches too short to reach the immense wooden shoes—they came out quite abashed with the ridiculous dress they had assumed. The very first step of the prisoner within the prison walls was thus to be wrapped up in a dress which is in itself a story of degradation.

I did not see much of the relations between the administration and the common-law prisoners at Lyons. But I saw enough to perceive that the warders—mostly old police-soldiers—maintained all the well-known brutal features of the late Imperial police. As to the higher administration, it is pervaded with the hypocrisy which characterizes the ruling classes at Lyons. To quote but one example. The Director of the prison had reiterated to me on many occasions the formal promise of never sequestrating any of my letters, without letting me know that such letters had been confiscated. It was all I claimed. Notwithstanding that, several of my letters were confiscated, without any notice, and my wife, ill at that time, remained anxious without news from me. One of my letters, stolen in this way, was even transmitted to the Procureur Fabreguettes, who read it before the Court of Appeal. I might quote several other examples, but this one will do.

There is in our system of prisons a feature well worthy of notice, but completely lost sight of, and which I would earnestly commend to the attention of all interested in penal matters. The leading idea of our penal system is obviously to punish those who have been recognized as "criminals;" while in reality the penalty of several years of imprisonment hurts much less the "criminal" than people quite innocent— that is, his wife and children. However hard the conditions of prison-life, man is so made that he finally accommodates himself to these conditions, and considers them as an unavoidable evil, as soon as he cannot modify them. But there are people—the prisoner's wife and his children—who never can accommodate themselves to the imprisonment of the man who was their only support in life. The judges and lawyers who so freely pronounce sentences of two, three, and five years of imprisonment—have they ever reasoned about the fate they are preparing for the prisoner's wife? Do they know how few are the women who can earn more than six or seven shillings per week? And do they know that to live with a family on such a salary means sheer misery with all its dreadful consequences? Have they ever reflected also about the moral sufferings which they are inflicting on the prisoner's wife—the despising of her neighbours, the sufferings of the woman who naturally exaggerates those of her husband, the pre-

occupations for the present and the future? ...
Who can measure all these sufferings, and count
the tears shed by a prisoner's wife?

If the slightest attention were ever given to
the sufferings of the prisoner's kinsfolk, surely the
inventors of schemes of civilized prisons would
not have invented the reception-halls of the
modern dungeons. They would have said to
themselves that the only consolation of the
prisoner's wife is to see her husband, and they
would not have inflicted on her new and quite
useless sufferings, and planned those halls
where everything has been taken into account
—everything excepting the wife who comes once
a week to cast a glance on her husband, and to
exchange a few words with him.

Imagine a circular vaulted hall, miserably
lighted from above. If you enter it at the
reception-hours, you are literally stunned. A
clamour of some hundred voices speaking, or
rather crying all at once, rises from all parts of
it towards the vault, which sends them back
and mingles them into an infernal noise, together with the piercing whistles of the warders,
the grating of the locks, and the clashing of
the keys. Your eyes must be first accustomed
to the darkness before you recognize that the

clamour of voices comes from six separate groups of women, children, and men crying all at once to be heard by those whom they address. Behind these groups, you perceive along the walls six other groups of human faces, hardly distinguishable in the darkness behind iron-wire networks and iron bars. You cannot divine at once what is going on in these groups. The fact is, that to have an interview with his kinsfolk the prisoner is introduced, together with four other prisoners, into a small dark coop, the front of which is covered with a thick network and iron bars. His kinsfolk are introduced into another coop opposite, also covered with iron bars, and separated from the former by a passage three feet wide, where a warder is posted. Each coop receives at once five prisoners; while in the opposite coop some fifteen men, women, and children—the kinsfolk of the five prisoners—are squeezed. The interviews hardly last for more than fifteen or twenty minutes; all speak at once, hasten to speak, and amidst the clamour of voices, each of which is raised louder and louder, one soon must cry with all his strength to be heard. After a few minutes of such exercise, my wife and myself were voiceless, and were compelled simply to look at each other without speaking, while I climbed on the iron bars of my coop to raise my face to the height of a small window which feebly lighted the coop from behind; and then my wife could perceive in the darkness my profile on the grey ground of the window. She used to leave the reception-hall saying that such a visit is a real torture.

I ought to say a few words about the *Palais de Justice* at Lyons, where we were kept for ten days during our trial. But I should be compelled to enter into such disgusting details that I prefer to go on to another subject. Suffice it to say that I have seen rooms where the arrested people were awaiting their turn to be called before the examining magistrate, amidst ponds of the most disgusting liquids; and that there are within this "Palace" several dark cells which have alternately a double destination: sometimes they are literally covered with human excretions; and a few days later, after a hasty sweep, they are resorted to for locking up newly arrested people. Never in my life had I seen anything so dirty as this Palace, which will always remain in my recollections as a palace of filth of all descriptions. It was with a real feeling of relief that I returned from thence to my *pistole*, where I remained for two months more, while most of my comrades addressed the Court of Appeal. This last confirmed, of course, the sentences pronounced by order of Government in the Police Correctionnelle Court; and a few days later, on March 17, 1883, we were brought in the night, in great secrecy, and with a ridiculous display of police force, to the railway-station. There we were packed up in cellular waggons to be transported to the "Maison Centrale" of Clairvaux.

· It is remarkable how so many improvements in the penitentiary system, although made with excellent intentions of doing away with some evils, always create, in their turn, new evils, and become a new source of pain for the prisoners. Such were the reflections which I made when locked up in a cell of the cellular waggon which was slowly moving towards Clairvaux. A French cellular waggon is an ordinary empty waggon, in the interior of which a light frame-work consisting of two rows of cells, with a passage between, has been constructed. But I am afraid of conveying a false and exaggerated impression to my readers when I write "two rows of cells." "Two rows of cupboards" would be more correct, for the cells are just the size of small cupboards, where one may sit down on a narrow bench, touching the door with his knees and the sides with his elbows. One need not be very fat to find it difficult to move within this narrow space ; and he need not be too much accustomed to the fresh breezes of the sea-side to find difficulties in breathing therein. A small window protected by iron bars, which is cut through the door of the cupboard, would admit enough air; but to prevent the prisoners from seeing one another and talking, there is an additional little instrument of torture in the shape of a Venetian blind, which the warders close as soon as they have locked up somebody in the cupboard. Another instrument of torture is an iron stove, especially when it runs at full speed to boil the potatoes and roast the meat for the warders' dinner. My fellow-prisoners, all workmen of a great city, accustomed to the want of fresh air in their small workshops, did not actually suffocate, but two of us were prevented from fainting only by being allowed to step out of our respective cupboards and to breathe some air in the passage between. Happily enough, our journey lasted only fifteen hours ; but I have Russian friends, who were expelled from France, and who have spent more

T

than forty-eight hours in a cellular waggon on their way from Paris to the Swiss frontier, the waggon being left in the night at some station, while the warders called at the Mâcon and other prisons.

The worst is, however, that the prisoners are completely given up to the mercy of the two warders; if the warders like, they put the cuffs on the hands of the prisoners already locked up in the cupboards, and they do that without any reason whatever; and if they like better, they, moreover, chain the prisoners' feet by means of irons riveted to the floor of the cupboards. All depends upon the good or bad humour of the warders, and the depth of their psychological deductions. On the whole, the fifteen hours which we spent in the cellular waggon remain among the worst reminiscences of all my comrades, and we were quite happy to enter at last the cells at Clairvaux.

The central prison of Clairvaux occupies the site of what formerly was the Abbey of St. Bernard. The great monk of the twelfth century, whose statue, carved in stone, still rises on a neighbouring hill, stretching its arms towards the prison, had well chosen his residence at the mouth of a fine little dale supplied with excellent water from a fountain, and at the entrance to a wide and fertile plain watered by the Aube. Wide forests cover still the gentle slopes of the hills, whose flanks supply good building-stone. Several lime-kilns and forges are scattered round about, and the Paris and Belfort railway runs now within a mile from the prison.

During the great Revolution the abbey was confiscated by the State, and its then extensive and solid buildings became, in the earlier years of our century, a *Dépôt de Mendicité*. Later on, their destination was changed, and now the former abbey is a "Maison de Détention et de Correction," which shelters about 1400 and occasionally 2000 inmates. It is one of the largest in France; its outer wall—the *mur d'enceinte*—a formidable masonry some twenty feet high, incloses, besides the prison proper, a wide area occupied by the buildings of the administration, barracks of the soldiers, orchards, and even corn-fields, and has an aggregate length of nearly three miles. The buildings of the prison proper, with its numerous workshops, cover a square about 400 yards wide, inclosed by another still higher wall—the *mur de ronde*.

With its lofty chimneys, which day and night send their smoke towards a mostly cloudy sky, and the rhythmical throbbing of its machinery, which is heard late in the night, it has the aspect of a little manufacturing town. In fact, there are within its walls more manufactures than in many small towns. There are a big manufacture of iron beds and iron furniture, lighted by electricity, and employing more than 400 men; workshops for weaving velvet, cloth, and linen; for making frames to pictures, looking-glasses, and meters; for cutting glass and fabricating all kinds of ladies' attire in pearl-shell; yards for cutting stone; flour-mills, and a variety of smaller workshops; all dress for the inmates is made by the men themselves. The whole machinery is set in motion by four powerful steam-engines and one turbine. An immense orchard and a corn-field, as also small orchards allotted to each warder and *employé*, are also comprised within the outer wall and cultivated by the prisoners.

Without seeing it, one could hardly imagine what an immense fitting up and expenditure are necessary for lodging and giving occupation to some 1400 prisoners. Surely the State never would have undertaken this immense expenditure, had it not found at Clairvaux, St. Michel, and elsewhere, ready-made buildings of old abbeys. And it never would have organized so wide a system of productive work, had it not attracted private undertakers by renting to them the prisoners' labour at a very low price, to the disadvantage of free private industry. And still, the current expenses of the State for keeping up the Clairvaux prison and the like must be very heavy. A numerous and costly administration, seventy warders, nourished, lodged, and paid from 45*l.* to 56*l.* per year, and a company of soldiers which are kept at Clairvaux, bear hard on the budget—not to speak of the expenses of the central administration, the transport of prisoners, the infirmary, and so on. It is obvious that the above-mentioned percentage, raised on the salaries of the prisoners, which does not exceed an average of 6*d.* per day and per head of employed men, falls very short of defraying all these heavy expenses.

Leaving aside the political prisoners who are occasionally sent thither, there are at Clairvaux two different categories of inmates. The great number are common-law prisoners condemned to more than one year of imprisonment but not to hard labour (these last being transported to New Caledonia); and there are, besides, a few dozen of soldiers condemned by martial courts—the so-called *détentionnaires*. These last are a sad product of our system of militarism. A soldier who has assaulted his corporal, or officer, is usually condemned to death; but if he has been provoked—which is mostly the case—the penalty is commuted into a twenty years' imprisonment, and he is sent to Clairvaux. I cannot explain how it happens, but there are *détentionnaires* who have to undergo two or three like condemnations— probably for assaults committed during their imprisonment. There was much talk, during our stay at Clairvaux, of a man, about forty years old, who had cumulated an aggregate penalty reaching sixty-five years of imprisonment; he could fulfil his sentence only if he could prolong his life beyond his hundredth year. On the 14th of July, twenty-five years of his term were taken off by a decree of the President of the Republic; but still the man had some forty years more to remain imprisoned. It may seem incredible, but it is true.

Everybody recognizes the absurdity of such

condemnations, and therefore the *détentionnaires* are not submitted to the usual regimen of the common-law prisoners. They are not constrained to compulsory labour, and they enter a workshop only if they like. They wear a better grey dress than other prisoners, and are permitted to take wine at the canteen. Those who do not go to the workshops occupy a separate quarter, and spend years and years in doing absolutely nothing. It is easy to conceive what some thirty soldiers, who have spent several years in barracks, may do when they are locked up for twenty years or so in a prison, and have no occupation of any kind, either intellectual or physical. Their quarter has so bad a reputation that the rains of brimstone which destroyed the two Biblical towns are invoked upon it by the administration.

As to the common-law prisoners, they are submitted to a regimen of compulsory labour, and of absolute silence. This last, however, is so adverse to human nature that it has in fact been given up. It is simply impossible to prevent people from speaking when at work in the workshops; and, without trebling the number of warders and resorting to ferocious punishments, it is not easy to prevent prisoners from exchanging words during the hours of rest, or from chattering in dormitories. During our stay at Clairvaux we saw the system abandoned more and more, and I suppose that the watchword is now merely to prohibit loud speaking and quarrels.

Early in the morning—at five in the summer, and at six in the winter—a bell rings. The prisoners must immediately rise, roll up their beds, and descend into the yards, where they stand in ranks, the men of each workshop separately under the command of a warder. On his order, they march in Indian file, at a slow pace, towards their respective workshops, the warder loudly crying out, *un, deux! un, deux!* and the heavy wooden shoes answering in cadence to the word of command. A few minutes later, the steam-engines sound their call, and the machines run at full speed. At nine (half-past eight in the summer) the work is stopped for an hour, and the prisoners are marched to the refectories. There they are seated on benches, all faces turned in one direction, so as to see only the backs of the men on the next bench, and they take their breakfast. At ten they return to the workshops, and the work is interrupted only at twelve, for ten minutes, and at half-past two, when all men less than thirty-five years old, and having received no instruction, are sent for an hour to the school.

At four the prisoners go to take their dinner; it lasts for half-an-hour, and a walk in the yards follows. The same Indian files are made up, and they slowly march in a circle, the warder always crying his cadenced, *un, deux!* They call that *faire la queue de saucissons*. At five the work begins again and lasts until eight in the winter, and until nightfall during the other seasons.

As soon as the machinery is stopped—which is done at six, or even earlier in September or March—the prisoners are locked up in the dormitories. There they must lie in their beds from half-past six until six the next morning, and I suppose that these hours of enforced rest must be the most painful hours of the day. Certainly, they are permitted to read in their beds until nine, but the permission is effective only for those whose beds are close to the gas-burners. At nine the lights are diminished. During the night each dormitory remains under the supervision of *prévôts* who are nominated from among the prisoners and who have the more red lace on their sleeves, as they are the more assiduous in spying and denouncing their comrades.

On Sundays the work is suspended. The prisoners spend the day in the yards, if the weather permits, or in the workshops, where they may read, or talk—but not too loud—or in the school-rooms, where they write letters. A band composed of some thirty prisoners plays in the yard, and for half-an-hour goes out of the interior walls to play in the *cour d'honneur*—a yard occupied by the lodgings of the administration—while the fire-brigade takes some exercise. At six all must be in their beds.

Besides the men who are at work in the workshops, there is also a *brigade extérieure*, the men of which do various work outside the prison proper, but still within its outer wall—such as repairs, painting, sawing wood, and so on. They also cultivate the orchards of the house and those of the warders, for salaries reaching but a few pence per day. Some of them are also sent to the forest for cutting wood, cleaning a canal, and so on. No escape is to be feared, because only such men are admitted to the exterior brigade as have but one or two months more to remain at Clairvaux.

Such is the regular life of the prison; a life running for years without the least modification, and which acts depressingly on man by its monotony and its want of impressions; a life which a man can endure for years, but which he cannot endure—if he has no aim beyond this life itself—without being depressed and reduced to the state of a machine which obeys, but has no will of its own; a life which results in an atrophy of the best qualities of man and a development of the worst of them, and, if much prolonged, renders him quite unfit to live afterwards in a society of free fellow-creatures.

As to us, the "politicals," we had a special regimen—namely, that of prisoners submitted to preventive incarceration. We kept our own dress; we were not compelled to be shaved, and we could smoke. We occupied three spacious rooms, with a separate small room for myself, and had a little garden, some fifty yards long and ten yards wide, where we did some gardening on a narrow strip of earth along the wall, and could appreciate, from our own experience, the benefits of an "intensive culture." One would suspect me of exaggeration if I enumerated all crops of vegetables we made in our kitchen-garden, less than fifty square yards. No compulsory work was imposed upon us; and my comrades—all workmen who had left at home their families without support—never could obtain any regular employment. They tried to sew ladies' stays for an undertaker of Clairvaux, but soon abandoned the work, seeing that with the deduction of three-tenths of their salaries for the State they could not earn more than from three to four pence a day. They gladly accepted the work in pearl-shell, although it was paid but a little better than the former, but the orders came only occasionally, for a few days. Over-production had occasioned stagnation in this trade, and other work could not be done in our rooms, while any intercourse with the common-law prisoners was severely prohibited.

Reading and the study of languages were thus the chief occupations of my comrades. A workman can study only when he has the chance of being imprisoned—and they studied earnestly. The study of languages was very successful, and I was glad to find at Clairvaux a practical proof of what I formerly maintained on theoretical grounds—namely, that the Russians are not the only people who easily learn foreign languages. My French comrades learned, with great ease, English, German, Italian, and Spanish; some of them mastered two languages during a two years' stay at Clairvaux. Bookbinding was among us the most beloved occupation. Some instruments were made out of pieces of iron and wood; heavy stones and small carpenters' presses were resorted to; and as we finally obtained—about the end of the second year—some tools worth this name, all learned bookbinding with the facility with which an intelligent workman learns a new profession, and most of us reached perfection in the art.

A special warder was always kept in our quarter, and as soon as some of us were in the yard, he regularly took his seat on the steps at the door. In the night we were locked up under at least six or seven locks, and, moreover, a round of warders passed each two hours, and approached each bed in order to ascertain that nobody had vanished. A rigorous supervision, never relaxed, and maintained by the mutual help of all warders, is exercised on the prisoners as soon as they have left the dormitories. During the last two years I met with my wife in a little room within the walls, and, together with some one of our sick comrades, we took a walk in the solitary little garden of the Director, or in the great orchard of the prison; and never during these two years was I left out of sight of the warder who accompanied us, for so much as five minutes.

No newspapers penetrated into our rooms, excepting scientific periodicals or illustrated weekly papers. Only in the second year of our imprisonment were we permitted to receive a halfpenny colourless daily paper, and a Government paper published at Lyons. No socialist literature was admitted, and I could not introduce even a book of my own authorship dealing with socialist literature. As to writing, the most severe control was exercised on the manuscripts I intended to send out of the prison. Nothing dealing with social questions, and still less with Russian affairs, was permitted to issue from the prison-walls. The common-law prisoners are permitted to write letters only once a month, and only to their nearest relatives. As to us, we could correspond with friends as much as we liked, but all letters sent or received were submitted to a severe censorship, which was the cause of repeated conflicts with the administration.

The food of the prisoners is, in my opinion, quite insufficient. The daily allowance consists chiefly of bread, 850 grammes per day (one pound and nine-tenths). It is grey, but very good, and if a prisoner complains of having not enough of it, one loaf, or two, per week are added to the above. The breakfast consists of a soup which is made with a few vegetables, water, and American lard—this last very often rancid and bitter. At dinner the same soup is given, and a plate of two ounces of kidney-beans, rice, lentils, or potatoes is added. Twice a week, the soup is made with meat, and then it is served only at breakfast, two ounces of boiled meat being given instead of it at dinner. The men are thus compelled to purchase additional food at the canteen, where they have for very honest prices, varying from three-farthings to twopence, small rations of cheese, or sausage, pork-meat, and sometimes tripe, as also milk, and small rations of figs, jams or fruits in the summer. Without this supplementary food the men obviously could not maintain their strength; but many of them, and especially old people, earn so little that, after deducting the percentage-money raised by the State, they cannot spend at the canteen even twopence per day. I really wonder how they manage to keep body and soul together.

Two different kinds of work are made by the prisoners at Clairvaux. Some of them are employed by the State, either in its manufactures of linen, cloth, and dress for the prisoners, or in various capacities in the house itself (joiners, painters, man-nurses in the infirmary, accountants, &c.). They are mostly paid from 8*d.* to 10*d.* a day. Most, however, are employed in the above-mentioned workshops by private undertakers. Their salaries, established by the *Chambre de Commerce* at Troyes, vary very much, and are mostly very low, especially in those trades where no safe scale of salaries can be established on account of the great variety of patterns fabricated, and of the great subdivision of labour. Very many men earn but from 6*d.* to 8*d.* per day; and it is only in the iron bed manufacture that the salaries reach 1*s.* 8*d.* and occasionally more; while I found that the average salaries of 125 men employed in various capacities reached only 11*d.* (1 franc 17 centimes) per day. This figure is, however, perhaps above the average, there being a great number of prisoners who earn but 7$d.$ or even 5$d.$, especially in the workshop for the fabrication of socks, where old people are sent to die from the dust and exhaustion.

Several reasons might be adduced as an apology for these small salaries; the low quality of prison-work, the fluctuations of trade, and several other considerations ought no doubt to be taken into account. But the fact is that undertakers who have rapidly made big fortunes in the prisons are not rare; while the prisoners consider with full reason that they are robbed when they are paid only a few pence for twelve hours' work. Such a payment is the more insufficient, as one half, or more, of the salaries is taken by the State, and the regular food supplied by the State is quite inadequate, especially for a man who is doing work.

If the prisoner has had a previous condemnation before being sent to a central prison—and this is very often the case—and if his salary is 10$d.$ per day, 6$d.$ are taken by the State, and the remaining 4$d.$ are divided into two equal parts, one of which goes to the prisoner's reserve-fund and is handed over to him only on the day of his delivery; while the other part—

that is, 2*d*. only—is inscribed on his "disposable" account, and may be spent for his daily expenses at the canteen. With 2*d*. per day for supplementary food a workman obviously cannot live and labour. In consequence of that a system of *gratifications* has been introduced; they mostly vary from two to five shillings, and they are inscribed in full on the prisoner's "disposable" account. It is certain that this system of *gratifications* has given rise to many abuses. Suppose a skilled workman who is condemned for the third time and of whose salary the State retains seven-tenths. Suppose further that the work he has made during the month is valued at 40*s*. The State taking from this salary 28*s*., there will remain only 6*s*. to be inscribed on his "disposable" account. He proposes then to the undertaker to value his work only at 20*s*. and to add a gratification of 10*s*. The undertaker accepts, and so the State has only 14*s*.; the undertaker disburses 30*s*. instead of 40*s*.; and the prisoner has on his disposable account 3*s*., as also the whole of the *gratification*—that is, 13*s*.; all are thus satisfied, and if the State is at loss of 14*s*.—*ma foi, tant pis!*

Things look still worse if the great tempter

of mankind—tobacco—be taken into account. Smoking is severely prohibited in prisons, and the smokers are fined from 5*d*. to 4*s*. every time they are discovered smoking. And yet everybody smokes or chews in the prisons. Tobacco is the current money, but a money so highly prized that a cigarette—a nothing for an accomplished smoker—is paid 2*d*., and the 5*d*. *paquet* of tobacco has a currency worth 4*s*. or even more in times of scarcity. This precious merchandise is so highly esteemed that each pinch of tobacco is first chewed, then dried and smoked, and finally taken as snuff, although reduced to mere ash. Useless to say that there are undertakers who know how to exploit this human weakness and who pay half of the work done with tobacco, valued at the above prices, and that there are also warders who carry on this lucrative trade. Altogether, the prohibition of smoking is a source of so many evils that the French Administration probably will be compelled soon to follow the example of Germany and to sell tobacco at the canteens of the prisons. This would be also the surest means for diminishing the number of smokers.

We came to Clairvaux at a propitious moment. All the old administration had been recently dismissed, and a new departure taken in the treatment of prisoners. A year or two before our arrival a prisoner was killed in his cell by the keys of the warders. The official report was to the effect that he had hanged himself; but the surgeon did not sign this report, and made another report of his own, stating the assassination. This circumstance led to a thorough reform in the treatment of prisoners, and I am glad to say that the relations between the prisoners and the warders at Clairvaux were without comparison better than at Lyons. In fact, I saw much less brutality and more human relations than I was prepared to see—and yet the system itself is so bad that it brings about most horrible results.

Of course the relatively better wind which now blows over Clairvaux may change in a day or two. The smallest rebellion in the prison would bring about a rapid change for the worse, as there are enough warders and inspectors who sigh for "the old system," which is still in use in other French prisons. Thus, while we were at Clairvaux, a man was brought thither from Poissy—a central prison close by Paris. He considered his condemnation as unjust, and cried loudly day after day in his cell. In fact, he already had the symptoms of a commencing madness. But, to silence him the Poissy authorities invented the following plan. They brought a fire-engine and pumped water on the man through the opening in the door of his cell; they then left him quite wet in his cell, notwithstanding the winter's frost. The intervention of the Press was necessary to bring about the dismissal of the Director. As to the numerous revolts which have broken out during the last two years in almost all French prisons, they seem to show that "the old system" is in full force still.

And now, what are these better relations between warders and prisoners which I saw at Clairvaux? Many chapters could be written about them, but I shall try to be as short as possible, and point out only their leading features. It is obvious that a long life of the warders in common and the very necessities of their service have developed among them a certain brotherhood, or rather *esprit de corps*, which causes them to act with a remarkable uniformity in their relations with the prisoners. In consequence of that *esprit de corps*, as soon as a prisoner is brought to the prison, the first question of the warders is whether he is a *soumis* or an *insoumis*—a submissive fellow, or an insubordinate. If the answer is favourable, the prisoner's life may be a tolerable one; if not, he will not soon leave the prison; and if he happens ever to leave it, he will do it with broken health, and so exasperated against society that he will be soon interned in a prison again, and finish his days there, if not in New Caledonia. If the prisoner is described as an insubordinate, he will be punished again and again. If he speaks in the ranks, although not louder than the others, a remonstrance will be made in such terms that he will reply and be punished. And each punishment will be so disproportionate that he will object to it, and the punishment be doubled. "A man who has been once sent to the punishment quarter, is sure to return thither a few days after he has been released from it," say the warders, even the mildest ones. And this punishment is not a light one.

The man is not beaten; he is not knocked down. No, we are civilized people, and the punished man is merely brought to the cellular quarter, and locked up in a cell. The cell is quite empty: it has neither bed nor bench. For the night a mattress is given, and the prisoner must lay his dress outside his cell, at the door. Bread and water are his food. As soon as the prison-bell rings in the morning, he is taken to a small covered yard, and there he must—walk. Nothing more; but our refined civilization has learned how to make a torture even of this natural exercise. At a formal slow pace, under the cries of *un, deux*, the patients must walk all the day long, round the building. They walk for twenty minutes; then a rest follows. For ten minutes they must sit down immovable, each of them on his numbered stone, and walk again for twenty minutes; and so on through all the day, as long as the engines of the workshops are running; and the punishment does not last one day, or two; it lasts for whole months. It is so cruel that the prisoner implores but one thing: "Let me return to the workshops." "Well, we shall see that in a fortnight or two," is the usual answer. But the fortnight goes over, and the next one too, and the patient still continues to walk for twelve hours a day. Then he revolts. He begins to cry in his cell, to insult the warders. Then he becomes "a rebel" —a dreadful qualification for any one who is in the hands of the brotherhood of warders—and as such he will rot in the cells, and walk throughout his life. If he assaults a warder, he will not be sent to New Caledonia: he will still remain in his cell, and ever walk and walk in the small building. One man, a peasant, seeing no issue from this horrible situation, preferred to poison himself rather than live such a life—a terrible story which I shall some day tell in full.

As we were walking with my wife in the garden, more than two hundred yards distant from the cellular quarter, we heard sometimes horrible, desperate cries coming from that building. My wife, terrified and trembling, seized my arm, and I told her that it was the man whom they had watered with the fire-pump at Poissy, and now, quite contrary to the law, had brought here, to Clairvaux. Day after day —two, three days without interruption, he cried, "*Vaches, gredins, assassins!*" (*vache* is the name of the warders in the prisoner's slang), or loudly called out his story, until he fell, exhausted, on the floor of his cell. He considered as unjust his detention at Clairvaux in the punishment quarter, and he declared loudly that he would kill a warder rather than remain all his life in a cell. For the next two months he remained quiet. An inspector had vaguely promised him that he might be sent into the workshops on the 14th of July. But the "Fête Nationale" came, and the man was not released. His exasperation then had no limits; he cried, insulted, and assaulted the warders, destroyed the wooden parts of his cell, and finally was sent to the black-hole, where heavy irons were laid upon his hands and feet. I have not seen these irons, but when he reappeared again in the cellular quarter, he loudly cried out that he was kept in the black-hole for two months, with irons on his hands and feet so heavy that he could not move. He already *is* half mad, and he will be kept in the cell until he becomes a complete lunatic, and then .... then he will be submitted to all those tortures which lunatics have to endure in prisons and asylums. . . .

And the immense problem of suppressing these atrocities rises at its full size before us. The relations between the administration and the prisoners are not imbued at Clairvaux with the brutality which I have spoken of in the preceding chapters. And yet our penitentiary system fatally brings about such horrible results as the above—the more horrible as they must be considered a necessary consequence of the system itself. But why are these sufferings inflicted on human creatures? What are the moral results achieved at the cost of such sufferings? In what direction lies the solution of the immense problem raised by our system of punishments and prisons? Such are the grave questions which necessarily rise before the observer.

CHAPTER IX.

ON THE MORAL INFLUENCE OF PRISONS ON PRISONERS.

THE central prison of Clairvaux, described in the preceding chapter, may be considered as a fair representative of modern prisons. In France, it is decidedly one of the best—I should say the best if I were not aware that the military prison at Brest is not inferior to the *Maison Centrale* of Clairvaux. In fact, the recent discussion about prisons in the French Chamber of Deputies, and the outbreaks of prisoners which have been witnessed last year in nearly all the chief penal establishments of France, have disclosed such a state of affairs in most French prisons that we must recognize them as much worse than the central prison with which I was enabled to make some acquaintance.

If we compare the prison discipline at

Clairvaux with that of English prisons—as it appears from the Reports of the Commission on Prisons of 1863, as well as from the works of Michael Davitt,[1] John Campbell,[2] the lady who signs herself "A Prison Matron,"[3] and Sir Edmund Du Cane,[4] from "Five Years' Penal Servitude,"[5] and the letters published last year in the *Daily News*, by "Late B 24,"—we must recognize that, national pride apart, prison discipline in the French Central prisons is not worse, and in some respects is more humane, than in this country. As to German prisons, it may be inferred from what we see in literature, and what I know from my Socialist friends, that the treatment to which prisoners are submitted in Germany is, without comparison, more brutal than in the Clairvaux prison. And, with regard to Austrian prisons, they may be said to be now in the same con-

---

[1] "Leaves from a Prison Diary." London, 1885.

[2] "Thirty Years' Experiences of a Medical Officer in the English Convict Service." London, 1884.

[3] "Prison Characters," by a Prison Matron. London, 1866.

[4] "The Punishment and Prevention of Crime." "English Citizen" series. London, 1885.

[5] "Five Years' Penal Servitude," by One who has endured it. (George Routledge and Sons.)

dition as they were in this country before the reform of 1863. We may thus safely conclude that the prison described in the preceding chapter is certainly not worse than thousands of like institutions spread all over Europe, but rather ranks among the best.

If I were asked, what could be reformed in this and like prisons, *provided they remain prisons*, I could really only suggest improvements in detail, which certainly would not substantially ameliorate them; and, at the same time, I should perfectly recognize the immense difficulties standing in the way of every amelioration, however insignificant, in institutions based on a false principle.

I might suggest, for instance, that the prisoners be more equitably remunerated for their labour—to which proposal the prison administration probably would reply by showing the difficulty of finding private employers ready to erect expensive workshops in prisons, and the consequent necessity of hiring out the convicts to them at very low prices. And I could not advocate that the State should undertake to supply prisoners with labour, because I know perfectly well that the State would pay the prisoners as badly, and even worse, than do some of the private employers at Clairvaux. The State would never risk sinking millions in workshops and steam engines, and without the use of a perfected machinery it would be unable to remunerate the prisoners' labour better; it would continue to pay from seven to ten pence a day. Besides, State enterprise could hardly introduce the variety of trades which I have mentioned in the above chapter, and this variety is one of the first conditions for supplying the prisoners with a regular occupation. In this country, where private employers are not admitted within the prisons as they are in France, the average production of each prisoner in 1877 did not exceed £3, and the maximum it had reached was only £22.[6]

I certainly should suggest that the system of prohibiting talk between prisoners should be frankly given up, because the prohibition remains in France, in England,[7] and in America, a dead letter and a useless vexation. And I should suggest also that the use of

---

[6] It rose to 70*l*. at the Lusk prison-farm, where forty-two convicts only were kept. See Edmund Du Cane's "Punishment and Prevention of Crime."

[7] Michael Davitt's "Leaves."

tobacco be permitted, because it is the only means to put an end to the disgraceful trade in this prohibited article which is carried on by the warders both in France and in England,[8] and sometimes also by the employers of labour. This measure has already been taken in Germany, where tobacco is, or shortly will be, sold at the canteen; and it obviously will be the most adequate means for reducing the number of smokers. It is, however, but a minor detail, which would not much improve our penal institutions.

In order to improve them substantially, I might suggest, of course, that each prison should be provided with a Pestalozzi for governor and sixty Pestalozzis more as warders. But I am afraid the prison administration would answer me as Alexander II. answered once on an administrative report: "Where shall I find the men?" Because really, as long as our prisons remain prisons, Pestalozzis will be exceptionally rare among the governors and warders, while retired soldiers will furnish the greater number.

And the more one reflects about the partial improvements which might be made; the more

[8] "Five Years' Penal Servitude," p. 61.

one considers them under their real, practical aspect, the more one is convinced that the few which can be made will be of no moment, while serious improvements are impossible under the present system. Some thoroughly new departure is unavoidable. The system is wrong from the very foundation.

One fact—the most striking in our penal institutions—is, that as soon as a man has been in prison, there are three chances to one that he will return thither very soon after his release. Of course, there are a few exceptions to the rule. In each prison there are persons who have got into trouble quite by chance. There has been, in their life, some succession of fatal circumstances which has resulted in an act of violence or weakness, and this has brought them within the prison walls. Nobody will contend, with regard to these persons, that if they had not been imprisoned at all, the results for society would not have been the same. They are tortured in prisons—none can say why? They themselves feel the wrongfulness of their acts, and would feel it more strongly if they had never been imprisoned. Their numbers are not so small as is often thought, and the injustice of their imprisonment is so obvious that authorized voices have been raised of late, asking that the judges be empowered to liberate them without any punishment.

But writers on criminal law will say that there is another numerous class of inmates of our prisons, for whom our penal institutions have been properly devised, and the question necessarily arises: How far do our prisons answer their purpose with regard to these inmates; how far do they moralize them, and how far do they deter them from further breaches of the law?

There cannot be two answers to this question. Figures tell us loudly enough that the supposed double influence of prisons—the deterring and the moralizing—exist only in the imagination of lawyers. Nearly one-half of all people condemned by the Courts are regularly released prisoners. In France, two-fifths to one-half of all brought before the assizes, and two-fifths of all brought before the *Police Correctionnelle* Courts, are released prisoners. No less than seventy to seventy-two thousand *récidivistes* are arrested every year; forty-two to forty-five per cent. of all assassins, seventy to seventy-two per cent. of all thieves condemned every year are *récidivistes*. In great towns the proportion is still more dreadful. Of all arrested at Paris in 1880, more than one-fourth had been condemned more than four times during the last ten years.[9] As to central prisons, twenty to forty per cent. of all prisoners released from them are retaken during the first year after their release, chiefly during the very first months which they spend at liberty; and the number of *récidivistes* would be still larger if so many liberated prisoners did not disappear, change their names and profession, emigrate, or die shortly after their liberation.[1]

In the French Central Prisons the return of liberated prisoners is so customary, that you may hear the warders saying: "Is it not strange that N. is not yet back? Has he had time, perchance, to go to another judicial district?" Several prisoners, when leaving the prison where they have succeeded, by their conduct, in obtaining some privileged occupa-

[9] *Compte Rendu général de l'Administration de la Justice Criminelle en France en* 1878 *et* 1879; Reinach, *Les Récidivistes.* Paris, 1882.

[1] "If those who die after liberation and those whose *récidive* crimes are not discovered be taken into account, it remains an open question whether the number of *récidivistes* is not equal to that of the liberated prisoners."—Lombroso, *L'Uomo delinquente.*

tion, used to ask that the post they occupied be kept open for them until their next return! The poor men are sure beforehand that they will not be able to resist the temptations they will meet with on release, and they are sure to return very soon, to end their life in prison.

In this country, as far as my knowledge goes, things do not stand much better, notwithstanding the recent development and endeavours of sixty-three Discharged Prisoners' Aid Societies. About forty per cent. of all condemned persons are still released prisoners, and we are told by Mr. Davitt that as much as ninety-five per cent. of all those who are kept in penal servitude have formerly received, on one or two occasions, a prison education.

More than that. It has been remarked throughout Europe that if a man has been kept in prison for some minor offence, his return to a prison will be under a graver charge. His theft will be more refined; and if he has been condemned, first for an assault, he has a serious chance of returning to the Court as a murderer. The *récidive* has grown to be an immense problem for European writers on criminal law, and we see that, in France, under the impression of the gravity of this problem, they are now devising schemes which surely do not fall very short of proposals for the wholesale extermination of recondemned people in the most unhealthy colony of the French Republic.

Just now, when I am writing these lines, I see in the Paris papers the tale of a murder committed by a man on the very second day after his release from a prison. Before being arrested and condemned to thirteen months' imprisonment (for some minor offence) he had been acquainted with a woman who kept a small shop. He knew her mode of life, and as soon as released—the second day after his release—he went to her in the evening, as she was shutting up the shop, stabbed her, and tried to take possession of the cash-box. The scheme had been devised down to the minutest detail whilst the man was kept in prison; he had worked it out during his thirteen months of incarceration.

Now, like cases are met with in considerable numbers in criminal practice, although they are not always as striking as that just mentioned. The most terrible schemes of brutal murder are mostly devised in prisons; and when public indignation is stirred by some exceptionally brutal deed, in most cases its origin may be traced, either directly or indirectly, to prison-education: the deed has been committed by a released prisoner, or at the instigation of such a man.

Whatever the schemes hitherto introduced either for the seclusion of prisoners, or for the prevention of conversation, prisons have remained nurseries of criminal education. The schemes of well-meaning philanthropists who fancied they could make so many reformatories out of our convict establishments, have proved a complete failure; and while official literature tries to make light of this characteristic feature of our penal institutions, those governors of prisons who see and tell the things as they are—not as it is desired they should be represented—frankly avow that prisons have not moralized anybody, but have more or less demoralized all those who have spent a number of years there.

It cannot be otherwise; and we cannot but acknowledge that it *must* be so, as soon as we analyse the effect the prison exercises on the prisoner.

First of all, none of the condemned people—a few exceptions apart—recognize that their condemnation is just. It is a secret to nobody;

but we are inclined to accept it too lightly, while in reality this circumstance is a condemnation of the very first principles of what we now call justice. The Chinese who is condemned by his "compound family" Court to expatriate himself;[2] the Tchuktchi who is boycotted by his fellow-men; the man who is condemned to a fine by a Water Court of Valencia or of Turkestan, almost always recognizes the justice of the verdict pronounced by his judges. But no such sense is awakened in the inmate of our modern prison.

Here is a man of the "Upper Prison Ten" condemned for having "run a long firm," that is, for having started some business to exploit "the cupidity and ignorance of the public," as one of the heroes of the admirable prison-sketches by Michael Davitt used to say. Try to convince him that he was not right in starting his "business." His answer probably will be: "Sir, the small thieves are here, but the big ones are free, and they enjoy the respect of those very same judges who condemned me." And he will mention to you one of those companies which were started for robbing the naive people who thought to enrich themselves with gold-mines in Devon-

---

[2] Compare Eugène Simon's *La Cité Chinoise*.

shire, with lead-mines under the Thames, or with electric lighting. We all know these companies; we know their pompous circulars; we know how they rob the poorest classes of their savings. . . . What shall we reply to the representative of the Upper Ten?

Or, take this other person who has been condemned for what the French *argot* describes as having *mangé la grenouille*, that is, for having spent public money. He would answer you: "I was not sufficiently cunning, sir, that is all." What will you, what can you reply when you know perfectly well, and he knows much better than yourself, how many small and still more big "frogs" are "eaten" every year without ever bringing the eaters before a judge? "I was not cunning enough," that is the sentence he will repeat to himself as long as he wears the prisoner's coat; and let him lie in a cell, or clear the Dartmoor moors, his brain will work in the direction of meditating the injustice of a society which pardons the most cunning and punishes those who were not cunning enough. As soon as he is out, he will necessarily try to occupy the highest steps in the ladder; he will try to be cunning; he will conceal the "swag" better.

I do not affirm that each prisoner considers

his deeds as a quite honourable pursuit; but it is undoubtedly true that he does not consider himself as less honourable than those who sell turnips instead of orange marmalade, and fuchsine-coloured, alcoholized water instead of wine, who rob shareholders, who also traffic by a thousand means "on the cupidity and ignorance of the public," and who, nevertheless, enjoy the esteem of society. "Steal, but do not be caught!" is a common saying in prisons all over the world; and it is useless to try to combat this watchword as long as in the wide world of "business" transactions the borderland between honourable and dishonourable remains as wide as it is now.

The teaching which the prisoner receives within the prison is not much better than that given by the outer world. I have mentioned in the preceding chapter (page 291) the scandalous traffic in tobacco which is carried on in French prisons, but I thought it a feature which had disappeared from the prisons of this country until I found the same traffic mentioned in a book on English prisons. Nay, the figures and the proportions are the same: in the first place, ten shillings out of twenty for the warder; and then, exorbitant prices charged for tobacco and other things which the warder brings to the prisoner—such is the Millbank tariff.[3] The French tariff is twenty-five francs out of fifty for the warder, and then the above-mentioned exorbitant prices for tobacco.

In fact, both in the administration and in the commercial undertakings which are carried on in big prisons, there are unavoidably so many small frauds that I often heard at Clairvaux: "The real thieves, sir, are those who keep us here—not those who are in." Of course, it will be said that even the least possibility of pronouncing such a judgment ought to disappear, and that much improvement has been already made in that direction. I gladly admit that it is so. But it is another question as to whether it *can* completely disappear. The very fact that it still remains true of so many prisons in Europe shows how difficult it is to get rid of bribery in the administration. At any rate, the above remark is still fully justified in the case of a very great number of European prisons.

While mentioning this factor of demoraliza-

[3] "Five Years' Penal Servitude," by One who has endured it, p. 61.

tion in prisons, I shall not, however, lay too much stress on it; not because I do not realize its exceedingly bad and wide influence; but because, even if it completely disappeared from prison-life, there would still remain in our penal institutions so many demoralizing factors, which cannot be got rid of as long as a prison remains a prison, that I prefer rather to insist upon them.

Much has been written about the moralizing effects of labour—of manual labour,—and surely I should be the last to deny them. To keep prisoners without any occupation, as they are kept in Russia, means utterly to demoralize them and to inflict on them a quite useless punishment, to kill their last energy, and to render them quite unable later to earn their living by work. But there is labour and labour. There is the free labour, which raises the man, which releases his brain from painful or morbid thoughts—the free labour which makes man feel himself a part of the immense life of the world. And there is the forced labour of the slave which degrades man, which is done reluctantly, only from fear of a worse punishment, and such is prison-labour. I do not speak of so wicked an invention as the treadmill, which a man must move like a squirrel in a wheel, supplying a motive power which could be supplied otherwise at a much cheaper rate. I do not speak also of picking oakum, which permits a man to produce in the course of a day the value of a farthing.[4] As to these kinds of labour the prisoners are fully entitled to consider them merely as the base revenge of a society which has done so little since their childhood to show them better ways towards a higher, more human life. Nothing is more revolting than to feel that one is compelled to work, not because somebody wants one's work, but merely to be punished. While all humanity work for the maintenance of their life, the man who picks oakum is condemned to perform a work which nobody needs. He is an outcast. And if he treats society as an outcast would, we can accuse nobody but ourselves.

Things do not stand better, however, with productive labour in prisons. In the world-market where produce is bought only for the bargains that can be realized on sale and purchase, the State can seldom be a successful competitor. So it has been compelled to invite private employers to give occupation to

[4] Du Cane, *l.c.*, p. 176.

prisoners. But, to attract such employers and to induce them to sink money in factories, and to guarantee a certain amount of labour to a certain number of convicts, notwithstanding the fluctuations of the market—and this under such unfavourable circumstances as a prison and the prison-work of untrained labourers— the State has been compelled to concede the prisoners' labour for nearly nothing—not to speak of the *pots de vin*, which certainly have something to do with the low prices at which prisoners are hired out to employers. Therefore, the wages paid to prisoners, both by the State and private employers, are merely nominal.

We have seen in the preceding chapter that the highest full wages paid by private employers at Clairvaux rarely exceed 1s. 8d., and in most cases are below 10d. for twelve hours' work, while one-half, and more, of these wages are kept by the State. At Poissy, the average wages in a private enterprise are 3d. (29 centimes) a day, and less than 2d. (19 centimes) in the workshops of the State.[5]

In this country, since the Prison Commission

[5] Speech of M. Dupuy (de l'Aisne) at the French Chamber of Deputies on January 18, 1887.

of 1863 discovered that convicts earn too much in penal servitude, the prisoner earns nearly nothing but a very small diminution of the term of imprisonment; and the trades carried on in prisons are such that the average daily value of the prisoner's work exceeds 1s. only in skilled labour (shoemaking, tailoring, and basketmaking).[6] As to the other trades, the market-value of the prisoner's work mostly varies from 3d. to 10d.

It is obvious that, under such circumstances, the work which has no attractiveness in itself, because it gives no exercise to the mental faculties of the labourer, and is paid so badly, comes to be considered as a mere punishment. When I saw my Anarchist friends at Clairvaux making ladies' stays, or pearl-shell buttons, and earning sixpence for ten hours' work—out of which twopence were retained by the State (threepence, and more, with common-law prisoners)—I fully understood what disgust must be inspired by such work in the man who is condemned to do it. What pleasure can he find in such toil? What moralizing effect can it exercise, when the prisoner repeats again and again to himself that he is working merely

[6] "The Punishment and Prevention of Crime," p. 176.

to enrich his employer? When he has been paid eighteenpence at the end of the week, he and his comrades exclaim: "Decidedly, the real thieves are those who keep us in—not we!"

But still, my comrades who were not compelled to work, used to do this kind of work; and sometimes, by assiduous labour, some of them managed to realize as much as tenpence per day, instead of six, when the work implied some skill or artistic feeling. They did so, however, because they had an inducement to labour. Those who were married were in continual correspondence with their wives, who had a hard time of it as long as their husbands were in prison. Letters from home kept coming in; they could be answered. The bands which connected the prisoners with home were not broken. As to those who were not married, or had no mother to support, they had a passion —study; and they scooped away at pearl-shell in the hope of being able, at the end of the month, to order some long-desired book.

They had a passion. But what a passion can inspire the common-law prisoner, secluded from his home—from all attachments which might have connected him with the outer world?

For, with a refinement of cruelty, those who schemed our prisons did all in their power to cut all the threads which might keep up the prisoner's connection with Society. They trampled under foot all the best feelings that the prisoner has, like other men. His wife and children are not permitted in this country to see him more than once every three months, and the letters he may write are a mere mockery. The philanthropists who have schemed our prison discipline have pushed their cold contempt for human nature so far as to permit the prisoner only to sign a printed circular! A measure the more despicable, as each prisoner, however low his intellectual development, fully understands the petty feeling of revenge which lies at the bottom of this measure, whatever be the excuses as to the necessity of preventing communication with the outer world.

In French prisons—at least, in the Central prisons—the visits of relatives are not so severely limited, and the governor of the jail is even entitled in exceptional cases to allow visits in a common parlour without gratings. But the Central prisons are far from the great cities; and, as the great cities supply the largest numbers of convicts, and the condemned people chiefly belong to the poorest classes, only very few women have the means to make the journey to Clairvaux for a few interviews with their husbands.

And thus the best influence to which the prisoner might be submitted, the only one which might bring a ray of light, a softer element into his life—the intercourse with his relatives and children—is systematically secluded. The prisons of old were less clean; they were less "orderly" than the modern ones; but, at any rate, under this aspect, they were more humane.

In a prisoner's greyish life, which flows without passions and emotions, all those best feelings which may improve human character soon die away. Even those workmen who like their trade and find some æsthetic satisfaction in it, lose their taste for work. Physical energy is very soon killed in prison. I remember the years passed in prison in Russia. I entered my cell in the fortress with the firm resolution not to succumb. To maintain my bodily energy, I regularly every day walked my five miles in my cell, and twice a day I performed some gymnastics with my heavy oak chair. And, when pen and ink were allowed to enter my cell, I had before me the task of recasting a large work—a great field to cover—that of submitting to a systematic revision the Indices of Glaciation. Later on, in France, another passion inspired me—the elaboration of the bases of what I consider a new system of philosophy—the bases of Anarchy. But, in both cases, I soon felt lassitude overtaking me. Bodily energy disappeared by-and-by. And I can think of no better comparison for the state of a prisoner than that of wintering in the Arctic regions. Read reports of Arctic expeditions—the old ones, those of the good-hearted Parry, or of the elder Ross. When going through them you feel a note of physical and mental depression pervading the whole diary, and growing more and more dreary, until sun and hopes reappear on the horizon. That is the state of a prisoner. The brain has no longer the energy for sustained attention; thought is less rapid, or, rather, less persistent: it loses its depth. An American report mentioned last year that while the study of languages usually prospers with the prisoners, they are mostly unable to persevere in mathematics ; and so it is.

It seems to me that this depression of healthy nervous energy can be best accounted for by the want of impressions. In ordinary life thousands of sounds and colours strike our senses; thousands of small, varied facts come within our knowledge, and spur the activity of the brain. Nothing of the kind strikes the prisoner; his impressions are few, and always the same. Therefore—the eagerness of the prisoners for anything new, for any new impression. I cannot forget the eagerness with which I observed, when taking a walk in the fortress yard, the changes of colour on the gilt needle of the fortress, its rosy tints at sunset, its bluish colours in the morning, its changing aspects on cloudy and bright days, in the morning and evening, winter and summer. It was the only thing which changed its aspect. The appearance of a parrot in the yard was a great event. It was a new impression. This is probably also the reason that all prisoners are so fond of illustrations; they convey new impressions in a new way. All impressions received by the prisoner, be they from his reading or from his own thoughts, pass through the medium of his imagination. And the brain, already poorly fed by a less active heart and impoverished blood, becomes tired, worried. It loses its energy.

This circumstance probably explains also the striking want of energy, of ardour, in prison work. In fact, each time I saw at Clairvaux the prisoners lazily crossing the yards, lazily followed by a lazy warder, my imagination always transported me back to my father's house and his numerous serfs. Prison-work is slavish work; and slavish work cannot inspire a human being with the best inspiration of man—the need to work and to create. The prisoner may learn a handicraft, but he will never learn to love his work. In most instances he will learn to hate it.

There is another important cause of demoralization in prisons which cannot be too much insisted upon, as it is common to all prisons and inherent in the system of deprivation of liberty itself. All transgressions against the established principles of morality can be traced to a want of firm Will. Most of the inmates of our prisons are people who have not had firmness enough to resist the temptations that surrounded them, or to master a passionate impulse that momentarily overpowered them. Now, in prison, as in a monastery, the prisoner is secluded from all temptations of the outer world; and his intercourse with other men is so limited and so regulated that he seldom feels the influence of strong passions. But, precisely in consequence of that he has almost no opportunity for exercising and reinforcing the firmness of his Will. He is a machine. He has no choice between two courses of action; the very few opportunities of free choice which he has, are of no moment. All his life has been regulated and ordered beforehand; he has only to follow the current, to obey under the fear of a cruel punishment. In these conditions such firmness of Will as he may have had before entering the prison, disappears. And, where shall he find the strength to resist the temptations which will suddenly arise before him, as by enchantment, as soon as he has stepped outside the walls? Where will he find the strength to resist the first impulse of a passionate character, if, during many years, everything has been done to kill in him the interior force of resistance, to make him a docile tool in the hands of those who govern him?

This fact, in my opinion—and it seems to me that there can be no two opinions in the matter—is the strongest condemnation of all systems based on depriving the condemned man of his liberty. The origin of the systematic suppression of all individual will in the prisoners, the systematic reduction of men to the level of unreasoning machines, carried on throughout the long years of imprisonment, is easily explained. It grew from the desire of preventing any breaches of discipline, and of keeping the greatest number of prisoners with the least possible amount of warders. And we may see throughout the bulky literature of "prison-discipline" that the greatest admiration is bestowed precisely on those systems which have obtained the results of discipline with the least possible number of warders. The ideal of our prisons would be a thousand automatons, rising and working, eating and going to bed, by electric currents transmitted to them from a single warder. But our modern and perfected systems of prisons, although realizing perhaps some immediate economies for the State Budget, are also the most appropriate for bringing *récidive* to the strikingly high figures it attains now. The less prisons approximate to their present ideal, the less the *récidive*.[7] And it is not to

[7] In Russia the number of *récidivistes* is only eighteen

be wondered at that men accustomed to be mere machines do not prove to be the men whom society needs.

As soon as the prisoner is released, the comrades of his former life wait upon him. They receive him in brotherly guise, and, as soon as liberated, he is taken up by the current which already once has brought him to a prison. Guardians and Prisoners' Aid Societies cannot help. All they can do is to undo the bad work done by the prison, to counterbalance its bad effects in some of the released prisoners. While the influence of honest men who could have tendered a brotherly hand to the man *before* he was brought into the prisoner's dock, would have prevented him from committing the faults he has committed, now, after he has undergone the prison education, their efforts will remain fruitless in most cases.

And what a contrast between the fraternal reception of the brotherhood of " magsmen " and the reception on behalf of " respectable people," who conceal under a Christian exterior a Pharisaic egotism! For them the liberated prisoner is something plague-stricken. Who

per cent., as against forty to fifty per cent. in Western Europe.

of them would invite him into his own house, and merely say, "Here is a room, there is work for you; sit at this table, and be one of our family"? He needs most fraternal support, he is most in need of a brotherly hand stretched out to him. But, after having done all in our power to make of him a foe of society, after having inoculated him with the vices which characterize prisons, who will tender him the brotherly hand he is in need of?

And who is the woman who would like to marry a man who has been once in a prison? We know how often women marry men "to save them;" but, apart from a very few exceptions, they instinctively refuse those who have received prison education. And so the liberated prisoner is compelled to search for a partner in life among those women—the sad products of an abominably organized society—who have most contributed to bring him into trouble. No wonder that most of the released prisoners return to prison again after having spent but a few months at liberty!

There are few who would now dare to affirm hat prisons ought only to exercise a deterrent influence without caring for the moral improvement of the prisoners. But what are we doing to achieve this last end? Our prisons are made for degrading all those who enter them, for killing the very last feelings of self-respect.

Everybody knows the influence of a decent dress. Even an animal is ashamed to appear amidst its like if its coat renders it conspicuous and ridiculous. A cat, which a boy would have painted with yellow and black stripes, would be ashamed to appear in this guise amidst other cats. But men begin by giving a fool's dress to those whom they pretend to moralize. When at Lyons I often saw the effect produced on prisoners by the prison dress. Mostly workmen, poorly but decently clad, they crossed the yard where I was taking my walk, and entered the room where they had to throw off their own dress and take the prison costume. And as they went out, wearing the ugly prison-dress mended with pieces of multi-coloured rags, with a round ugly cap, they felt quite ashamed of appearing before men in such ugly attire. And there are plenty of prisons, especially in this country, where the dress of the prisoner, made out of parti-coloured pieces, resembles more the dress of a mad jester of old than that of a man whom our prison philanthropists pretend to improve.

That is a convict's first impression, and throughout his life in a prison he will be submitted to a treatment which is imbued with the utmost contempt for human feelings. At Dartmoor, for instance, convicts will be considered as people who dare not have the slightest feeling of decency. They will be compelled to parade in gangs, quite naked, before the prison authorities, and to perform in this attire a kind of gymnastics before them. "Turn round! Lift both arms! Lift the right leg! Hold up the sole of the left foot with the right hand!" And so on.[8]

The prisoner is no longer a man in whom any feeling of self-respect is permitted to exist. He is a thing, a mere number B 24, and he will be treated as a numbered thing. No animal could bear such treatment year after year without being utterly abashed; but those human beings, who in a few years ought to become useful members of society, are treated in this way. If the prisoner is permitted to have a walk, his walk will not be like that of other men. He will be marched in a file,

[8] "Dartmoor," by late B 24, in the *Daily News*, 1886.

with a warder standing in the middle of the yard, and loudly crying, "*Un-deusse, un-deusse, arch-fer, arch-fer!*" If he yields to the most human of all desires—that of communicating an impression, or a thought, to a fellow-creature—he will commit a breach of discipline. And, however docile, he will do this. Before he entered the prison he may have felt reluctance to lie and deceive anybody; here he *will* learn to lie and deceive, until lying and deceit become his second nature.

He may be sad or gay, good or bad tempered; he must not show it. He is a numbered thing, which must move about according to regulations. Tears may choke him; he must suppress them. Throughout the years of servitude he never will be alone; even in the solitude of his cell an eye will spy his movements and surprise the feeling he wished to keep to himself, because it was a human feeling, and human feelings are not allowed in prisons. Be it compassion for a fellow-sufferer, or love for his relatives, which awakens in him; be it a desire of speaking out his sorrows to somebody beyond the persons officially appointed for that purpose; be it any of those affections which render man better, all is crushed by the force which denies him the right to be a man. Condemned to a bestial life, all that might suggest better feelings will be carefully suppressed. He must *not* be a man, so it is ordained by the prison rules.

He must have no feelings. But woe betide him if by ill-luck the feeling of human dignity awakens within him! Woe to him if he is annoyed by a disbelief in his word; if the searching of his dress, repeated several times a day, humiliates him; if the hypocrisy of going to the chapel, when nothing attracts him there, is repugnant to him; if he betrays by a word, by the tone of his voice, the contempt he feels for a warder who carries on the traffic in tobacco and steals the last coppers of a fellow-prisoner; if the need of showing compassion to somebody makes him take pity upon a feebler comrade and share his bread with him; if he has maintained enough of human dignity to revolt against an unmerited reproach, an unmerited suspicion, a rough taunt; if he is honest enough to rebel against the small intrigues, the favouritism of the warders;—then, the prison will become a hell to him. He will be crushed by labour beyond his strength, if he is not sent to rot in the black cell.

The most trifling breach of discipline, which would pass unnoticed in the hypocrite who makes his way up the prison-ladder by his base conduct, will call down a punishment upon his head; it will be treated as insubordination. And each punishment will lead to a new one. He will be brought to madness by small persecutions, and may be happy if ever he leaves the prison except in a coffin.

It is easy to write to the newspapers that the warders ought to be under severe control; that governors ought to be chosen amongst the very best men. Nothing easier than to build Administrative Utopias! But man is man; the warder as well as the prisoner. And when men are condemned all their life to false relations with other men, they become false themselves. Prisoners themselves, the warders become as fastidious as the prisoners. Nowhere in my life, except around the Russian monasteries, have I seen such a spirit of petty intrigue as we saw amidst the warders and the surroundings of Clairvaux. Compelled to move within a small and limited world of trivial interests, the prison authorities feel its influence. Small tittle-tattle, narrow discussions about a word said by such a prisoner and a gesture made by another, supply the material for their conversations.

Men are men; and you cannot give so immense an authority to men over men without corrupting those to whom you give the authority. They will abuse it; and their abuses of it will be the more unscrupulous, and the more felt by the abused, the more limited and narrow is the world they live in. Compelled as they are to live in the midst of a hostile camp of prisoners, the warders cannot be models of kindness and humanity. To the league of the prisoners, they oppose the league of the warders. And, as they hold the power, they abuse it like all those who hold power in their hands. The institution makes them what they are, petty and vexatious persecutors of the prisoners. Put a Pestalozzi in their place (if only a Pestalozzi would accept the function), and he also would soon become a prison warder. And, when I take all the circumstances into consideration, I really am inclined to say that still the men are better than the institution.

And a rancorous feeling against a society which always was but a step-mother to him grows within the prisoner. He accustoms himself to hate—cordially to hate—all those "respectable" people who so wickedly kill his best feelings in him. He divides the world into two parts: that to which he and his comrades belong, and the outer world represented by the governor, the warders, the employers. A brotherhood rapidly grows between all the inmates of a prison against all those who do not wear the prisoner's dress. These are the enemies. Everything which may be done to deceive them is right. The prisoner is an outlaw to them; they become outlaws to him. And, as soon as he is free, he will put this morality into practice. Before having been in prison, he may have committed faults without reflection. Prison education will make him consider society as an enemy: now he will have a philosophy of his own—that which Zola summed up in the following words: "Quels gredins les honnêtes gens!"

Not only exasperation against Society does the prison develop in its inmates; not only does it systematically kill in them every feeling of self-respect, dignity, compassion and love, and favour the growth of opposite feelings,—it inoculates the prisoner with vices which belong to the most abject category of reprobates. It is known in what threatening proportions crimes against decency are growing all over the Continent, as well as in this country. Many causes contribute towards this growth; but amidst these various causes one occupies a marked rank ; it is the pestilential influence of our prisons. In this direction, the deteriorating influence of prisons on society is felt perhaps more strongly than in any other.

I do not speak only about those unhappy creatures—the boys whom we saw at Lyons. We were told in sober earnestness that day and night the whole atmosphere of their life is permeated throughout with one foul breath of depravity. It is there, in such nests of corruption as the boys' department of the Prison of St. Paul, that we must look for the growth of what the lawyers describe as "the criminal classes," not to the laws of heredity. But the same is true with regard to prisons where fully grown people are kept. The facts which we came across during our prison life surpass all that the most frenzied imagination could invent. One must have been for long years in a prison, secluded from all higher influences and abandoned to one's own and that of a thousand convicts' imaginations, to come to the incredible state of mind which is witnessed among some prisoners. And I suppose that I shall say only what will be supported by all intelligent and frank governors of prisons, if I say that the prisons are *the* nurseries for the most revolting category of breaches of moral law.[9]

I shall not enter into details upon this subject, only too lightly treated now in a certain kind of literature. I only wish to add that those fall into gross error who imagine that the complete seclusion of prisoners and cellular imprisonment can promise any improvement in that special direction. A perverse turn of imagination is the real cause of all like cases, and the cell is the best means for giving to imagination such a turn. As to how far imagination can go in that direction, even alienists, I suppose, do not suspect it: to know it one must spend several months in a prisoner's cell, and enjoy a full confidence of his neighbours.

On the whole, cellular imprisonment, which has so many advocates now, would be merely a useless cruelty, and a powerful instrument in weakening still more the bodily and mental energy of the prisoners. Experience all over Europe, and the dreadful proportion of cases of insanity which have been witnessed everywhere that cellular imprisonment has been resorted to

[9] Mr. Davitt's remarks in his "Leaves from a Prison Diary," show that the same thing is true with regard to the prisons of this country.

for any length of time, are conclusive in this respect, and one cannot but wonder how little this experience has profited. For a man who has some occupation which may be a source of enjoyment to him, and whose mind is by itself a rich source of impressions ; for a person who has nothing outside the prison to worry him, whose family life is happy, and who has no such mental preoccupations as might become a source of continuous pain to the mind, seclusion from human society may not be fatal, if it lasts only for a few months. But for those who cannot live with their own thoughts, and especially for those whose relations with the outer world are not quite smooth, and who are worried by their own thoughts, even a few months of cellular imprisonment may prove a most fatal experiment.

CHAPTER X.

ARE PRISONS NECESSARY?

IF we take into consideration all the influences briefly indicated in the above rapid sketch, we are bound to recognize that all of them, separately and combined together, act in the direction of rendering men who have been detained for several years in prisons less and less adapted for life in society; and that none of them, not a single one, acts in the direction of raising the intellectual and moral faculties, of lifting man to a higher conception of life and its duties, of rendering him a better, a more human creature than he was.

Prisons do *not* moralize their inmates; they do *not* deter them from crime. And the question arises: What shall we do with those who break, not only the written law—that sad growth of a sad past—but also those very principles of morality which every man feels in his own heart? That is the question which now preoccupies the best minds of our century.

There was a time when Medicine consisted in administering some empirically-discovered drugs. The patients who fell into the hands of the doctor might be killed by his drugs, or they might rise up notwithstanding them, the doctor had the excuse of doing what all his fellows did; he could not outgrow his contemporaries.

But our century which has boldly taken up so many questions, but faintly forecast by its predecessors, has taken up this question too, and approached it from the other end. Instead of merely curing diseases, medicine tries now to prevent them; and we all know the immense progress achieved, thanks to the modern view of disease. Hygiene is the best of medicines.

The same has to be done with the great social phenomenon which has been called Crime until now, but will be called Social Disease by our children. Prevention of the disease is the best of cures: such is the watchword of a whole younger school of writers, which grew up of late, especially in Italy, represented by Poletti,[1] Ferri,[2] Colajanni,[3] and, to some limited extent, by Lombroso; of the great school of psychologists represented by Griesinger,[4] Krafft-Ebbing,[5] Despine[6] on the Continent, and Maudsley[7] in this country; of the sociologists like Quételet and his unhappily too scanty followers; and finally, in the modern schools of Psychology with regard to the individual, and of the social reformers with regard to society. In their works we have already the elements of a new position to be taken with regard to those unhappy people whom we have hanged, or decapitated, or sent to jails until now.

Three great causes are at work to produce

[1] *Il Delinquente;* Udine, 1875.

[2] *Nuovi orizzonti del Diritto e della Procedure penale; Socialismo e Criminalità,* and several others.

[3] *L'Alcoolismo, sue consequenza morali e sue cause;* Catania, 1887. A study which I cannot but warmly recommend to those writers on the subject who so often mistake the effects for causes.

[4] *Gesammelte Abhandlungen,* Berlin, 1882. *Pathologie der Psychischen Krankheiten.*

[5] *Zweifelhafte Geistzustände,* Erlangen, 1873; *Grundzüge der Criminal-Psychologie,* 1872; *Lehrbuch der gerichtlichen Psychopatie,* Stuttgart, 1875.

[6] *Psychologie Naturelle,* Paris, 1868; *Congrès Pénitentiaire de Stockholm en* 1878, vol. ii.

[7] "Insanity with Relation to Crime," London, 1880.

what is called crime: the social causes, the anthropological, and, to use Ferri's expression, the cosmical.

The influence of these last is but insufficiently known, and yet it cannot be denied. We know from the Postmaster-General's Reports that the number of letters containing money which are thrown into the pillar-boxes without any address is very much the same from year to year. If so capricious an element in our life as oblivion of a certain given kind is subject to laws almost as strict as those which govern the motions of the heavenly bodies, it is still more true with regard to breaches of law. We can predict with a great approximation the number of murders which will be committed next year in each country of Europe. And if we should take into account the disturbing influences which will increase, or diminish, next year the number of murders committed, we might predict the figures with a still greater accuracy.

There was, some time ago, in *Nature*, an essay on the number of assaults and suicides committed in India with relation to temperature and the moisture of the air. Everybody knows that an excessively hot and moist temperature renders men more nervous than they are when the temperature is moderate and a dry wind blows over our fields. In India, where the temperature grows sometimes exceedingly hot, and the air at the same time grows exceedingly moist, the enervating influence of the atmosphere is obviously felt still more strongly than in our latitudes. Mr. S. A. Hill, therefore, calculate from figures extending over several years, a formula which enables you, when you know the average temperature and humidity of each month, to say, with an astonishing approximation to exactitude, the number of suicides and wounds due to violence which have been registered during the month.[8] Like calculations may seem very strange to minds unaccustomed to treat psychological

[8] S. A. Hill, "The Effects of the Weather upon the Death-Rate and Crime in India," *Nature*, vol. 29, 1884, p. 338. The formula shows that the number of suicides and acts of violence committed each month is equal to the excess of the average monthly temperature over 48° Fahr. multiplied by 7·2, *plus* the average moistness, multiplied by 2. The author adds :—" Crimes of violence in India may therefore be said to be proportional in frequency to the tendency to *prickly heat*, that excruciating condition of the skin induced by a high temperature combined with moisture. Any one who has suffered from this ailment, and knows how it affected his temper will really understand how the conditions which produce it may sometimes lead to homicide and other crimes." Under cold weather the influence is the reverse.

phenomena as dependent upon physical causes, but the facts point to this dependence so clearly as to leave no room for doubt. And persons who have experienced the effects of tropical heat accompanied by tropical moisture on their own nervous system, will not wonder that precisely during such days Hindoos are inclined to seize a knife to settle a dispute, or that men disgusted with life are more inclined to put an end to it by suicide.[9]

The influence of cosmical causes on our actions has not yet been fully analyzed; but several facts are well established. It is known, for instance, that attempts against persons (violence, murders, and so on) are on the increase during the summer, and that during the winter the number of attempts against property reaches its maximum. We cannot go through the curves drawn by Professor E. Ferri,[1] and see on the same sheet the curves of

---

[9] See also Mayr, *Gesetzmässigkeit in Gesellschaftsleben*, as also E. Ferri in *Archivio di Psychiatria*, fasc. 2nd; *La Teoria dell' imputabilità e la Negazione del libero arbitrio*, Bologna, 1881; and many others.

[1] *Das Verbrechen in seiner Abhängigkeit von Temperatur*, Berlin, 1882. Also, Colajanni's *Oscillations thermométriques et délits contre les personnes*, in *Bibl. d'Anthropologie Criminelle*, Lyons, 1886.

temperature and those showing the number of attempts against persons, without being deeply impressed with their likeness: one easily mistakes them for one another. Unhappily, this kind of research has not been prosecuted with the eagerness it deserves, so that few of the cosmical causes have been analyzed as to their influence on human actions.

It must be acknowledged also that the inquiry offers many difficulties, because most cosmical causes exercise their influence only in an indirect way; thus, for instance, when we see that the number of breaches of law fluctuates with the crops of cereals, or with the wine-crops, the influence of cosmical agents appears only through the medium of a series of influences of a social character. Still, nobody will deny that when weather is fine, the crops good, and the villagers cheerful, they are far less inclined to settle their small disputes by violence than during stormy or gloomy weather, when a spoiled crop spreads moreover general discontent. I suppose that women who have constant opportunities of closely watching the good and bad temper of their husbands could tell us plenty about the influence of weather on peace in their homes.

The so-called 'anthropological causes' to which much attention has been given of late, are certainly much more important than the preceding. The influence of inherited faculties and of the bodily organization on the inclination towards crime has been illustrated of late by so many highly interesting investigations, that we surely can form a nearly complete idea about this category of causes which bring men and women within our penal jurisdiction. Of course, we cannot endorse in full the conclusions of one of the most prominent representatives of this school, Dr. Lombroso,[2] especially those he arrives at in one of his writings.[3] When he shows us that so many inmates of our prisons have some defect in the organization of their brains, we must accept this statement as a mere fact. We may even admit with him that the majority of convicts and prisoners have longer arms than people at liberty. Again, when he shows us that the most brutal murders have been committed by men who had some serious defect in their bodily structure, we have only to incline before this statement and recognize its accuracy. It is a statement—not more.

[2] *L' Uomo delinquente*, 3rd edition, Torino, 1884.
[3] *Sull' Incremento del Delitto*, Roma, 1879.

But we cannot follow Mr. Lombroso when he infers too much from this and like facts, and considers society entitled to take any measures against people who have like defects of organization. We cannot consider society as entitled to exterminate all people having defective structure of brain, and still less to imprison those who have long arms. We may admit that most of the perpetrators of the cruel deeds which from time to time stir public indignation have not fallen very far short of being sad idiots. The head of Frey, for instance, an engraving of which has made of late the tour of the Press, is an instance in point. But *all* idiots do not become assassins, and still less all feeble-minded men and women; so that the most impetuous criminalist of the anthropological school would recoil before a wholesale assassination of all idiots if he only remembered how many of them are free—some of them under care, and very many of them having other people under their care—the difference between these last and those who are handed over to the hangman being only a difference of the circumstances under which they were born and have grown up. In how many otherwise respectable homes, and palaces, too, not to speak of lunatic asylums, shall we not find the very same features which Dr. Lombroso considers characteristic of " criminal madness " ? Brain diseases may favour the growth of criminal propensities; but they may *not*, when under proper care. The good sense, and still more the good heart of Charles Dickens have perfectly well understood this plain truth.

Certainly we cannot follow Dr. Lombroso in all his conclusions, still less those of his followers ; but we must be grateful to the Italian writer for having devoted his attention to, and popularized his researches into, the medical aspects of the question. Because, for an unprejudiced mind, the only conclusion that can be drawn from his varied and most interesting researches is, that most of those whom we treat as criminals are people affected by bodily diseases, and that their illness ought to be submitted to some treatment, instead of being aggravated by imprisonment.

Mr. Maudsley's researches into insanity with relation to crime are well known in this country.[4] But none of those who have seriously read his works can leave them without

[4] " Responsibility in Mental Disease," London, 1872; "Body and Will," London, 1883.

being struck by the circumstance that most of those inmates of our jails who have been imprisoned for attempts against persons are people affected with some disease of the mind; that the "ideal madman whom the law creates," and the only one whom the law is ready to recognize as irresponsible for his acts, is as rare as the ideal "criminal" whom the law insists upon punishing. Surely there is, as Mr. Maudsley says, a wide "borderland between crime and insanity, near one boundary of which we meet with something of madness but more of sin (of conscious desire of doing some harm, we prefer to say), and near the other boundary of which something of sin but more of madness." But "a just estimate of the moral responsibility of the unhappy people inhabiting this borderland" will never be made as long as the idea of "sin," or of "bad will," is not got rid of.[5]

[5] Maudsley's "Responsibility in Mental Disease." On page 27, Mr. Maudsley says: "In like manner, though a criminal might be compassionated it would still be necessary to deprive him of the power of doing further mischief; society has clearly the right to insist on that being done; and though he might be kindly cared for, the truest kindness to him and others would still be *the enforcement of that kind of discipline which is best fitted to bring him, if possible, to a*

Unhappily, hitherto our penal institutions have been nothing but a compromise between the old ideas of revenge, of punishment of the " bad will" and " sin," and the modern ideas of " deterring from crime," both softened to a very slight extent by some notions of philanthropy. But the time, we hope, is not far distant when the noble ideas which have inspired Griesinger, Krafft-Ebbing, Despine, and some of the modern Italian criminalists, like Colajanni and Ferri, will become the property of the general public, and make us ashamed of having continued so long to hand over those whom we call criminals to hangmen and jailers. If the conscientious and extensive labours of the writers just named were more widely known, we should all easily understand that most of those who are kept now in jails, or put to death, are merely people in need of the most careful fraternal treatment. · I do not

healthy state of mind, even if it were hard labour within the measure of his strength." Leaving aside the "right" of society to enforce hard labour, which might be doubted upon, because Mr. Maudsley recognizes himself that society has ' manufactured its criminals," we wonder that so open a mind admits, even for a moment, that imprisonment with hard labour *may be* best fitted to bring anybody to a healthy state of mind.

mean, of course, that we ought to substitute lunatic asylums for prisons. Far be it from me to entertain this abhorrent idea. Lunatic asylums are nothing else but prisons; and those whom we keep in prisons are not lunatics, nor even people approaching the sad boundary of the borderland where man loses control over his actions. Far be from me the idea which is sometimes brought forward as to maintaining prisons by placing them under pedagogists and medical men. What most of those who are now sent to jail are in need of is merely a fraternal help from those who surround them, to aid them in developing more and more the higher instincts of human nature which have been checked in their growth either by some bodily disease—anemia of the brain, disease of the heart, the liver, or the stomach—or, still more, by the abominable conditions under which thousands and thousands of children grow up, and millions of adults are living, in what we call our centres of civilization. But these higher faculties cannot be exercised when man is deprived of liberty, of the free guidance of his actions, of the multifarious influences of the human world. Let us carefully analyze each breach of the moral unwritten law, and we shall always find—as good old Griesinger said—that it is not due to something which has suddenly sprung up in the man who accomplished it: it is the result of effects which, for years past, have deeply stirred within him.[6] Take, for instance, a man who has committed an act of violence. The blind judge of our days comes forward and sends him to prison. But the human being who is not overpowered by the kind of mania which is inculcated by the study of Roman jurisprudence—who analyzes instead of merely sentencing—would say, with Griesinger, that although in this case the man has not suppressed his affections, but has left them to betray themselves by an act of violence, this act has been prepared long since. Before this time, probably throughout his life, the same person has often manifested some anomaly of mind by noisy expression of his feelings, by crying loudly after some trifling disagreeable circumstance, by easily venting his bad temper on those who stood by him; and, unhappily, he has not from his childhood found anybody who was able to give a better direction to his

[6] *Vierteljahrsschrift für gerichtliche und öffentliche Medicin*, 1867.

nervous impressibility. The causes of the violence which has brought him into the prisoners' dock must be sought long years before. And if we push our analysis still deeper, we discover that this state of mind is itself a consequence of some physical disease either inherited or developed by an abnormal life; some disease of the heart, the brain, or the digestive system. For many years these causes have been at work before resulting in some deed which falls within the reach of the law.

More than that. If we analyze ourselves, if everybody would frankly acknowledge the thoughts which have sometimes passed through his mind, we should see that all of us have had —be it as an imperceptible wave traversing the brain, like a flash of light—some feelings and thoughts such as constitute the motive of all acts considered as criminal. We have repudiated them at once; but if they had had the opportunity of recurring again and again; if they were nurtured by circumstances, or by a want of exercise of the best passions—love, compassion, and all those which result from living in the joys and sufferings of those who surround us; then these passing influences, so brief that we hardly noticed them, would have degenerated into some morbid element in our character.

That is what we ought to teach our children from the earliest childhood, while now we imbue them from their tenderest years with ideas of justice identified with revenge, of judges and tribunals. And if we did this, instead of doing as we do now, we should no longer have the shame of avowing that we hire assassins to execute our sentences, and pay warders for performing a function for which no educated man would like to prepare his own children. Functions which we consider so degrading cannot be an element of moralization.

Fraternal treatment to check the development of the anti-social feelings which grow up in some of us—not imprisonment—is the only means that we are authorized in applying, and can apply, with some effect to those in whom these feelings have developed in consequence of bodily disease or social influences. And that is not a Utopia; while to fancy that punishment is able to check the growth of anti-social feelings is a Utopia—a wicked Utopia; the Utopia of "leave me in peace, and let the world go on as it likes."

Many of the anti-social feelings, we are told by Dr. J. Bruce Thompson [7] and many others, are inherited; and facts amply support this conclusion. But what is inherited? Is it a certain bump of criminality, or something else? What is inherited is insufficient self-control, or a want of firm will, or a desire for risk and excitement,[8] or disproportionate vanity. Vanity, for instance, coupled with a desire for risk and excitement, is one of the most striking features amidst the population of our prisons. But vanity finds many fields for its exercise. It may produce a maniac like Napoleon the First, or a Frey; but it produces also, under some circumstances—especially when instigated and guided by a sound intellect—men who pierce tunnels and isthmuses, or devote all their energies towards pushing through some great

[7] *Journal of Mental Science*, January, 1870, p. 488 sq.

[8] The importance of this factor, well pointed out by Ed. Du Cane, is proved by the circumstance that what they call "the criminal age" is the age between twenty-five and thirty-four. After that age, a desire for a quieter life makes the breaches of law suddenly decrease. The proposal of Ed. Du Cane ("if those persons whose career evidences in them marked criminal tendencies could either be locked up or kept under supervision until they had passed, say, the age of forty") is typical · of the peculiar logics developed in those people who have been for some time superintendents of prisons.

scheme for what they consider the benefit of humanity; and then it may be checked, and even reduced almost to nothingness, by the parallel growth of intelligence. If it is a want of firmness of will which has been inherited, we know also that this feature of character may lead to the most varied consequences according to the circumstances of life. How many of our "good fellows" suffer precisely from this defect? Is it a sufficient reason for sending them to prison?

Humanity has seldom ventured to treat its prisoners like human beings; but each time it has done so it has been rewarded for its boldness. I was sometimes struck at Clairvaux with the kindness bestowed on sick people by several assistants in the hospital; I was touched by several manifestations of a refined feeling of delicacy. Dr. Campbell, who has had much more opportunity of learning this trait of human nature during his thirty years' experience as prison-surgeon, goes much farther. By mild treatment, he says, "with as much consideration as if they had been delicate ladies [I quote his own words], the greatest order was generally maintained in the hospital." He was struck with that "esteemable trait in the character of prisoners—observable even among the roughest criminals; I mean the great attention they bestow on the sick." " The most hardened criminals," he adds, " are not exempt from this feeling." And he says elsewhere: "Although many of these men, from their former reckless life and habits of depredation might be supposed to be hardened and indifferent, they have a keen sense of what is right or wrong." All honest men who have had to do with prisoners, can but confirm the experience of Dr. Campbell.

What is the secret of this feature, which surely cannot fail to strike people accustomed to consider the convict as very little short of a wild beast? *The assistants in hospitals have an opportunity of exercising their good feelings.* They have opportunities of feeling compassion for somebody, and of acting accordingly. Moreover, they enjoy within the hospital much more freedom than the other convicts ; and those of whom Dr. Campbell speaks were under the direct moral influence of a doctor like himself—not of a soldier.

In short, anthropological causes—that is, defects of organization—play a most important part in bringing men to jail; but these causes are not causes of "criminality," properly speaking. The same causes are at work amidst millions and millions of our modern psychopathic generation; but they lead to anti-social deeds only under certain unfavourable circumstances. Prisons do not cure these pathological deformities, they only reinforce them; and when a psychopate leaves a prison, after having been subjected for several years to its deteriorating influence, he is without comparison less fit for life in society than he was before. If he is prevented from committing fresh anti-social deeds, that can only be attained by undoing the work of the prison, by obliterating the features with which it inculcates those who have passed through its ordeal—a task which certainly is performed by some friends of humanity, but a task utterly hopeless in so many cases.

There is something to say also with regard to those whom criminalists describe as qualified assassins, and who in so many countries imbued with the old Biblical principle of a tooth for a tooth, are sent to the gallows. It may seem strange in this country, but the fact is that throughout Siberia—where there is ample opportunity to judge different categories of exiles—the "murderers" are considered as the best class of the convict population; and I was very happy to see that Mr. Davitt, who has so acutely analyzed crime and its causes, has also been able to make a like observation.[2] It is not known as generally as it ought to be that the Russian law has not recognized capital punishment for more than a century. However freely political offenders have been sent to the gallows under Alexander II. and III., so that 31 men have been put to death during the preceding reign[1] and about 25 since 1881, capital punishment does not exist in Russia for common-law offences. It was abolished in 1753, and since that time murderers are merely condemned to hard-labour from eight to twenty years (parricides for life), after the expiration

[2] He says: "Murders occasionally occur in connection with robbery, it is true; but they are as a rule accidental to the perpetration of the latter crime, and scarcely ever premeditated. The most heinous of all offences—murder deliberately intended and planned before its commission—is ordinarily the offspring of the passions of revenge and jealousy, or the outcome of social or political wrongs; and is more frequently the result of some derangement of the nobler instincts of human nature than traceable to its more debased orders or appetites."—*Leaves from a Prison Diary*, vol. i., page 17.

[1] Nobody knows exactly how many scores, or hundreds, of Poles were executed in 1863-65.

of which term they are settled free for life in Siberia. Therefore, Eastern Siberia is full of liberated assassins; and, nevertheless, there is hardly another country where you could travel and stay with greater security. During my very extensive journeys in Siberia I never carried with me a defensive weapon of any kind, and the same was the case with my friends, each of whom every year travelled something like ten thousand miles across this immense territory. As mentioned in a preceding chapter the number of murders which are committed in East Siberia by liberated assassins, or by the numberless runaways, is exceedingly small; while the unceasing robberies and murders of which Siberia complains now, take place precisely in Tomsk and throughout Western Siberia, whereto no murderers, and only minor offenders are exiled. In the earlier parts of this century it was not uncommon to find at an official's house that the coachman was a liberated murderer, or that the nurse who bestowed such motherly care upon the children bore imperfectly obliterated marks of the branding-iron. As to those who would suggest that probably the Russians are a milder sort of men than those of Western Europe, they have only to remember the scenes which have accompanied the outbreaks of peasants; and they might be asked also, how far the absence of executions and of all that abominable talk which is fed by descriptions of executions— the talk in which English prisoners delight most—has contributed to foster a cold contempt for human life.

The shameful practice of legal assassination which is still carried on in Western Europe, the shameful practice of hiring for a guinea an assassin[2] to accomplish a sentence which the judge would not have the courage to carry out himself—this shameful practice and all that hardly-imaginable amount of corruption it continues to pour into society, has not even the excuse of preventing murder. Nowhere has the abolition of capital punishment increased the number of murders. If the practice of putting men to death is still in use, it is merely a result of craven fear, coupled with reminiscences of a lower degree of civilization when the tooth-for-a-tooth principle was preached by religion.

But if the cosmical causes—either directly or indirectly—exercise so powerful an influence

[2] 'Du Cane's "Punishment and Prevention of Crime," p. 23.

on the yearly amount of anti-social acts; if physiological causes, deeply rooted in the intimate structure of the body, are also a powerful factor in bringing men to commit breaches of the law, what will remain of the theories of the writers on the criminal law after we have also taken into account the social causes of what we call crime?

There was a custom of old by which each commune (clan, Mark, Gemeinde) was considered responsible as a whole for any anti-social act committed by any of its members. This old custom has disappeared like so many good remnants of the communal organization of old. But we are returning to it; and again, after having passed through a period of the most unbridled individualism, the feeling is growing amongst us that society is responsible for the anti-social deeds committed in its midst. If we have our share of glory in the achievements of the geniuses of our century, we have our part of shame in the deeds of our assassins.

From year to year thousands of children grow up in the filth—material and moral—of our great cities, completely abandoned amidst a population demoralized by a life from hand to mouth, the incertitude of to-morrow, and a misery of which no former epoch has had even an apprehension. Left to themselves and to the worst influences of the street, receiving but little care from their parents ground down by a terrible struggle for existence, they hardly know what a happy home is; but they learn from earliest childhood what the vices of our great cities are. They enter life without even knowing a handicraft which might help them to earn their living. The son of a savage learns hunting from his father ; his sister learns how to manage their simple household. The children whose father and mother leave the den they inhabit, early in the morning, in search of any job which may help them to get through the next week, enter life not even with that knowledge. They know no handicraft; their home has been the muddy street ; and the teachings they received in the street were of the kind known by those who have visited the whereabouts of the gin-palaces of the poor, and of the places of amusement of the richer classes.

It is all very well to thunder denunciations about the drunken habits of this class of the population, but if those who denounce them had grown up in the same conditions as the children of the labourer who every morning conquers by means of his own fists the right of being admitted at the gate of a London dockyard,—how many of them would not have become the continual guests of the gin-palaces? —the only palaces with which the rich have endowed the real producers of all riches.

When we see this population growing up in all our big manufacturing centres we cannot wonder that our big cities chiefly supply prisons with inmates. I never cease to wonder, on the contrary, that relatively so small a proportion of these children become thieves or highway robbers. I never cease to wonder at the deep-rootedness of social feelings in the humanity of the nineteenth century, at the goodness of heart which still prevails in the dirty streets, which are the causes that relatively so few of those who grow up in absolute neglect declare open war against our social institutions. These good feelings, this aversion to violence, this resignation which makes them accept their fate without hatred growing in their hearts, are the only real barrier which prevents them from openly breaking all social bonds,—not the deterring influence of prisons. Stone would not remain upon stone in our modern palaces, were it not for these feelings.

And at the other end of the social scale, money that is representative signs of human work, is squandered in unheard-of luxury, very often with no other purpose than to satisfy a stupid vanity. While old and young have no bread, and are really starving at the very doors of our luxurious shops,—these know no limits to their lavish expenditure.

When everything round about us—the shops and the people we see in the streets, the literature we read, the money-worship we meet with every day—tends to develop an unsatiable thirst for unlimited wealth, a love for sparkish luxury, a tendency towards spending money foolishly for every avowable and unavowable purpose; when there are whole quarters in our cities each house of which reminds us that man has too often remained a beast, whatever the decorum under which he conceals his bestiality; when the watchword of our civilized world is: "Enrich yourselves! Crush down everything you meet in your way, by all means short of those which might bring you before a court!" When apart from a few exceptions, all—from the landlord down to the artisan—are taught every day in a thousand ways that the *beau-ideal* of life is to manage affairs so as to make others work for you; when manual work is so despised that those who perish from want of bodily exercise prefer to resort to gymnastics, imitating the movements of sawing and digging, instead of sawing wood and hoeing the soil; when hard and blackened hands are considered as a sign of inferiority, and a silk-dress and the knowledge of how to keep servants under strict discipline is a token of superiority; when literature expends its art in maintaining the worship of richness and treats the " impractical idealist" with contempt—what need is there to talk about inherited criminality when so many factors of our life work in one direction— that of manufacturing beings unsuited for a honest existence, permeated with anti-social feelings!

Let us organize our society so as to assure to everybody the possibility of regular work for the benefit of the commonwealth—and that means of course a thorough transformation of the present relations between work and capital; let us assure to every child a sound education and instruction, both in manual labour and science, so as to permit him to acquire, during the first twenty years of his life, the knowledge and habits of earnest work—and we shall be in no more need of dungeons and jails, of judges and hangmen. Man is a result of those conditions in which he has grown up. Let him grow in habits of useful work ; let him be brought by his earlier life to consider humanity as one great family, no member of which can be injured without the injury being felt by a wide circle of his fellows, and ultimately by the whole of society ; let him acquire a taste for the highest enjoyments of science and art—much more lofty and durable than those given by the satisfaction of lower passions,—and we may be sure that we shall not have many breaches of those laws of morality which are an unconscious affirmation of the best conditions for life in society.

Two-thirds of all breaches of law being so-called " crimes against property," these cases will disappear, or be limited to a quite trifling amount, when property, which is now the privilege of the few, shall return to its real source—the community. As to " crimes against persons," already their numbers are rapidly decreasing, owing to the growth of moral and social habits which necessarily develop in each society, and can only grow when common interests contribute more and more to tighten the bonds which induce men to live a common life.

Of course, whatever be the economical bases of organization of society, there will always be in its midst a certain number of beings with passions more strongly developed and less easily controlled than the rest; and there always will be men whose passions may occasionally lead them to commit acts of an anti-social character. But these passions can receive another direction, and most of them, can be rendered almost or quite harmless by the combined efforts of those who surround us. We live now in too much isolation. Everybody cares only for himself, or his nearest relatives. Egotistic—that is, unintelligent—individualism in material life has necessarily brought about an individualism as egotistic and as harmful in the mutual relations of human beings. But we have known in history, and we see still, communities where men are more closely connected together than in our Western European cities. China is an instance in point. The great "compound family" is there still the basis of the social organization: the members of the compound family know one another perfectly; they support one another, they help one another, not merely in material life, but also in moral troubles; and the number of "crimes" both against property and persons, stands at an astonishingly low level (in the central provinces, of course, not on the seashore). The Slavonian and Swiss agrarian communes are another instance. Men know one another in these smaller aggregations: they mutually support one another; while in our cities all bonds between the inhabitants have disappeared. The old family, based on a common origin, is disintegrating. But men cannot live in this isolation, and the elements of new social groups—those ties arising between the inhabitants of the same spot having many interests in common, and those of people united by the prosecution of common aims—is growing. Their growth can only be accelerated by such changes as would bring about a closer mutual dependency and a greater equality between the members of our communities.

And yet, notwithstanding all this, there surely will remain a limited number of persons whose anti-social passions—the result of bodily diseases—may still be a danger for the community. Shall humanity send these to the gallows, or lock them up in prisons? Surely it will not resort to this wicked solution of the difficulty.

There was a time when lunatics, considered as possessed by the devil, were treated in the most abominable manner. Chained in stalls like animals, they were dreaded even by their keepers. To break their chains, to set them free, would have been considered then as a folly. But a man came—Pinel—who dared to take off their chains, and to offer them brotherly words, brotherly treatment. And those who were looked upon as ready to devour the human being who dared to approach them, gathered round their liberator, and proved that he was right in his belief in the best features of human nature, even in those whose intelligence was darkened by disease. From that time the cause of humanity was won. The lunatic was no longer treated like a wild beast. Men recognized in him a brother.

The chains disappeared, but asylums—another name for prisons—remained, and within their walls a system as bad as that of the chains grew up by-and-by. But then the peasants of a Belgian village, moved by their simple good sense and kindness of heart, showed the way towards a new departure which learned students of mental disease did not perceive. They set the lunatics quite free. They took them into their families, offered them a bed in their poor houses, a chair at their plain tables, a place in their ranks to cultivate the soil, a place in their dancing-parties. And the fame spread wide of "miraculous cures" effected by the saint to whose name the church of Gheel was consecrated. The remedy applied by the peasants was so plain, so old—it was liberty—that the learned people preferred to trace the result to Divine influences instead of taking things as they were. But there was no lack of honest and good-hearted men who understood the force of the treatment invented by the Gheel peasants, advocated it, and gave all their energies to overcome the inertia of mind, the cowardice, and the indifference of their surroundings.[2]

Liberty and fraternal care have proved the best cure on our side of the above-mentioned wide borderland "between insanity and crime." They will prove also the best cure on the other

---

[2] One of them, Dr. Arthur Mitchell, is well known in Scotland. Compare his "Insane in Private Dwellings," Edinburgh, 1864; as also "Care and Treatment of Insane Poor," in *Edinb. Med. Journal* for 1868.

boundary of the same borderland. Progress is in that direction. All that tends that way will bring us nearer to the solution of the great question which has not ceased to preoccupy human societies since the remotest antiquity, and which cannot be solved by prisons.

APPENDIX A.

(*Page* 109.)

EXTRACTS FROM THE "ACT OF ACCUSA-
TION" BROUGHT BEFORE A COURT
MARTIAL AGAINST THE SOLDIERS
CHARGED WITH HAVING CARRIED
CORRESPONDENCE BETWEEN THE PRI-
SONERS OF THE ALEXIS RAVELIN AND
THEIR ACQUAINTANCES.

THE accused, who were brought before the court under this charge in December, 1882, were :—Eugene Dubrovin, student of the Medical Acadamy; the artillery sub-officers Alexander Filipoff, and Alexei Ivanoff; the soldiers of the St. Petersburg dépôt-troops; Andrei Oryekhoff, Egor Kolibin, Kir Byzoff, Timofei Kuznetsoff, Vlas Terentieff, Grigori Yushmanoff, Ivan Shtyrloff, Yakov Kolodkin, Adrian Dementieff, Grigori Petroff, Ivan Tanyshoff, Emelian Borisoff, Leon Arkhipoff, Platon Vishnyakoff, Ivan Gubkin, and of the 38th Tobolsk regiment Prokopi Samoiloff.

"In the last days of December, 1881," the official document of accusation says, " disorders were discovered in the Alexeievskiy ravelin of the St. Petersburg Petropavlovsk fortress, which disorders consisted chiefly in the circumstance, that the soldiers appointed to mount the guard at the ravelin carried correspondence between the state's criminals detained there as also with their co-religionaries outside. A special inquiry was than made, by order of the Minister of the Interior, by the chief of the St. Petersburg gendarms. It appeared from the inquiry that the just-mentioned state's criminals, numbering four, were detained in separate cells of a special building situated in the Alexis ravelin. Until November, 1879, there were in the cells only two prisoners, namely, in cells Number Five and Number Six; in November, a third prisoner was brought in and imprisoned in cell Number One; and a fourth on November 19th (o.s.), 1880, who was put into cell Number Thirteen.

"The military watch was maintained by soldiers under the orders of the Chief of the ravelin. For that purpose one or two sub-officers were commissioned, and a number of soldiers who mounted the guard at each cell, and moreover five gendarmes, who were instructed with keeping the strongest watch on the soldiers themselves and with prohibiting any intercourse between the prisoners.

"Nevertheless, notwithstanding these strong measures, it was discovered in March, 1881, from letters found on the executed state's criminals Jelaboff and Sophie Perovskaya, that the state's criminals who were kept in the Alexis ravelin, carried on a lively correspondence with members of the Criminal Secret Society at St. Petersburg through the intermediary of the ravelin soldiers.

"The intercourse, as proved by the inquiry, consisted in the following: (1) conversation of criminal content was carried on by the soldiers with the prisoner of cell Number Five; (2) letters were exchanged between the cells Number One, Five, and Thirteen; (3) different periodicals were brought to the prisoners; (4) letters were carried from the prisoners to persons living in town, and to these letters answers were brought to the prisoners, as also money.

"It was impossible to ascertain when this intercourse began, because the state's prisoner of cell Number Five tried to convert to his ideas every soldier who entered the ravelin, and said that since the very beginning of his seclusion (1873?) everybody had conversations with him. As to carrying letters, it seems that this began since the end of 1879, when a new prisoner was brought to the ravelin and confined in cell Number One; because all soldiers have testified that no letters were carried between the cells Number Five and Six,[1] but only between cells Number One, Five and Thirteen. When a fourth prisoner, confined to cell Number Thirteen, was brought to the ravelin, letters began to be carried to the town; it was about December, 1880, when one of the soldiers transmitted a letter from the ravelin to medical student Dubrovin, arrested on February 2nd this year (1882)."

[1] That is, between Netchaieff and Shevitch.

It would be too long to give here in full this very interesting document, which describes in detail the intercourse which was carried on between the prisoners, and the conversation between the soldiers and the prisoner of the cell Number Five. The above is already sufficient to prove that the government itself has avowed the existence of some *oubliettes* within the fortress. I may add that the whole document has been published in Russian in the *Vyestnik Narodnoi Voli*, No. 1; and that the St. Petersburg court martial, sitting on December 1st and 2nd, in the Petropavlovskaya fortress, condemned: student Dubrovin to four years' hard-labour; sub-officer Ivanoff to six months' imprisonment; sub-officer Filipoff to five years hard-labour; and fifteen soldiers to imprisonment in the *ispravitelnyia roty* (military convicts' companies); two soldiers more died during the preliminary detention which lasted about eighteen months. This sentence must have been published in the *Official Messenger*.

APPENDIX B.

(*Page* 176.)

PART PLAYED BY THE EXILES IN THE COLONIZATION OF SIBERIA.

WITH the disorder which reigns in the statistics of Siberia it is very difficult, indeed, to estimate in how far the exiles contribute in increasing the population of Siberia. The following reliable figures published in 1886 by the official *Tobolsk Gazette*, and reproduced by the *Vostochnoye Obozrenie* (March 20th), are well worthy of notice. During the ten years 1875 to 1885, 38,577 men and 4285 women were transported to the Government of Tobolsk. They were followed by 23,721 free women and children, making thus a total of 66,583. During the same ten years 11,758 exiles died, and 10,094 ran away; 4735 were recondemned and sent, or have been transferred on demand, to other parts of Siberia; 1854 were returned to Russia; and 28,670 only entered the regular ranks of peasants and *town-bürgers* in Tobolsk; total, 57,111. The total population of exiles in Tobolsk consisted in 1875 of 35,100 males, and about one-third of that of women.

The mortality of these is included in the above figure of 11,758 dead. But even if this deduction be made, it appears that at least 20,000, out of 66,583, have been transported to Tobolsk only to die there very soon after their arrival, or to run away. The population of the Government of Tobolsk in 1875 being 1,131,246, and its increase having been 187,626 in ten years, while the natural growth of population ought to be less than 100,000, it appears that the exiles have contributed to that increase by less than 45,000, while the remainder were free immigrants from Russia.

As to the working power of this population it will be best seen from the fact that in 1875 only 10,798 exiles were householders. During ten years, 5588 were added to this number, but 3775 abandoned their houses, so that in 1885 only 12,611 exiles had permanent houses. Besides, out of 20,846 exiles belonging to the peasantry, 8525 were wanting in 1875; they had disappeared.

In 1881, the Governor of Tomsk reported that out of the 28,828 exiles settled in the province, only 3400 were carrying on agriculture ; about two-thirds were without any means of subsistence, and were living from hand to mouth; while 9796 had run away.

APPENDIX C.

(*Page* 194.)

EXTRACTS FROM THE REPORT READ BY M. SHAKÉEFF AT THE SITTING OF THE REPRESENTATIVES OF THE ST. PETERSBURG NOBILITY ON FEBRUARY 17TH, 1881 (O.S.).

It is known that after the Winter Palace explosion, Loris Melikoff was nominated chief of the Executive, with nearly dictatorial powers. In fact, Alexander II. abdicated in his hands. One of the first steps of Loris Melikoff was to permit the Provincial Assemblies to express their wishes. So they did; and one of the first wishes expressed was for the abolition of the system of "Administrative exile." The St. Petersburg nobility were among the first to protest against this abominable system, and in their sitting of February 17th (March 1st), 1881, they carried the following resolution: "To address the Emperor a petition in order to ask that the law which warrants the inviolability of the person of each citizen, be not violated."

During the discussion, E. A. Shakéeff read a report on the system of Administrative exile, in which report he wrote :—

"If we revert to the Russian code, we see that no kind of punishment can be applied otherwise than by a sentence of a tribunal. . . . It seemed that after the promulgation of the Law of 1864 there could be no interference of the administrative authorities with the function of the judicial authorities, and that no punishment could be inflicted otherwise than by a sentence of a court. Such punishment without judgment was considered by the State's Council as an act of arbitrariness. . . . But of late we have seen something quite new. The rights given to each citizen by law have become illusory. Under the pretext of clearing Russia from men politically 'unreliable,' the Administration began to exile on a small scale; but later on it enlarged the scale more and more. . . . At the beginning, society was angry against such proceedings. But in the long run it became accustomed to these acts of arbitrariness, and the sudden disappearance of people from their families ceased to be considered as something extraordinary.

"The prosecution was chiefly directed against young men and women, most not having reached their majority. *Often for a single acquaintance, for kinship, for being related with some school which had a bad reputation in the eyes of the Administration, for an expression in a letter, or for keeping a photograph of some political exile, young people were exiled.*"

"The *Law Messenger* gave, some time ago, the numbers of persons thus exiled (to Siberia) by mere orders of the Administration, and the figures varied from 250 to 2500 every year; but, if we add to these figures those of persons exiled in the same way to the interior provinces of European Russia, which figures we may only guess at, the whole will appear as a real hecatomb of human beings."

M. Shakéeff concluded by proposing to sign the above-mentioned petition. His speech was often interrupted by cries of "Bravo! Quite right!" The President of the Assembly, Baron P. L. Korff, supported the proposal of M. Shakéeff, and added that it had a very deep meaning for all Russia.

The Assembly, "considering that the system of Administrative exile is not justified by the law," signed the petition and sent it to the Emperor. Of course, all remained as it was. The only change made was that there is now a special committee which periodically revises all cases of Administrative exile, and periodically adds three or five years more of exile to those persons whom they consider dangerous. Those exiles who are permitted to return to Russia are prohibited to stay in any of the larger cities where they might find their livings.

APPENDIX D.

(*Page* 262.)

ON REFORMATORIES FOR BOYS IN FRANCE.

THE revolt of the boys who were kept at the reformatory colony of Porquerolles, has disclosed the abominable treatment to which they were submitted. The facts brought last February before a court, have shown that the food they received was of the worst imaginable description, and absolutely insufficient. In fact, they were kept hungry throughout. As to the treatment, it was really horrible. The *crapaudine*—a mediæval instrument of torture—was freely resorted to by the warders and the lady-proprietor of the colony.

As to the colony of Mettray, which was often represented as a model colony, it appears from a discussion at the French Chamber of Deputies on March 31st, 1887, that there also the treatment of children is most cruel. The facts brought forward during the discussion quite agree with my private information as to the barbarous treatment of children at that colony.

INDEX.

ADMINISTRATION at Clairvaux, 293; *vers.* jurors in Russia, 31; of Russian prisons, 81.
Administrative exile, 33, 134; exiles in Siberia, 191; numbers of in hamlets, 193, 195; report by Shakéeff on, 194 and Appendix C; misery of, 197; in Yakut encampments, 199.
Alcoholism, 340.
Alexeievsky ravelin, 109.
Anthropological causes of crime, 345.
Arrestantskiya roty, 46.
Arrestations of innocent in Russia, 48.
Avvakum, nonconformist priest, 128.

BARGES for transportation of convicts, 138.
Bastions, ravelins, 87.
Bodily diseases, their influence, 345.
Borderland between insanity and crime, 348.
Brotherly treatment of convicts, 356.
Brodyaghis, see Runaways.
Byelgorod prison, 71.

CAMPBELL, Dr., on prisoners, 355.
Canteen in French prisons, 264.
Capital punishment, 358.
Cells at Lyons, 259.

Cellular department at Clairvaux, 294.
Cellular imprisonment no remedy, 336; in the fortress, 99.
Central prison of Clairvaux, 274 *sq.*
Central prisons in Russia, 20, 46, 65.
Children growing in neglect, 363; in French prisons, 261 and Appendix D; of exiles in Siberia, 148.
Clairvaux, central prison, 274; manufactures, 276; military convicts, 278; walk, 280; exterior brigade, 282; political prisoners, 283; food, 287; labour and earnings, 288.
Coal-mines on Sakhalin, 211.
Committee of inquiry into Russian prisons, 13 *sq.*
Commune, responsible for its members, 361.
Cosmical causes of crime, 341.
Courtine of Catherine, 88.
'Criminal age,' 354.

DAVITT, Mich., "Leaves," 300; the "Upper Ten," 310; on re-convictions, 307; on immorality, 336; on murderers, 358.
Decency, crimes against, 263, 279, 335.
Despine, 340.

Détentionnaires at Clairvaux, 278.
Deterring influence of prisons, 305.
Disobedience, punishments, 293.
Dress, influence of, 331.
Drugs given in St. Petersburg fortress, 91.
Du Cane, on English prisons, 300; on "criminal age," 354.
Dué on Sakhalin, 211.

EARNINGS of prisoners in France, 288.
Economical organization as a cause of crime, 363.
Emancipation of serfs in Russia, 9, 10.
Emperor's mines, 63, 155; cheap labour for, 203.
Energy destroyed in prisoners, 320.
Etapes in Siberia, 22, 140.
Executioners, hired, 360.
Executions in secrecy in Russia, 41.
Exile by order of Administration, *see* Administrative exile.
Exiles in Siberia, 154—201; earlier, 127; Poles, 129, 131; numbers and categories of, 133; journey on foot, 135; on their march through Siberia, 140—142; their wives and children, 144; their charity-song, 145; political exiles, 150; settled exiles, enlistment of, 163; numbers, 173; their present position, 174, and Appendix B; disappearance of, 175; misery, 179; transportation to, 124—153.

FERRI, Prof., 340, 343.
Flogging in Russian central prisons, 69.
Food in French prisons, 265, 287.

Fortress of St. Peter and St. Paul, 84 *sq.*; history, 85; plan of, 87; writers imprisoned there, 89; Trubetskoi bastion, 91; courtine of Catherine, 91; cellular imprisonment before trial, 92; fortress bells, 95; interviews, 100; famine-strike, 101; condemned prisoners, 104; Trubetskoi ravelin, 104; Alexis ravelin, 107; Netchaieff, 109, *sq.*; soldiers condemned for carrying correspondence, 109 and Appendix A; Shevitch, 114; Shiryaeff, 110, 113.
French prisons, 257—298; departmental prisons, 257; Lyons prisons of St. Paul, 257; cells at, 258; children in, 261; *récidive*, 263; undertakers in, 265; warders, 267, 293; interviews with kinsfolk, 269; Lyons' Palais de Justice, 271; cellular waggons, 272; Clairvaux central prison, 275 *sq.*; military prisoners, 278; labour, 280; political prisoners, 283; food, 287; earnings of convicts, 288; traffic in tobacco, 290; administration, 293; punishments, 294.

GAOLERS in Russia, 54.
Gheel, cure of insane, 369.
Gold-washings in Siberia, character of work, 162; enlistment of workers 163; *see also* Kara.
Gradovsky, Prof., on Vera Zassoulitch's case, 35.
Gratifications for work in French prisons, 290.
Griesinger, 340; on the slow growth of mental disease, 351.
Groth, State's Secretary, report on prisons, 62.

Index. 385

HANGING in Russia, 40.
Hard-labour in Siberia, 154 sq.; mines, 156; numbers of convicts, 158; Kara mines, 161; food, 164; punishments, 167—170; salt works, 172.
Hard-labour prisons in Russia, 46; also central prisons.
Heredity, 354.
Herzen's *Prison and Exile*, 240.
Hill, S. A., on the influence of weather in India, 342.
Houses of correction in Russia, 46.
Hygiene *vers.* Medicine, 339.

IDIOTS, 346.
Impressions, want of, 322.
Improvements possible in prisons, 301.
India, influence of temperature and moistness on suicides and murders, 342.
Instruction, preliminary, in Russia, 27, 30.
Interviews with kinsfolk, at Lyons, 269.

JUDICIAL procedure, law of, in Russia, 26.
Jurors in Russia, 30.

KAMOLOFF, runaway, 225.
Katkoff's review, on prisons, 238.
ara gold-washings, 47, 81; scurvy-epidemics, 156; rotten buildings, 161; work, 162; food, 164; punishments, 167; liberated convicts, 166; superintendents, 168; torture, 170.
Katorga (hard-labour), 155 sq.
Kharkoff central prisons, 71.
Kieff, typhus epidemics, 57, 246.
Kowno, prison, 51.

Krafft-Ebbing, 340.
Kutuzoff, Mme., experience in prisons, 49.

LABOUR in prisons; incitements to, 317; moral effects of, 314; remuneration of, 288—291, 316; state *vers.* private undertakers, 289.
Lansdell, on Russian prisons, 229 sq.; hasty visits to, 233; ignorance of Russian literature on subject, 239; accusations against Herzen, 240; on the St. Petersburg fortress, 247; Count Tolstoi's promises not kept 249; on *oubliettes*, 252.
Law of Judicial procedure in Russia, 26; encroachments on, 30.
Letters to kinsfolk, 319; stolen, 267.
Litovskiy Zamok, 59, 236, 238, 243.
Loghishino, land-robbery at, 38.
Loshkareff's affair, 35.
Lombroso, Dr., on anthropological causes of crime, 340, 345; on re-convicted prisoners, 306.
Lyons, prisons at, 257—270; children, 262; letters, 267; "Palace of Justice," 271.

MAUDSLEY, on insanity, 347; on hard-labour, 348.
Maximoff's "Hard-labour and Siberia," 153.
Mikhailoff, poet, 19.
Military convicts at Clairvaux, 278.
Mitchell, Dr., on insane, 370.
Mortality in Russian prisons, 55 sq., 218.
Mtsensk dépôt-prison, 78.
Murderers in Siberia, 358.

C C

NERTCHINSK mining distret, 157.
Netchaeff, his circles, 90; in an *oubliette*, 108.
Nikitin, on Russian prisons, 237.

OSTROGS, Russian, 49, 236.
Oubliettes in St. Petersburg fortress, 107; in Solovetsk monastery, 115 *sq.*
Overcrowding in Russian prisons, 55, 237 *sq.*, 243, 244.

PARTIES of convicts, 140, 147.
Petri, Dr., on Sakhalin, 213.
Petropavlovskaya fortress, 87—123; 246—252.
Pinel and the insane, 369.
Pissaref in fortress, 89.
Pistole in French prisons, 258.
Plète in Russia, 62.
Poletti, 340.
Police Correctionnelle condemnation of children, 261.
Political prisoners, at Kharkoff, 75; in Siberia, 184—201; in hard-labour, 186—189; in administrative exile, 191 *sq.*; at Clairvaux, 283.
Polyakoff, on Sakhalin, 210.
Poselentzy, see Exiles, settled.
Preliminary detention in Russia, 98.
"Prison Matron," 300.
Punishments of prisoners in Russia, 67; at Kara, 167; at Clairvaux, 293.
Pushkin, religious reformer, in an *oubliette*, 115.

RAVELIN, Alexeievskiy, 109; soldiers condemned for correspondence carried, 109, and Appendix C; Trubetskoi, 104; inmates of transported to Siberia, 106; ravelins of the St. Petersburg fortress, 87.
Récidive, reconvictions, 305—308.
Reinach, on re-convictions, 306.
Runaways in Siberia, 180 *sq.*; on Sakhalin, 222.
Russian prisons, 24—84; committee of improvement, 13; nothing done, 43; organization of, 45; numbers of inmates, 47; state of, 49 *sq.*; mortality in, 55; overcrowding, 55, 238—244; typhus epidemics, 55, 57; St. Petersburg chief prison, 58; House of Detention, 59; Central prisons, 65—68, 71—78; punishments in, 68; Kharkoff prisons, 71; Mtsensk depôt, 77; superintendents, 79; *see also* Fortress, and Exile to Siberia.
Russian revolutionary party, 5.
Ryssakoff tortured, 40.

SABUROFF, drugs given to, in fortress, 91.
St. Paul prison at Lyons, 257 *sq.*
St. Petersburg prisons, 236—238; committee for prisons, 237; fortress, 84 *sq.*; House of Detention, 59.
Sakhalin, exile on, 202—226; physical characters, 207; climate, 209; unfit for agriculture, 211; coal-mines, 215; convicts, 217; mortality of, 218.
Salt-works, 47, 172.
Schlüsselburg fortress, 121.
Scurvy epidemics at Kara, 156; at Kharkoff, 56; at Perm, 55.
Seasons, their influence on breaches of law, 341, 343.
Self-respect killed in prisoners, 328—331.

Shevitch in an *oubliette*, 114.
Siberia, transportation to, 124—153; *see* Exile; population of, 205; proportion of exiles, Appendix B.
Social causes of breaches of law, 360.
Society responsible for its criminals, 361.
Solovetsk monastery, *oubliettes* of, 115.
Solovioff, 91.
State as a purveyor of labour in prisons, 264, 289.
Stepniak, quoted, 102.

TCHERNYSHEVSKIY in fortress, 89; sent to Viluisk, 190.
Temperature, its influence on attempts against persons, 341, 343.
Tetenoff acquitted by jury, re-arrested by police, 32.
Thompson, J. B., on heredity, 354.
Tobacco, traffic in, 291, 312.
Tokareff's affair, 35.
Transbaikalia, 12.
Transportation to Siberia, 21 *sq.*
Trials in Russia, 34.
Trubetskoi bastion, 91 *sq.*, 248; ravelin, 104, 249.

Typhus epidemics in Russian prisons, 56, 57.

UNDERTAKERS in French prisons, 265, 316.
Urussoff, exiled, 31.

VISITS of relatives, in fortress, 100; at Lyons, 269; their influence, 319.

WAGGONS, cellular, 272.
Warders in prisons, 331; in French prisons, 292.
Wilno prison, 49.
Will, firmness of, destroyed by prisons, 323.
Wives of prisoners, 267; of exiles in Siberia, 145.
Wolkowijsk prison, 52.

YADRINTSEFF on Siberian prisons, 239.

ZASSOULITCH, VERA, her trial, 35; attempts to re-arrest, 32.

THE END.

www.ingramcontent.com/pod-product-compliance
Lightning Source LLC
Chambersburg PA
CBHW032022220426
43664CB00006B/330